EMINENT
ASTORIANS

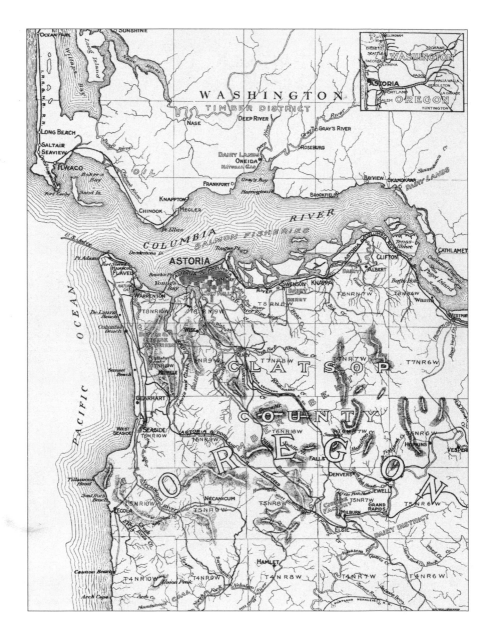

Map from *Astoria, Oregon, Homeseekers Edition*, published by the
Astoria Chamber of Commerce, Astoria, Oregon, ca. 1911, p. 48. CCHS 91.04.01.

EMINENT
ASTORIANS

FROM JOHN JACOB ASTOR
TO THE SALMON KINGS

STEPHEN DOW BECKHAM

HISTORICAL ADVISER

EDITED BY KAREN KIRTLEY

East Oregonian Publishing Company

Salem, Oregon

We are grateful to Michael Bales for exercising his editorial wisdom
throughout these pages and to Sam Rascoe for organizing a high-resolution
image catalog. Tom Booth of OSU Press made many excellent suggestions.
Thanks are due also to John Bruijn, McAndrew Burns, John Goodenberger,
Alex Pajunas, Dave Pearson, John Perry, and Matt Winters for their
help in bringing this book to fruition.

Distributed by Oregon State University Press, 121 The Valley Library, Corvallis, OR 97331
541-737-3166
    Toll-free orders: 1-800-426-3797

Library of Congress Cataloging-in-Publication Data

Eminent Astorians : from John Jacob Astor to the salmon kings / edited by
Karen Kirtley ; Stephen Dow Beckham, historical advisor.
        p. cm.
    Includes bibliographical references and index.
    ISBN 978-0-87071-631-7 (pbk. : alk. paper)
    1. Astoria (Or.)--Biography. I. Kirtley, Karen. II. Beckham, Stephen Dow.
    F884.A8E45 2010
    979.5'46--dc22
    [B]
                                2010028547

Editor: Karen Kirtley
Designer: Elizabeth M. Watson
Production Coordinator: Dick Owsiany
Photo research by Liisa Penner
Directed by Stephen Aldrich Forrester of the East Oregonian Publishing Company

Printed in the United States

Contents

Introduction

BY STEPHEN DOW BECKHAM

Image from the *Illustrated London News,* February 10, 1849.
"On Fort George, or Astoria, Columbia River—Site of the Hudson's Bay
Company's Establishment." CCHS 33854.906.

THE NAME ASTORIA rings with elegance. A term derived from the surname of America's first multi-millionaire—John Jacob Astor—it is a city, the title of a book by Washington Irving, and the location of two communities on the far reaches of the continent. Astoria, Oregon, is at the crossroads of the Pacific Ocean and the entry to the Columbia River, the great "River of the West." Astoria, New York, is near the entrance of the Hudson River and the harbor of New York City. Both communities were products of the enterprise of John Jacob Astor (1763–1848), a man of business acumen and vision.

The essays in this volume concern several figures who spent their energies and talents at Astoria, Oregon. All but one—John Jacob Astor—lived part of their lives in Astoria or Clatsop County. In various ways, all cast their fortunes, at least for a time, in the town. These figures came to a community founded in 1811 as a fur-trading post of the Pacific Fur Company.

Bold in his grasp of potentials, Astor secured partners to invest in a venture of remarkable daring. In 1810 he dispatched expeditions by land and by sea via Cape Horn to establish a post on the Northwest Coast of North America. The Pacific Fur Company was to trap and trade for furs and export them from the mouth of the Columbia. Astor's vision was to import blankets, cotton cloth, beads, brass kettles, metal tools, and weapons to outfit his men in the field and to trade with Native Americans. His vessels then carried furs to the markets of the Pearl River on the south coast of China to exchange them for cargoes of tea, porcelain tableware, cloth (nankeen and silk), Chinese Chippendale furniture, fans, and other luxury goods for the residents of the East Coast of the United States. The ships returned to New York City to unload the imports and take on a new cargo of trade goods for the distant Oregon Country.

The mouth of the Columbia was a landscape of deep but undocumented historical antecedents. For ten thousand years (or longer), Native Americans resided in the Pacific Northwest. Their tools found in archaeological excavations date to the late Pleistocene. They hunted mastodons, mammoths, camels, and other mega-fauna that lived in the region thirteen thousand and more years ago.

In the eighteenth century, their descendants, speakers of Chinookan languages, resided from the Pacific Ocean east to Celilo Falls on the Columbia Plateau. The employees of the Pacific Fur Company settled among the Clatsop (on the Oregon shore) and the Chinook (on the Washington shore), speakers of Lower Chinookan and arbiters in the maritime fur trade that developed since 1792, when Captain Robert Gray entered the Columbia River. The Lewis and Clark Expedition spent the winter of 1805–1806 in close proximity to Chief Coboway's people, the Clatsops. The Pacific Fur Company dealt primarily with Chief Comcomly's band, the Chinooks, whose villages lined the north shore of the estuary west of Gray's River and on nearby Willapa Bay.

Fort Astoria, subsequently Fort George of the North West Company and the Hudson's Bay Company, became the nucleus of Astoria, Oregon, the region's oldest Euro-American community. The outpost, founded in March 1811, went through decades of trial, its population dropping at times to a single family and a few bachelor employees of the Hudson's Bay Company, but it endured.

The location was a geographical anomaly. On the positive side, the fort and subsequent town lay in the lea of Coxcomb Hill, a site protected from the prevailing southwesterly storms and the incessant, driving rain. On the negative side, the nascent community was hacked out of a rain forest of towering conifers that grew in miry clay. The hillsides rolled down to the margin of the river, leaving little level ground for streets and public areas. Astoria emerged captive between a steep hillside and a tidal estuary. Its most redeeming feature was the deep shipping channel and good anchorage that hugged the southern shore of the broad Columbia. Its worst moments came when unstable hillsides gave way and slipped toward the river, sometimes carrying streets and houses in the muddy cascade.

The Oregon Treaty of 1846 resolved the issue of sovereignty in the Pacific Northwest. Great Britain accepted the 49th parallel as the international boundary between the United States and Canada. The Hudson's Bay Company moved its headquarters from Fort Vancouver in Oregon to Fort Victoria on Vancouver Island in British Columbia, and began withdrawing its personnel and closing down its operations in Oregon Territory. This change of tenure at Fort George (Astoria) and affirmation of American prospects gave the small settlement new magnetism. Hopes grew that the former fur-trading station had a fabulous future as the gateway city to the Pacific Northwest.

⊚ The Oregon Treaty of 1846 resolved the issue of sovereignty in the Pacific Northwest. Great Britain accepted the 49th parallel as the international boundary between the United States and Canada. ☙

As Astoria, New York, witnessed the development of the greatest city in the country, so might Astoria, Oregon, become its counterpart and port of call for the commerce of the vast Pacific Ocean. The deep harbor, safe anchorage, and navigable connections to the fertile Willamette Valley, along with the resources of the sprawling interior plateau east of the Cascade Mountains, appeared to confirm Astoria's site as ideal for commerce. The tremendous stands of timber along the Columbia estuary suggested potentials for logging, the manufacture of forest products, and shipyards. The silvery flood of salmon that entered the river between March and September, as well as sturgeon, crabs, clams, and oysters, held the promise that marine food resources also had a future in the town's economy.

Pioneers in the 1840s settled west of Astoria on the Clatsop Plains. Any country that could grow lush grass and stands of spruce and fir, they reasoned, could surely be transformed into farms. A generation filed on donation land claims, homesteads, and cash-entry purchases of public lands only to discover that the country south of Point Adams to Tillamook Head was a vast deposit of sand churned out of the mouth of the Columbia River. The Clatsop Plains lacked fertile soil and received far too much rain to sustain successful farming, except for modest dairy operations.

The next generation hatched other plans for the lands west of Youngs Bay and Astoria. It founded its dreams on construction of a railroad to open the coastline south of the Columbia's mouth. These investors platted New Astoria and Flavel, progenitors of Warrenton and Hammond, and beach resort communities subsequently called Gearhart and Seaside. The cities they imagined—to be serviced by the stores, banks, and government offices of Astoria—developed only slowly, taking decades to draw inhabitants. The imagined towns looked good on paper, but attracted few residents and investors.

Astoria's development was a product of natural resources as well as a function of the town's location. The federal government took notice and, over the past 160 years, invested in a variety of projects that have developed and sustained Astoria. Uncle Sam's role at the mouth of the Columbia has been of immense benefit to the town and surrounding communities.

A port of call, Astoria in 1850 became the site of a customs house. The designation led to the construction of a federal building, appointment of a collector of customs, and hiring of support staff. The dangers of the harbor entrance inspired significant congressional appropriations for lighthouses: at Cape Disappointment (1856), Point Adams (1875), Tillamook Rock (1881), North Head (1898), and Desdemona Sands (1902). In 1892 the U.S. Light-House Service also placed a lightship equipped with a fog signal in the ocean off the bar and established a system of buoys, range lights, and navigation markers. In time, federal investments led to U.S. Life-Saving Service stations at Ilwaco and Hammond. Today, the U.S. Coast Guard in the Department of Homeland Security is the successor agency for these assignments.

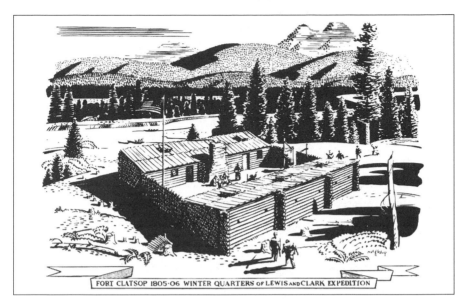

FORT CLATSOP 1805-06 WINTER QUARTERS of LEWIS and CLARK EXPEDITION

Fort Clatsop, the 1805–1806 winter quarters of Lewis and Clark's Corps of Discovery.
Based on a sketch of the floor plan in William Clark's journal, a replica was built in 1955.

DRAWING BY ROLF KLEP, CA. 1956. CCHS 23909.796.

Because the Columbia River had great strategic importance, the federal government invested heavily in its defense. Congress funded projects that created payrolls for laborers and the sale of supplies from local stores to build and staff fortifications from the Civil War to World War II. The facilities included Fort Stevens (and Battery Russell), Fort Canby, Fort Columbia, Tongue Point Naval Air Station, and the U.S. Army airfield at Youngs Bay, today the Astoria airport.

Between 1886 and 1896, the U.S. Army Corps of Engineers spent over $2 million to build a south jetty. The project sought to create a viable channel for the Columbia River over its dangerous bar, the entry to the Pacific Ocean. In later years, further harbor improvements included a north jetty, repeated dredging operations, and the construction of pile dikes and a boat basin at Hammond.

The U.S. Immigration Service operated the Columbia River Quarantine Station at Knappton from 1899 to 1938 on the site of a former Hume brothers salmon cannery. Since 1958, the National Park Service has administered the Fort Clatsop National Memorial, a reconstruction of the Lewis and Clark

Expedition's winter camp of 1805–1806. These diverse federal initiatives have drawn immigrants and visitors and helped sustain the local economy.

By 1900 Astoria had become the most important city on the coast between San Francisco and Victoria. It was a fascinating community of multi-ethnic, multi-lingual residents. Swedes, Norwegians, Finns, Danes, and Germans engaged in fishing, logging, and lumbering. Older-stock Americans from the East, and a few of the immigrant generation, owned canneries, banks, retail stores, newspapers, and subsistence farms. More than two thousand Chinese worked in the three dozen salmon canneries along the estuary, many of them residing in dormitory bunkhouses on Astoria's waterfront. Astoria was coming of age and aspired to greatness with the advent of railroad connections to the east and the south.

Salmon fishing and canning generated substantial wealth for a select set of Astoria investors. Grasping the potentials of steam pressure cooking, soldered tin cans, and bright-colored paper labels, and selling their product to a world market, the "Salmon Kings" thrived from the 1870s to the 1910s, even though the catch peaked in 1892. They created a web of business connections through the Columbia River Packers and Alaska Packers Associations, combining their resources to build canneries along the Columbia, the coast of Oregon, the west coast of Canada, and from southeast Alaska to Bristol Bay south of the Arctic Circle.

Astoria in 1870, an engraving published by Captain J. G. Hustler.

Photo by E. A. Coe. CCHS 1254.900.

The port of Astoria, ca. 1970. CCHS 23879.900.

Astoria's development proceeded unevenly. The disastrous fire of 1922 destroyed most of the town's business district, a loss estimated at $15 million. It proved a setback from which some investors never recovered. The city built a port dock and a huge warehouse to handle freight, only to endure for decades the frustration of watching ships enter the harbor and sail on to upstream cities that continued to grow and flourish. Astoria's transit through the twentieth century was a long glide. The city neither grew nor shrank as the salmon fishing and canning industry declined and closed and, ultimately, the great stands of timber in the nearby coastal mountains were exhausted.

By the 1990s, Astoria had discovered its most wonderful resources—its setting and, especially, its heritage. The city's attractions were numerous. The Astoria Column, erected in 1926–1927 atop Coxcomb Hill, was decorated with *sgraffito* (incised) murals of Oregon history and rose 125 feet above the ridge to provide stunning vistas of the town, river, and harbor entrance. Captain George Flavel's home, a gem in the Queen Anne style erected by the city's first million-aire, is maintained on its city-block setting by the Clatsop County Historical Society. The Society also has its museum in the former Astoria City Hall, where thematic exhibits tell the story of the town's development. The Columbia River Maritime Museum on Astoria's waterfront includes fascinating collections of artifacts, paintings, small vessels, and a lightship—all associated with development of the community and its international maritime connections.

Restoration projects enhanced civic pride with the repair and stabilization of the Astoria Column, the renovation of old hotels and saloons, and the transformation of the Liberty Theater, a jewel of 1920s architecture, for multiple civic uses. Residents of Astoria realized that they and the surrounding area possessed a critical mass of cultural sites. The arrival of cruise ships in the harbor since 1982 affirmed the town's potential as a tourist attraction. Nearby Fort Clatsop, reconstructed per the drawing of its footprint in William Clark's journal of 1805–1806 and administered by the National Park Service, is a popular destination. The site includes an interpretive center, a replica of the fort, and extensive hiking trails linking west to the shores of the Pacific.

The biographical profiles in this volume cover the lives of a dozen individuals who helped create modern Astoria. The cast of characters is intriguing.

The biographical profiles in this volume cover the lives of a dozen individuals who helped create modern Astoria.

Chief Comcomly was the one-eyed Chinook leader who for nearly thirty years in the early nineteenth century became a major arbiter in the fur trade. John Jacob Astor, who never visited the city but gave it his name, earned millions through the fur trade and real-estate speculation. George Gibbs, the scion of a wealthy East Coast family, became the first member of the Oregon bar to practice in Astoria and found his lifework studying the languages and customs of the Pacific Coast Indians. Ranald MacDonald, son of a trader and a Chinook woman, contrived to enter Japan, study Japanese, and teach English during the time its rulers barred foreigners from its shores. George Flavel dropped anchor in the city and established a lucrative bar-pilot service. He and his family built landmark homes in Astoria and invested extensively in commercial properties. Bethenia Owens-Adair (Oregon's first woman with a hyphenated surname) was an early doctor, essayist, and controversial advocate of eugenics. Silas Bryant Smith, grandson of Clatsop chief Coboway, became Oregon's first Native

American lawyer and advocate of tribal land claims. DeWitt C. Ireland, a racist foe of the Chinese living in the city, and Merle Chessman of the *Evening Budget*, who stood up to the powerful Ku Klux Klan, molded public opinion for decades through their voices as newspaper writers and editors. Astoria was also the home of the "Salmon Kings," an assortment of investors who grasped the potential of catching, canning, and selling salmon on a national and international market. Each in his or her way became an "Eminent Astorian" whose personality, labors, adventures, and ambitions became part of the daily life that shaped a community.

Eminent Astorians provides glimpses into the development of a city, a state, and a region through the diverse life stories of these individuals. Most were immigrants who arrived hungry but with a drive to succeed. They tested the natural resources of a rich land. They engaged in townsite speculation, captured and processed resources, and—in the cases of Smith and Owens-Adairs—sought to right wrongs, both individual and societal. Quintessential Oregonians, not all found wealth or happiness. A stream of human failings and frailties flows through these biographies like the surge of the nearby great river on its final journey to the sea.

Comcomly

Chinook Nation CEO

By John Terry

*And yet the owner of that skull when it pulsated
with life was a man of considerable intelligence, ability
and leadership. He was a great man not only among his own
people but also among all the neighboring tribes, and as
their chief he ruled over a wide extent of territory.*

—A. G. Harvey (1939, 161)

O NCE AGAIN THERE were sails on the horizon. By now The People were well
aware of what they were.

Years before, the sight was mysterious, mystical, frightening—huge *canim*
(canoes) topped with billowing wings carrying strange, bearded creatures. Some
thought they were bears; others saw them as demigods come to check on their
earthly *tenas tillikums* (children).

But in time The People came to know neither of those was true. The hair-
shrouded beings aboard the big vessels were men such as themselves, come from
faraway places to exchange wonderful new things—shiny trinkets, metal knives,
cooking pots, pretty cloth, firearms—for the furs The People routinely collected
and used for clothing, bedding, and other everyday comforts.

But this day it was different.

The ship, as they now knew such vessels were called, did not pass by, as
all others had done. Instead, it hesitated just outside the surging, white-topped
waves that guarded the entrance to the *Hyas Cooley Chuck* (Big River), as it was
called in Chinook Jargon, the language increasingly used by The People and
outsiders alike.

Early Morning View of Tongue Point from Astoria, by Cleveland Rockwell
(American, 1837–1907), watercolor on paper, 19⅜" by 27⅛", ca. 1883.
Courtesy of the Columbia River Maritime Museum.

The Columbia River Bar, oil painting by Cleveland Rockwell, 1884. CCHS 282.

Then slowly, methodically, the ship made its way across the angry waters
and lowered its heavy iron anchor in the large bay. A sweeping crescent of land
separated the river from the vast, salty water, *hyas salt chuck,* stretching endlessly beyond.

The sails were lowered and tied into neat bundles along stout branches extending outward from soaring tree trunks—"ship sticks" or "masts," they were called—rising high above the great body of the vessel. Men, women, and children alike took to their *canims* for a closer look.

Surely among them, perhaps in the lead, was a young *tyee* (chief) named Comcomly, also known as Madsu, or Thunder (Ruby and Brown 1976, 340).

Chief Comcomly, from Duncan McDougal's Astoria Journal (1811–1813).

Given his age, high station, and temperament, it's a good bet that nothing as significant as the arrival of Robert Gray—the first *ship tyee* (captain) to venture into the waters of the Big River—would escape his attention. Comcomly would not only become the chief among chiefs on the Lower Columbia, but he would play a central role in historic events on the river over the next thirty-four years.

The People traveled the coast in great canoes, forty to fifty feet long, carrying thirty, forty, even fifty people plus many items for trading. They made their way along the *illahe wake siah kopa chuck* (Northwest Coast) long before Gray sailed the *Columbia Rediviva* into the river on May 11, 1792.* For The People, the arrival of the great ship ushered in a new, at first wondrous, but ultimately disastrous era.

Chinook historian and lexicographer Edward Harper Thomas described the natives of the Northwest coast:

> Aboriginally the mouth of the Columbia River, on both the
> Washington and Oregon sides, was occupied by natives of the
> Chinookan linguistic stock. Those residing on the Oregon side
> were known as the Clatsop, those on the Washington side, the
> Chinook. The latter extended up the Washington coast as far as the
> northern shore of Willapa Bay, formerly known as Shoalwater Bay.
> Adjoining the Chinook and Clatsop in the river valley on the east
> were the Cathlamet in speech. These three groups occupied a signally
> important position in the cultural setting of the Northwest, for within
> their territory four great streams of travel fused.
>
> Seagoing canoes from British Columbia and even Alaska met
> vessels from the southern Oregon coast, while cruder dugouts
> carrying traders from the Plateau east of the Cascades reached this
> great commercial center via the Columbia waterway. The fourth route,

---

*In honor of the occasion, Gray renamed the *Hyas Cooley Chuck* after his ship, thus guaranteeing his own prominence in the Big River's history.

least important, led overland through the Cascade passes from the interior of southern Washington (Thomas 1969, 5).

The earliest reports of outsiders arriving on the Northwest coast tell of Chinese junks blown off course and across the Pacific. There is no real evidence of Chinese sailors surviving such a journey.*

European exploration began in the 1540s, when Spanish ships started inching up the coast from Mexico and South America. Ferdinand Magellan opened the Pacific rim with his voyage around South America and on to Asia starting in 1519.

There are theories that Sir Francis Drake, in the summer of 1579, sailed north to (today's) Oregon Coast and spent five weeks repairing his ship, the *Golden Hinde,* though San Francisco Bay has long laid claim to that distinction. Drake called wherever it was he landed "New Albion," an ancient, now mostly poetic, term for "England."

In 1603, the Spaniard Martin d'Aguilar sailed up the coast. Russian ships in the 1740s ventured across the Bering Sea and eventually traded down the Gulf of Alaska as far south as Vancouver Island and the coast of Washington.** Juan Perez explored the coast in 1774, Bruno Heceta and Juan Francisco de Bodega y Quadra in 1775, Captain James Cook in 1778.

Between 1784 and 1795, thirty-five British vessels traded on the Northwest Coast. Two American vessels pioneered U.S. trade in the area in 1788. French, Russian, and Spanish ships added to the mix. It's estimated that more than 311 vessels worked the coast between 1774 and 1800 (Cook 1973, Appendix E).

For Comcomly and the Chinooks, as well as for other tribes along the coast—the Clatsop and the Tillamook south of the great river, the Willapa and the Quinault farther north—the sight of sails against the western horizon grew increasingly familiar. But it wasn't until Gray sailed into the mouth of the Columbia that the Chinooks played host to one of the great ships. The *Columbia*

---

*Much later, in 1834, a shipwreck cast three Japanese sailors ashore on the Olympic Peninsula. Because of the exclusion rule, the men were unable to return to Japan, and eventually they were taken to China. The wreck was mentioned in John McLoughlin's letters of May 16 and May 20, 1834 (*The Letters of John McLoughlin from Fort Vancouver to the Governor and Committee,* ed. by E. E. Rich, Toronto: The Champlain Society, 1941–1944).

**Russia owned Alaska until 1867, when the United States bought it for $7.2 million.

Rediviva was a relatively modest 85 feet long and 220 tons, but it was a giant vessel in their eyes, and it was literally parked in their front yard.

Chronicling Comcomly and his people, as with all native peoples at the time, is difficult in that they had no written language. All we have to go on are oral descriptions passed down by native generations, and a few accounts written by outsiders, some sympathetic but many others self-centered and showing minimal, even distorted, interest in native ways. Most visitors neither cared for their hosts nor made an effort to understand them. In telling Comcomly's story, I quote liberally from the work of historians who have attempted to separate truth from myth and painted pictures that are both vivid and accurate.

What meager biographies there are agree that Comcomly was born sometime in the middle or late 1760s, making him twenty-five to thirty years old when Gray arrived at the Columbia. His father was Komkomis, a top Chinook chief and a fearsome individual in his own right.

According to historians Robert H. Ruby and John A. Brown, the Chinooks told of the time Komkomis "led some thousand warriors into battle against the upriver peoples, who were weakened from battles on their way downstream. In one version of the encounter the Chinooks were said to have tricked the enemy into pursuing them through waist-high sword grass, where hidden defenders suddenly sprang from concealment to slay the invaders. For years their bones would litter an eroding Columbia shoreline" (Ruby and Brown 1976, 17).

Another time, "about 1789, one hundred large and one hundred small Chinook canoes traveled twenty days up the Columbia past 'some great falls' [maybe Celilo] to a lake to destroy the men of a large tribe inhabiting its shores, enslaving their women and children" (Ruby and Brown 1976, 17).

Slavery was part and parcel of Chinook commerce. As Edward Harper Thomas says, "Among the tribes along all this coast and far into the interior, slavery was an established and time-honored institution. Taking and selling slaves was a commercial pursuit. The Chinooks dignified it by making it the one great business in which they engaged. They were the profiteers in this particular trade. They made raids upon their neighbors, conquered tribes and villages and sold the victims to other warlike masters living in the wildernesses to the north and northwest" (Thomas 1969, 12).

For the most part, however, the Chinooks were peaceful, more interested in profits from trade than in war. Their success in business had rendered them rich by native standards even before Gray and company made their entrance.

"Intervillage quarrels and slave raids produced warlike posturing—war dances and the massing of war canoes," writes historian Dorothy O. Johansen. "Lower Columbia River warriors encased themselves in *clamons*, armor of thick elkskin that could turn an arrow, and carried small round shields of skins hardened in fire. Their weapons were bows and arrows and stout clubs. But the purpose of battle was to save face rather than to slaughter or reduce the enemy; after a casualty or two, peace was restored" (Johansen 1967, 9).

While one group might ally itself with one or more others against another alliance, there was no concept of tribe or nation. "The governmental unit was the village, which was sometimes simply an extended family," Johansen writes. "Leadership was inherited, but was affected by possession or lack of wealth. Through personal prestige the chief man of one village might exert influence over other villages. Nevertheless each village was independent. It had its own fishing area and hunting sites and lands for berry-gathering, and within a given area a village moved from summer to winter habitations as the seasonal economy required. There seems to have been no intervillage competition for possession of these locations" (Johansen 1967, 8).

Such was the society into which Comcomly had been born and Gray sailed on that fateful day in 1792. Gray was terse in describing his discovery in the *Columbia Rediviva* log: "At eight a.m. being a little windward of the entrance of the Harbor, bore away, and run in east-north-east between the breakers, having from five to seven fathoms of water. When we were over the bar, we found this to be a large river of fresh water. At one p.m. came to with the small bower, in ten fathoms, black and white sand. . . . Vast numbers of natives came alongside; people employed in pumping the salt water out of our water casks, in order to fill fresh, while the ship floated in" (Stephenie Flora, *The Oregon Territory and Its*

Pioneers, http://www.oregonpioneers.com/gray.htm, accessed October 12, 2009).

Among the *Columbia*'s crew was a young fifth mate, John Boit, of both curious and poetic nature. He kept a detailed journal and in doing so provided a graphic description of the ship's arrival.

> This day saw an appearance of a spacious harbour abreast the Ship, haul'd wind for it, observ'd two sand bars making off, with a passage between them to a fine river. . . . The river extended to the N.E., as far as eye could reach, and water fit to drink as far down as the Bars, at the entrance. We directed our course up this noble river in search of a village. Soon after, about 20 Canoes came off, and brought a great lot of Furs and Salmon, which last they sold two for a board Nail. . . .
>
> They appeared to view the Ship with the greatest astonishment and no doubt we was the first civilized people that they ever saw. . . . The tide set down the whole time and was rapid, whole trees sometimes came down with the stream. The Indians inform'd us there was 50 villages on the banks of this river (Boit 1921, 30).

A few days later, on May 18, Boit wrote:

> Captain Gray names this river Columbia's, and the North entrance Cape Hancock, and the South Point, Adams. The River, in my opinion, wou'd be a fine place for to set up a factory. The Indians are very numerous, and appear'd very civil (not even offering to steal). . . . The river abounds with excellent Salmon, and most other River fish, and woods with plenty of Moose, and Deer, the skins of which was brought us in great plenty, and Banks produced a ground nut, which is an excellent substitute for either bread or Potatoes. We found plenty of Oak, Ash, and Walnut trees, and clear ground in plenty, which with little labor made fit to raise such seeds as necessary for the sustenance of inhabitants (Boit 1921, 32).

Boit gave no indication Comcomly was among the ship's visitors, but the Chinooks as a whole rendered a positive impression.

The Men, at Columbia's River, are strait limb'd, fine looking fellows, and the Women are very pretty. They are all in a state of Nature, except the females, who wear a leaf Apron (perhaps 'twas a fig leaf. But some of our gentlemen . . . reported that it was not a leaf, but a nice wove mat in resemblance!) (Boit 1921, 29).

Gray sailed the *Columbia* out of the river on May 20, 1792, bound for Nootka Sound on the western shore of what is today Vancouver Island, the informal headquarters of the West Coast fur trade. There he shared a map of his discovery with the Spaniard Bodega y Quadra, who passed it along to British Captain George Vancouver.

On an earlier voyage, Vancouver, under orders to survey the West Coast for the British, had missed the mouth of the river. Straightaway he sailed south to confirm Gray's find. Leery of risking his large ship, the *Discovery,* on the treacherous bar, Vancouver dispatched Lt. William Broughton in a small ship, the *Chatham,* to have a look.

Broughton took the *Chatham* as far upriver as he dared, then launched a longboat and rowed roughly a hundred miles upstream as far as the mouth of the Sandy River east of Portland. As he went, he freely named various geographic points, including Mount Hood. We have no indication Broughton met Comcomly. But again, it is unlikely such a visit escaped the young chief's attention.

In May 1795, the British trader *Jane,* under Captain John Myers, sailed into the river. Ruby and Brown report that the *Jane* was "fitted out as a virtual floating hardware and department store, with a multifarious cargo of axes, brandy, iron bars, paints, clothing, chisels, hammers, copper sheets, small bells, tobacco, china beads, buckets, looking glasses, firearms, and ammunition" (Ruby and Brown 1976, 66). Comcomly and his people no doubt were among the Indians who traded with the *Jane.*

The *Jane*'s cargo was evidence of the Chinooks' and other coastal tribes' growing sophistication when it came to trading furs. In especially high demand by the traders was the lush fur of the sea otter, which translated into huge profits when shipped to China. There otter furs were prized as the ultimate in luxury, as they were by the Chinooks and other natives as well. Only Indians of the highest rank were allowed to wear them.

The natives' discernment prompted Myers to comment, in an account published twenty-two years later, that

> the disposition of the rude Indian is subject to the same fluctuation
> and caprice as the more cultivated natives of Europe: that experience
> and observation on the manners and customs of others, without
> addressing the rational or sensitive faculties, have given them the
> opportunity of judging between articles of necessity and superfluity;
> and that they would now prefer a Blanket, or a piece of Cloth, to the
> unprofitable possession of a ring or necklace (Myers 1817, quoted in
> Ruby and Brown 1976, 66).

A musket shot fired by a Chinook lookout on May 22, 1795, resounded with triple import. First, Chinook armaments had advanced to the point where firearms were commonplace. Second, the shot signaled the arrival of the trading ship *Ruby*, out of Bristol, England, under Captain Charles Bishop. And third, it heralded the first recorded appearance of Comcomly, at the time in alliance with another Chinook chief, Shelathwell.

Bishop stayed in Baker's Bay, the stretch of water sheltered by the horn-shaped north shore of the Columbia, for eleven days, trading for furs from sea otters and a variety of other animals. When the furs ran out, he traded for the *clamons,* the body armor that was the specialty of Chinook arms dealers. These he took north to trade with tribes farther up the coast, where he found them in great demand. In early December, when his supply ran out, he hurried back to the Columbia in search of more. He noted in his journal:

> The Sea Otter skins procured here, are of an Excellent Quality and
> large size, but they are not in abundance and the Natives themselves
> set great value on them. Beaver and two or three kind of Fox Skins,
> Martin and River Otter are also bought here—but the best trade is the

Leather War Dresses, articles to be disposed of, on other parts of the Coast, to great advantage, we procured such a Quantity, that at the least estimation is expected will procure us near 700 prime Sea Otter Skins. These dresses are . . . a complete defense against a Spear or an Arrow, and sufficient almost to resist a Pistol Ball (quoted in Ruby and Brown 1976, 70).

Bishop placed his order with Comcomly and Shelathwell. So eager was the captain to earn the chiefs' favor that he invited Comcomly to be his overnight guest aboard the *Ruby* and presented him with a fine coat and trousers.

The chiefs in turn accommodated him with a three-hundred-mile upriver journey to obtain more *clamons*. They left December 6 and returned December 20 with the items requested. Only after Bishop noticed a couple of bullet holes in the merchandise did he learn the full story of their acquisition. As Bishop told the story, Comcomly and Shelathwell

took their departure on the Expidition before alluded to they [were] in a single cannoe paddled with 10 men, each arm'd with a musket. Comcomally had one of his Wives and a Child, and we dressed him in his Jackett and trowsers and appurtenances of European cloathing their mode of trade is somewhat curious, and afforded us an hearty laugh as he more curiously described it they go up the River Chinook [Columbia] two or three hundred miles and come to strange villages, where they land and offer trade with some trifling pieces of Copper or Iron the Strangers naturally demand more, the chief then gives the Signal and they all discharge their pieces laden with powder, into the air, these people never having heard or seen such a strange phenomena, throw off their Skins and Leather War Dresses and fly into the woods, while the others pick them up, and leave on the spot the articles first offered, then they proceed to other places in like manner and thus for the Quantity of goods we pay for one of these dresses they get sometimes twenty, but we suppose this mode cannot last long, as they will naturally be aware of a second visit of the kind (quoted in Ruby and Brown 1976, 71).

Harmony did not always prevail between the visitors and Comcomly. For the most part, Bishop and his men regarded the Chinooks, including their chief, as ignorant savages. In turn, Comcomly and company looked on the ship's crew as arrogant and uppity.

On January 13, 1796, Comcomly got into a scuffle with one of Bishop's officers over some trifle, sustaining a blow to his face as well as his royal ego. He wisely left the ship, hiding his outrage. But that evening, still smarting from the insult, he fired off a couple of musket shots in the direction of the ship.

By the next day he had cooled off and regretted his actions. He sent a delegation of his wives to the ship to invite Bishop to dinner, but Bishop allowed he had other fish to fry. Instead, Comcomly visited the captain to plead that he had merely been shooting at ducks in the twilight. Bishop wrote in his journal:

> We gave this story (in our minds) the credit it deserved, nevertheless as I ever have determined to avoid as much as possible, committing any hostility amongst these savage nations, we appeared satisfied with it and a small Present was mutually exchanged—he is going tomorrow in his canoe up the River to kill Wild Geese and procure some Fresh fish for us previous to our Sailing and Shelathwell is going away to get "Wapatoes" (wild potatoes) as his parting gift (quoted in Ruby and Brown 1976, 73).

Exactly how Comcomly went about cementing his authority over his people and extending his empire to territories bordering his base of operation is a matter of speculation. Suffice it to say that over the next decade, through business acumen, battle, and shrewd diplomacy, he emerged as the chief operating officer of an efficient and profitable monopoly.

"He was the principal chief of the confederacy of all the Chinook tribes along the Columbia between the Cascade Range and the sea except the Clatsops," A. G. Harvey writes. "Pursuant to Indian custom, he had a wife from nearly every tribe within the confederacy, and also additional wives from some of the outside tribes. With these wives he acquired a large family and to provide for them all he had many slaves, so that altogether he maintained quite an establishment" (Harvey 1939, 162–163).

When Meriwether Lewis, William Clark, and the Corps of Discovery made their way down the Columbia in November 1805, Comcomly and his retinue were not on hand to greet them. Most likely, the chief and his people had vacated their fair-weather lodgings on the shore of Baker's Bay in favor of more substantial inland dwellings, shielded by hills from the lashing winds and bone-chilling rains of winter on the waterfront.

On November 18, Clark left the corps' miserable "Station Camp" on the shore of Baker's Bay to search for a decent site to spend the winter. Clark got as far as the western slope of Cape Disappointment (named by British explorer John Meares after he failed to identify the Columbia), where he carved "Capt William Clark December 3rd 1805. By Land. U. States in 1804 & 1805" in the bark of a fir tree.

Expedition chronicler Stephen Ambrose describes the expedition leaders' first meeting with Comcomly:

> On his return from his reconnaissance, Clark found Lewis with a group of Chinooks, including two chiefs. They all sat for a smoke. The captains handed medals and an American flag to the chiefs. Some trading was done.
>
> One of the chiefs [most likely Comcomly] had on a robe made of sea-otter skins that Clark declared "more beautiful than any fur I had ever Seen." Lewis agreed. In his turn, each man tried to strike a bargain for the robe, offering different articles.
>
> "No," said the chief. He pointed at Sacagawea's belt of blue beads, the most highly prized beads of all. The captains looked at her, questioningly. She made it clear that if she had to turn over the belt she wanted something in return. One of the captains brought her a coat of blue cloth, and she handed over the belt. Clark's journal fails to say who ended up with the fur coat, but it surely wasn't Sacagawea (Ambrose 1996, 314–315).

Had Lewis and Clark sought Comcomly's counsel on a salubrious place to winter, they would have stayed dryer and better fed. Their journals reflect no request for assistance, but only mistrust and contempt for both the Chinooks and the Clatsops. Lewis wrote:

> Notwithstanding their apparent friendly disposition, their great avarice and hope of plunder might induce them to be treacherous, at event we determined allways to be on our guard . . . and never place ourselves at the mercy of any savages, we well know, that the treachery of the aborigenes of America and the too great confidence of our countrymen in their sincerity and friendship, has caused the distruction of many hundreds of us (Lewis and Clark journals, February 20, 1806).

Instead of asking the natives for advice, Lewis called the famous meeting in which each member of the company expressed his or her preference (Sacagawea had her say along with the others). The result was the move across the Columbia to the banks of the (now) Lewis and Clark River and the construction of soggy Fort Clatsop.

Comcomly apparently returned the explorers' distrust with distance and contempt of his own. While the expedition journals reflect frequent visits to the fort by numerous Chinooks and Clatsops, there is no indication that Comcomly himself ever bothered to make the trip.

⚜ ⚜ ⚜

Lewis and Clark's negative attitude toward the Columbia River natives in general and the Chinooks, including Comcomly, in particular, is reflected in other reports over ensuing decades. Washington Irving, whose 1836 book *Astoria* was in its day accepted as the last word on the subject, depicts Comcomly as little more than a native eccentric who shows up for the party in funny garb, eager to amuse the guests.

At one point Irving, who never visited the region and based his books on the reports of others, refers to Comcomly as "a shrewd old savage with but one eye [who] certainly possessed great sway, not merely over his own tribe, but over the neighborhood" (Irving 1836, Chapter 8).

The old chief held great authority over a large number of people for forty years, kept enemies at bay and often in subjugation, and consistently out-maneuvered money-grubbing outsiders. He was far more than a "shrewd old savage."

Historian J. F. Santee notes that "the adjectives 'shrewd,' 'crafty,' and 'wily,' so frequently applied to Comcomly, may indicate the ability of the great Chinook chief to act with foresight in matters affecting his own welfare and that of his people. Such enlightened self-interest on the part of white leaders is dignified by the name of statesmanship" (Santee 1932, 271).

A prime illustration of Comcomly's statesmanship took place in 1810. Boston's Winship brothers, Abel, Jonathan, and Nathan, sent their ship *Albatross*, with Nathan in command, to the Columbia to set up a permanent trading post. The Winships were old hands at the Pacific trade. Their reputation came from exploits "not only in their home port but far regions which took their men and ships below the equator, to the Orient, the Pacific Coast and up to the Arctic Circle," writes historian Anna Jerzyk (1940, 176). But they were unprepared to deal with Comcomly's intense territoriality.

Nathan entered the Columbia on May 26, 1810, heedlessly sailing the *Albatross* past Comcomly's trading headquarters at the mouth of the river and upriver forty-five miles, where he began building a fortress whence to do business with upriver natives, thereby circumventing Comcomly's enterprise.

The garden was under two feet of water. . . . The fortress would have to be torn down and rebuilt on ground that would not be flooded.

The first blow was delivered by the river itself. "On the morning of [June 7] a heavy rain started falling. The next morning it was still falling." Jerzyk continues: "The river had spread over the entire operation. The garden was under two feet of water. . . . The fortress would have to be torn down and rebuilt on ground that would not be flooded. . . . Winship ordered the fort dismantled and the timbers floated downriver to higher ground" (Jerzyk 1940, 177).

Scarcely had work begun in the new location a quarter mile downstream than the second, ultimately persuasive, blow was delivered. A large, unruly delegation of Chinooks, abetted by nearby confederates, all armed to the teeth, paddled into view. "The crafty Chinooks had . . . developed a rather profit-able business with the up-river tribes and those of the north by buying first from them and selling at a profit to the trader ships. If the white men put their settlement so far up the Columbia, this commerce would go to them and the Chinooks would be losers" (Jerzyk 1940, 179).

According to Jerzyk, after some hostile confrontations—"There was a lot of shooting and shouting"—Winship decided to pack it in. His assistant, William A. Gale, noted in his journal: "Much to our chagrin we find it impossible to prosecute the business as we intended, and we have concluded to pass farther down. On making this known to the Chinooks they appeared quite satisfied and sold us some furs" (Jerzyk 1940, 179).

Winship goats, pigs, and trade goods went back aboard the *Albatross,* and on June 12, the ship departed downriver and out across the bar. Oregon's first "permanent" settlement lasted just eight days.

Again, records fail to single out Comcomly as the strategist behind the *Albatross* ouster. But given his economic interest and power base, he was most likely its instigator, tactician, and commander.

The Winships continued to trade "up and down the coast from California to Alaska, to Hawaii, China, and back again to Boston" (Jerzyk 1940, 181). For the next year, they talked of having another go at a Columbia River fort. By that time, however, word of John Jacob Astor's Northwest venture was out, and they decided not to challenge such a formidable competitor.

The arrival of Astor's Pacific Fur Company in 1811 would herald a new and fateful era for Comcomly and his domain.

❧ ❧ ❧

J. F. Santee writes: "The facts appear to indicate that the aboriginal inhabit-ants of the lower Columbia region scarcely merited the epithet of 'savage' so commonly applied to them. The cultural status of these people more nearly approximated that of semi-civilization. . . . The lower Columbia Indians lived in houses made of split cedar boards. These houses were from 30 to 40 feet in length and were often as much as 20 feet in width. Incredible as it may seem, the

Photographic image from a 2004 painting by Roger McKay, showing a
Clatsop longhouse and canoes. CCHS HERITAGE MUSEUM.

boards used in the construction of the houses were sometimes 20 feet or more
in length, two or three feet in width, and varied from three to six inches in thick-
ness" (Santee 1932, 272).

Just as remarkable were the Chinooks' waterborne means of conveyance,
typically two types. One was a small canoe built from a single log about fifteen
feet long. Called the "shovel-nose canoe" after its rounded stern and prow, it
was suitable for one or two people on the relatively calm inland waterways and
common on the Columbia and its tributaries. The Chinooks constructed these
of native timber.

The other was a large canoe "obtained by trade from Nootkas of Vancouver
Island, since Chinook country produced white cedar too small for such craft.
[Decorated] with carved animals or human effigies, or inlaid with bits of shells,
the large canoe had a vertical bow and stern with an elongated prow to break
sea or rough water, as was often experienced on the lower Columbia" (Ruby and
Brown 1976, 18). It is said that visiting New England traders carried the details
of these craft home with them, where shipbuilders incorporated the design into
the famously swift Yankee Clipper ships.

As Philip Drucker pointed out, "The number of these canoes on the lower river attested not only to the industry of the Chinook but to their trading abilities" (Drucker 1965, quoted in Ruby and Brown 1976, 18).

It was likely a small Chinook canoe that first ingratiated Comcomly to members of John Jacob Astor's company after the ill-fated *Tonquin** arrived in Baker's Bay on March 23, 1811, to set up Astor's trading post.

On April 5, not long after the *Tonquin*'s arrival, two partners in Astor's enterprise, Duncan McDougal (often spelled McDougall) and David Stuart, took a small boat to survey the south shore of the river and pick out a suitable spot for their fort. They settled on a spot called Point George, with easy access to large vessels.

Washington Irving writes in *Astoria:*

> After a day thus profitably spent, they recrossed the river, but landed on the northern shore several miles above the anchoring ground of the *Tonquin* in the neighborhood of Chinooks, and visited the village of that tribe. Here they were received with great hospitality by the chief, who was named Comcomly. . . .
>
> With this worthy tribe of Chinooks the two partners passed a part of the day very agreeably. M'Dougal . . . had given it to be understood that they were two chiefs of a great trading company, about to be established here, and the quick-sighted, though one-eyed chief, who was somewhat practiced in traffic with white men, immediately perceived the policy of cultivating the friendship of two such important visitors. He regaled them, therefore, to the best of his ability, with abundance of salmon and wappatoo (Irving 1836, Chapter 8).

On the morning of April 7, McDougal and Stuart set out to return to the *Tonquin*. Comcomly pointed out the rough conditions on the river and warned them their small vessel wasn't up to the trip.

---

*After dropping off most of the party at what is now Astoria, the *Tonquin*'s autocratic captain Jonathan Thorn sailed up the coast, ostensibly to trade. At Clayoquot harbor, his behavior so outraged the natives that they massacred his whole crew except one who survived to carry the bad news back to the new Fort Astoria.

Photographic image from a 2004 painting by Roger McKay illustrating the
seasonal round of life of the Clatsop Indians. The berry-picker at front left has a flattened
forehead and carries a baby in a head-flattening cradleboard. CCHS Heritage Museum.

The two traders weren't about to be dissuaded and pushed off into the
whitecaps. Comcomly, knowing full well what was about to happen, followed in
one of his canoes. They had gone scarcely a mile when a wave washed over the
traders' boat and capsized it.

"They were in imminent peril of drowning, especially Mr. M'Dougal, who
could not swim," Irving recounts. "Comcomly, however, came bounding over
the waves in his light canoe, and snatched them from a watery grave" (Irving
1836, Chapter 8).

Comcomly's crew paddled them ashore, built a fire, dried their clothes, took
them back to the Chinook village, and bade them bide their time until calmer
conditions prevailed.

In his *Early Voyages in the North Pacific, 1813–1818*, Peter Corney, who
worked for both the Pacific Fur Company and the North West Company,
described the scene awaiting Stuart and McDougal: "About five miles up the

river, on the north side, stands the Chinook village. The king of this tribe is called Com Comley. . . . The village consists of about thirty houses, built of wood, and very large; they are formed of boards with the edges resting on each other, and fastened with strips of bark to upright posts, which are stuck in the ground on either side of them" (Corney 1896, 145).

According to Irving, "Here everything was done that could be devised for their entertainment. . . . Comcomly made his people perform antics before them; and his wives and daughters endeavored, by all the soothing and endearing arts of women, to find favor in their eyes. Some even painted their bodies with red clay, and anointed themselves with fish oil, to give additional lustre to their charms" (Irving 1836, Chapter 8).

After three days, conditions improved. Comcomly loaded his guests into his royal canoe, and his slaves paddled the traders back to their ship in grand style.

Irving continues: "They were welcomed with joy, for apprehensions had been felt for their safety. Comcomly and his people were then entertained on board of the *Tonquin*, and liberally rewarded for their hospitality and services. They returned home highly satisfied, promising to remain faithful friends and allies of the white men" (Irving 1836, Chapter 8).

Astoria in 1811. From an 1854 edition of Franchère's *Narrative* published by G. P. Putnam's Sons. CCHS 511-900.

Which they did, particularly Comcomly, who watched with great interest as Fort Astoria rose from the ground. He no doubt profited greatly as goods from his empire began flowing through his hands into the fort.

For his part, McDougal, whether through skepticism wrought by his Scottish blood or infatuation first experienced at the lavish party Comcomly threw following McDougal's brush with death in the frigid waters of the Columbia, sought to enhance the business relationship by seeking the hand of one of the chief's daughters in matrimony.

Irving writes that "this alliance . . . would infallibly rivet Comcomly to the interests of the Astorians, and with him the powerful tribe of the Chinooks." McDougal therefore "dispatched two of the clerks as ambassadors extraordinary, to wait upon the one-eyed chieftain, and make overtures for the hand of his daughter" (Irving 1936, Chapter 56).

Comcomly was more than happy to oblige. He had, after all, a surfeit of both wives and daughters. Wrote Corney:

Com Comley, king of the Chinook nation . . . is the richest and most powerful chief on the river; he is a short, elderly man, blind in one eye; he has three wives, and many children. His eldest son (Cassacas) is a strong, well-made man, about 5 feet 6 inches high; he succeeds his father in the government of the Chinooks; he is no friend to white men; he styles himself Prince of Wales. Selechel is the next son; he styles himself Duke of York; he is a small man, and well disposed towards the whites (Corney 1896, Chapter 7).

On July 20, 1813, the chief and his entourage made their way in royal state to Fort Astoria, where the ceremony was slightly delayed by the condition of the bride.

Irving recounts: "Her bridal adornments, it is true, at first caused some little dismay, having painted and anointed herself for the occasion according to the Chinook toilet; by dint, however, of copious ablutions, she was freed from all adventitious tint and fragrance, and entered into the nuptial state, the cleanest princess that had ever been known, of the somewhat unctuous tribe of the Chinooks" (Irving 1936, Chapter 56).

As both sides had envisioned, the marriage further codified the relationship between Comcomly and the Astorians, at least for a time.

"From that time forward," Irving says, "Comcomly was a daily visitor at the fort, and was admitted into the most intimate councils of his son-in-law. He took an interest in everything that was going forward, but was particularly frequent in his visits to the blacksmith's shop; tasking the labors of the artificer in iron for every state, insomuch that the necessary business of the factory was often postponed to attend to his requisitions" (Irving 1936, Chapter 56).

Comcomly enjoyed his own quarters in the fort, which he frequently occupied in warmth and comfort while most of his entourage was left to shiver in the rain and gales outside the stockade. The business and personal relationship was amenable to both Comcomly and the Astorians.

> @ *Comcomly enjoyed his own quarters in the fort, which he frequently occupied in warmth and comfort while most of his entourage was left to shiver in the rain and gales outside the stockade.* ⑤

Astor's people who arrived after the first contingent found Comcomly and his people considerably less attractive as associates. When the supply ship *Beaver* arrived to restock the fort in May 1812, Astorians and Chinooks alike, notified of its approach, turned out in greeting.

Historian Charles Carey writes: "The ship was met at the bar by these representatives of the company, in a barge with eight rowers, preceded by old Chief Concomly [a once commonly used spelling] in a canoe with six Indians, whom [arriving clerk Ross] Cox describes as 'the most repulsive looking beings that ever disgraced the fair form of humanity'" (Carey 1971, 206).

Cox's description, so different from earlier descriptions of Comcomly's people, may reflect the depredations of smallpox and other devastating diseases brought by the crews of trading ships, diseases to which the native population had little or no immunity. Despite the negative first appraisal, the Astorians continued their profitable relations with Comcomly and company until 1813, when a roadblock of a different stripe arose.

Word that the United States and Britain were at war arrived simultaneously with a contingent of traders from the Canada-based, British-affiliated North West Company, dispatched to set up operations at the mouth of the Columbia. The Astorians were understandably concerned. After learning that a British warship was on its way to overtake Fort Astoria by force if necessary, they hastily sold out to the Nor'Westers, as the interlopers from Canada were called.

Comcomly volunteered to help son-in-law McDougal send the Nor'Westers packing.

"See those few King George people who come down the river?" Comcomly said. "They were poor; they have no goods, and were almost starving; yet you were afraid of them, and delivered your fort and all your goods to them; and now King George's ships are coming to carry you all off as slaves. We are not afraid of King George's people. I have got eight hundred warriors, and we will not allow them to enslave you. The Americans are our friends and allies" (Ross 1849, quoted in Ruby and Brown, 148).

McDougal firmly advised Comcomly to hold off: the deal was done, and it was too late to fight it. As a reward for his loyalty, McDougal gave the chief some clothes.

Comcomly lost no time in switching allegiance. In October 1813, the British warship *Raccoon* sailed into the Columbia to reinforce the takeover of Fort Astoria, soon to be rechristened Fort George.

As historian David Peterson del Mar recounts, "Comcomly was soon on board the *Raccoon,* telling its captain that he was delighted to again see a British ship on the river. He departed with a British flag, coat, hat, and sword. The Chinook leader wore this new regalia to Fort Astoria the following day, and became, as a disgusted Astorian put it, 'as staunch a Briton as ever he had previously been an American partisan'" (Peterson del Mar 2003, 38).

Others followed his lead, primarily son-in-law McDougal, who stayed on to work as a Nor'Wester. After the pattern set by McDougal, other Comcomly daughters married Nor'Westers, helping to perpetuate Comcomly's influence.

But again, harmony did not always prevail between the new traders and the Chinook chief. Ruby and Brown write, for example, that "when Comcomly in late 1813 brought two sea otter skins to Fort George, the parties haggled vigorously over their value in trade. 'Mercenary brute,' 'troublesome beggar,' and 'niggardly fellow' were epithets Alexander Henry, a Nor'Wester partner, used for the chief. When McDougal accidentally broke one of the chief's dentalia [shells natives used as money], not even the son-in-law's gift of forty grains of large china beads could satisfy the chaffering chief" (Ruby and Brown 1976, 152).

Comcomly also became increasingly concerned about his people's use of alcohol. "The arrival of the *Raccoon* had occasioned the consumption of more spirits than had been consumed at the takeover ceremonies at the fort. Aboard the ship there had been an extended period of conviviality with considerable quantities of wine and grog consumed by all" (Ruby and Brown 1976, 152), including, presumably, the natives.

On one occasion, one of Comcomly's sons visited the fort, overindulged in rum, and returned home drunk, much to the amusement of the chief's household, especially the slaves, and the displeasure of the chief. "The angry father, his pride injured, wasted little time or words in reprimanding those who had sold his son the head-befuddling commodity" (Ruby and Brown 1976, 152).

Another time, a son visiting the fort with his father got so drunk he could neither walk nor talk straight and staggered around foaming at the mouth. Comcomly concluded he had gone crazy and declared, "Let him be shot!" (Ruby and Brown 1976, 152). The chief relented and was relieved when the young man sobered up.

The chief endured still other indignities. In January 1814, the Nor'Westers ordered Comcomly to dispose of a slave girl dead from venereal disease, probably inflicted by one of their company. "The natives disposed of the corpse by tying a cord around its neck and dragging it to the beach," say Ruby and Brown, "where with a wooden paddle they squeezed it into a hole, covering it with stones and dirt" (Ruby and Brown 1976, 155).

Then there was the laughable interlude provided by Jane Barnes, the first white woman in the Pacific Northwest.

Barnes arrived April 22, 1814, on the supply ship *Isaac Todd* and the arm of Donald McTavish, a retired Nor'Wester who had been reactivated to take charge of the company's Columbia Department. McTavish, stocking up for the long and tedious voyage to Fort George, came across Barnes in a Portsmouth, or maybe Plymouth, England, public house, where she was in service. He regarded her kindly, and she agreed to go along for the ride.

"Jane was a handsome strumpet," says regional storyteller Stewart Holbrook. "She dressed to kill in more ways than one. After a riotous few weeks, during which she seems to have dropped McTavish in favor of Nor'Wester clerk Alexander Henry, . . . both McTavish and Henry, while better or worse from drink, were drowned, along with five other men, almost in front of Fort George" (Holbrook 1956, 58).

> *"Jane was a handsome strumpet," says regional storyteller Stewart Holbrook. "She dressed to kill in more ways than one."*

That may or may not be the way the McTavish–Henry handoff happened. Other accounts have McTavish happily making Henry a gift of Barnes. In any case, the accident left her, the first white woman ever to grace these parts, up for grabs. Among those who sought to win her was Cassakas, the highest ranking of Comcomly's sons.

"[Cassakas] appeared one day at the fort, in full courting array, his features decorated with red paint and his body shining with whale oil," writes historian Kenneth W. Porter.

His truly princely offer was that "if she would become his wife, he would send 100 sea otters to her relations; that he would never ask her to carry wood, draw water, dig for roots or hunt for provisions; that he would make her mistress over his other wives (four in number), and permit her to sit at her ease from morning to night." He would allow her to wear her own clothing, rather than insist on her adopting the scanty bark garments of the Indian women, and "she should always have abundance of fat salmon, anchovies and elk, and be allowed to smoke as many pipes of tobacco during the day as she thought proper" (Porter 1930, 329).

Barnes declined not once but several times. Her offended suitor departed in extreme dudgeon, vowing "he would never more come near the fort while she remained there" (Porter 1930, 329).

He had but a short wait. From the start, Barnes was thoroughly put off by Fort Astoria, if not by the constant male attention. Further, the new Nor'Wester managers were eager to be rid of her and her distracting charms. They put her aboard the next ship to the Far East, and fare prepaid, she was off more or less in the direction of home.

※ ※ ※

The takeover by the North West Company also brought more serious issues for Comcomly and his business. The Nor'Westers were not content to go through the chief and began trading directly with tribes far up the Columbia at Fort Nez Perce, at the mouth of the Walla Walla River, and beyond. This brought far-flung tribal members to Fort George, which produced conflict and some-times bloodshed with the Chinooks. Comcomly's people resented the presence of long-standing enemies on their turf, except as slaves.

The Nor'Westers meanwhile faced tribulation on two fronts. Northwest tribes were increasingly hostile toward the company's fur-trapping brigades—white trappers in general as well as members of the Iroquois nation imported to poach on Chinook territory. In addition, the Nor'Westers and rival Hudson's Bay Company engaged in often bloody conflict over who would prevail in the fur-rich regions of the continent stretching from western Canada to the Northwest U.S. That conflict was resolved with the 1821 merger of the two companies, after which the North West Company faded into history. Hudson's Bay was now the law, and Comcomly entered a period that saw his decline and ultimate demise.

In 1824, George Simpson, the Hudson's Bay Company's governor for the Pacific Region, arrived at Fort George with his newly appointed chief factor, the redoubtable Dr. John McLoughlin. Simpson took a look around and came to two conclusions.

He saw the fort as "a large pile of buildings covering about an acre of ground well stockaded and protected by Bastions or Block houses, having two Eighteen Pounders mounted in front and altogether an air or appearance of Grandeur & consequence which does not become and is not at all suitable to an Indian Trading Post" (Simpson 1824–1825, quoted in Ruby and Brown, 167).

As for Comcomly and the Chinooks, Simpson said, "They never take the trouble of hunting and rarely employ their Slaves in that way, they are however keen traders and through their hands nearly the whole of our Furs pass, indeed so tenacious are they of this Monopoly that their jealousy would carry them the length of pillaging or even murdering strangers who come to the Establishment if we did not protect them" (Simpson 1824–1825, quoted in Ruby and Brown, 167).

Simpson and McLoughlin decided to remedy both problems by moving the operation ninety-odd miles upriver to a spot on the north bank of the Columbia that Lt. William Broughton a few years earlier had designated Belle Vue Point. On March 19, 1825, Simpson cracked a bottle of liquor on a newly installed flagpole and rechristened the spot Fort Vancouver. McLoughlin would reign over the fort, and the entire region, for the next twenty-one years.

The move delivered a crushing blow to Comcomly's empire as well as to his ego. It effectively ended his lucrative monopoly as middleman at the mouth of the Columbia. Simpson reported the chief so shaken by the decision that he "actually shed Tears when I shook hands with him at the Water side" (Morrison 1998, 137).

As it markedly diminished Comcomly's prestige, the move added greatly to that of a rival, Casino, a powerful chief with headquarters at the confluence of the Columbia and Willamette Rivers. "It must have angered the chief that after a decade and a half of pampering by white traders at Fort George, his position had passed upriver to Casino, who now had a trading post in his own front yard" (Ruby and Brown 1976, 179).

Comcomly searched diligently for ways to stay in McLoughlin's good graces and maintain his eminent position. He found the answer in piloting the ships that increasingly brought supplies and trade goods across the Columbia bar and upriver to the fort. As he had done with the Astorians and the Nor'Westers, the chief met each vessel at the river's mouth and guided it to its destination.

"His knowledge of the river channels, currents and sandbanks was so great that the Company made him its chief pilot—the first on the Columbia," says historian A. G. Harvey. "When a ship came in sight he had twenty of his slaves launch the royal canoe and take him out to the ship, which he would pilot up the river to Astoria" (Harvey 1939, 162).

"Sickness—probably malaria—spread with such deadly rapidity that whole villages were swept away, leaving the houses empty and the dead bodies strewn along the beach, while the air was rent with the howls of famished dogs."

Comcomly's skills as a pilot earned him the respect of both McLoughlin and Hudson's Bay ships' captains, not to mention the wherewithal to sustain his royal station. It is reported that at least one arrival at Fort Vancouver involved a retinue of three hundred slaves who disembarked before him to prepare his way by laying a path of furs to McLoughlin's doorstep, where he was entertained with the best the fort had to offer.

In 1830, an outbreak of what was variously described as "cold sick" or "intermittent fever"—probably malaria—swept the region, laying waste to the native population. "It spread with such deadly rapidity that whole villages were swept away, leaving the houses empty and the dead bodies strewn along the beach, while the air was rent with the howls of famished dogs," writes Harvey (1939, 162).

Its most illustrious victim was Comcomly, age sixty-five or sixty-six. "Pursuant to Indian custom his body was placed in a canoe raised on a platform at the family burial plot near Point Ellice, surrounded by his weapons, war and

Chinook Chief Comcomly's tomb, showing a box, not a canoe, held on
carved or painted posts. Wood engraving by Joseph Drayton from an 1841 drawing
by A. T. Agate, published in the fourth volume of Charles Wilkes' *Narrative of the
United States Exploring Expedition* (6 vols., 1844–1845), p. 321. CCHS 096.074.007.

ceremonial dresses and other possessions" (Harvey 1939, 162–163, citing W. S.
Lewis and N. Murakami, eds., *Ranald McDonald,* 1923, 74–78).

That in all reasonableness should have ended the saga of Comcomly, one of
the Northwest's greatest native leaders. But another chapter was yet to come, a
Gothic-tinged tale worthy of Edgar Allen Poe.

The year was 1835, five years after Comcomly was laid to rest. A young
Scotsman named Dr. Meredith Gairdner was toiling away for Dr. John
McLoughlin at Fort Vancouver. In addition to being a capable physician,
Gairdner was a naturalist of considerable ambition and ability. He had signed
on with Hudson's Bay "with the understanding that he would have time and
facilities for nature study," according to Harvey (1939, 163).

A Chinook cradle used for head-flattening. From *A History of Oregon*
by Robert Carlton Clark, Robert H. Down, and George V. Blue, Chicago and New York:
Row, Peterson and Company, 1926, p. 17. PENNER COLLECTION, CCHS.

McLoughlin had other ideas. The Hudson's Bay taskmaster insisted that business came first. Not only did he have Gairdner tending the fort's sick and lame, but he put the young man to work as a trader. Gairdner complained bitterly.

Perhaps as a result of his labors, Gairdner contracted tuberculosis. Restorative measures failed, and he decided to seek relief in Hawaii. Before he left, he resolved to do something extraordinary for the sake of science.

To understand Gairnder's decision, it is necessary to note the nineteenth century's fascination with craniometry, the measurement of skulls. Indians, considered inferior to whites, were thought to have a smaller brain capacity. Gairdner thought the Chinook and Clatsop Indians, with their flattened foreheads, would be interesting specimens to study.

He knew the location of the old chief's burial plot near Astoria. According to Harvey, "he also knew of the Indians' deep regard for their ancestors, evidenced by regular visits to their graves to see that their remains and property were undisturbed. . . . Desecration of . . . burial places was not uncommon, but offenders risked their very lives" (Harvey 1939, 164). Indeed, the Chinooks were so concerned that Comcomly's grave might be plundered that they removed his remains and buried them in a secret location.

Gairdner was not deterred. He somehow discovered the whereabouts of Comcomly's body. One dark night, he stole to the grave and began to dig.

Harvey describes the grisly scene:

> After great exertion, he reached a long box which served as a coffin,
> opened it, and found the body pretty much of a skeleton. The head
> was in good condition, the skin quite dry and the hair still on. The
> shape of the forehead, narrow and sloping back sharply, intrigued
> him. What a study in phrenology! Apparently Concomly's parents had
> done a good job of compressing his forehead when he was an infant,
> according to Chinook Indian custom. Was that then responsible for
> his genius? And were the Indians right in thinking that the flattening
> of the head signified superiority, in comparison with the round heads
> of the slaves, to whom the deformity was forbidden? Interesting
> questions these. The body must be decapitated and the head sent
> where scientists could study it at leisure.
>
> And decapitated it was, after much exertion. It was a bloodless
> affair as far as Concomly was concerned, but was not so much with
> Gairdner. The exertion brought on a severe hemorrhage, so that the
> ground was spattered not with stale, watery blood from Concomly's
> body as Gairdner had expected, but with fresh red life-blood from his
> own lungs. Nevertheless he managed to complete his gruesome job
> and got away with the head without being caught (Harvey 1939, 165).

Gairdner packed the head in a box he had brought along for the purpose
and hastened to Hawaii, where tuberculosis took its toll and he died in 1836. But
not before he had shipped the head to a good friend, fellow Scottish physician
and naturalist Dr. John Richardson, who had twice accompanied Captain John
Franklin in exploring the Arctic and was about to become chief medical officer
at the Royal Naval Hospital near Portsmouth.

"The head arrived in good condition except that the facial features were
greatly disfigured and pressed to one side," Harvey reports (1939, 165). "The
skin was so hard that a very sharp knife was required to cut it." After a few
months, however, "the moisture in the head became so offensive in odor that
notwithstanding a liberal application of corrosive sublimate it was found necessary to macerate it and remove the flesh and brain" (Harvey 1939, 165). Having

Burnby Bell with the repatriated skull of Chinook chief Comcomly,
March 1, 1953. CCHS History Scrapbook.

thus reduced the head to the basic skull, Richardson donated it to the hospital museum, where it was put on display.

With the head had come a letter from Gairdner. The original was lost, but in 1938, a copy was found, "screwed up and tucked away inside the skull, where it had been hidden for a hundred years," as Harvey notes (1939, 166). Gairdner wrote, in part: "You may have heard of this character for he is mentioned in most of the narratives relating to the Columbia. By his ability? cunning? or what you please to call it, he raised himself & family to a power & influence no Indian has since possessed in the district of the Columbia. . . . When the phrenologists look at this frontal development what will they say to this?"

If any phrenologists examined the skull, their conclusions are unknown. The artifact lay scarcely noticed in the Royal Naval Hospital's museum.

During World War II, a German bomb attack on the hospital complex blew Comcomly's lower jawbone to bits. In the interim between Gairdner and the Nazis, members of the Chinook Tribe and local historians lost track of the skull.

In 1952, Burnby Bell of the Clatsop County Historical Society came across Harvey's 1939 article in the *Oregon Historical Quarterly* about the skull's repose in the British Naval Museum. He wrote to museum officials asking if the skull might be sent home. The hospital's director, Rear Admiral J. H. Hamilton, replied in the affirmative.

The skull, what was left of it, arrived in Astoria in December 1953 and was put on display in the Flavel House Museum. In spring 1956, it was sent to the Smithsonian Institution in Washington, D.C., for brief study. Soon afterward, it was returned to the Astoria museum.

Comcomly's descendants requested that the skull be turned over to them for proper burial. In 1973, the Clatsop County Historical Society handed it over

Left: Marie Rondeau, granddaughter of Chinook Chief Comcomly and daughter of Margaret and Louis Rondeau, ca. 1898. Courtesy of Carolyn Shepherd. Right: Lucy Agnes Ducheney Elliott, born in 1852, the daughter of Rocque Ducheney and his wife Marie Rondeau. She was the great-granddaughter of Comcomly. Courtesy of Carolyn Shepherd.

Members of the Henry family ca. 1910—descendants of Comcomly
through his great-great-granddaughter Louise Elliott, who married Chris K. Henry.

COURTESY OF CAROLYN SHEPHERD.

to the Chinook Indian Tribe, which interred it beneath a handsome monument in Ilwaco, Washington. As Harvey concluded in 1939, "this is not the place to argue the right or wrong of his [Gairnder's] action: strange things have been and still are done in the cause of science" (Harvey 1939, 167).

❧ ❧ ❧

The concluding verse from a Umatilla song about the death of a young chief (quoted in Thomas 1935, 46) seems a fitting benediction to Comcomly, a great Chinook leader. Originally in Chinook Jargon, the song was translated by Hezekiah Butterworth. "Tamala" is the Chinook word for "tomorrow."

Forever and ever horizons are lifting—

Tamala, tamala, sing as we row;

    And life toward the stars of the ocean is drifting,

Through death will the morrow all endlessly glow—

    Tamala! Tamala!

    Ever and ever;

The morrows will come and the morrows will go.

    Tamala! Tamala!

Works Cited

Ambrose, Stephen E. 1996. *Undaunted Courage: Meriwether Lewis, Thomas Jefferson and the Opening of the American West.* New York: Simon and Schuster.

Boit, John. 1921. *A New Log of the Columbia, 1790–1792.* Seattle: University of Washington Press.

Carey, Charles H. 1971. *General History of Oregon.* Portland, OR: Binford & Mort.

Cook, Warren L. 1973. *Flood Tide of Empire: Spain and the Pacific Northwest, 1543–1819.* New Haven, CT: Yale University Press.

Corney, Peter. 1896. *Early Voyages in the North Pacific, 1813–1818.* Honolulu: Thomas G. Thrum. Reprinted in 1965 by Ye Galleon Press of Fairfield, WA.

Drucker, Phillip. 1965. *Cultures of the North Pacific Coast.* San Francisco: Chandler Publishing Company.

Edwards, Margaret Watt, ed. 1973. *Land of the Multnomahs: Sketches and Stories of Early Oregon.* Portland, OR: Binford & Mort.

Harvey, A. G. 1939. Chief Comcomly's Skull. *Oregon Historical Quarterly,* vol. 40, no. 2 (June).

Holbrook, Stewart. 1956. *The Columbia.* New York: Rinehart.

Irving, Washington. 1836. *Astoria; or, Anecdotes of an Enterprise Beyond the Rocky Mountains.* Various editions.

Jerzyk, Anna. 1940. Winship Settlement in 1810 Was Oregon's Jamestown. *Oregon Historical Quarterly,* vol. 41, no. 2 (June).

Johansen, Dorothy O. 1967. *Empire of the Columbia,* 2nd ed. New York: Harper & Row.

Morrison, Dorothy Nafus. 1998. *Outpost: John McLoughlin and the Far Northwest.* Portland, OR: Oregon Historical Society Press.

Myers, John. 1817. *The Life, Voyages and Travel of Capt. John Myers, Detailing His Adventures during Four Voyages Round the World: 1810–1813.* London. Various editions. (Note: This account was later debunked by at least one authority as "absolutely unreliable.")

Peterson del Mar, David. 2003. *Oregon's Promise: An Interpretive History.* Corvallis: Oregon State University Press.

Porter, Kenneth W. 1930. Jane Barnes, First White Woman in Oregon. *Oregon Historical Quarterly,* vol. 31, no. 2 (June).

Ross, Alexander. 1849. *Adventures of the First Settlers on the Oregon or Columbia River.* London. Various editions.

Ruby, Robert H., and John A. Brown. 1976. *The Chinook Indians.* Norman, OK: University of Oklahoma Press.

Santee, J. F. 1932. Comcomly and the Chinooks. *Oregon Historical Quarterly,* vol. 33, no. 3 (September).

Simpson, Sir George. 1824–1825. *Journals.* Various editions.

Thomas, Edward Harper. 1969. *Chinook: A History and Dictionary,* 2nd ed. Portland, OR: Binford & Mort.

Wilkes, Charles. 1844. *Narrative of the United States Exploring Expedition,* vol. 4. Philadelphia: C. Sherman.

John Jacob Astor I

"A Most Excellent Man"?

By Robert Michael Pyle

Anorth wind carried my cap out into the river as I walked the shoreline
toward the bridge. Little beaches of polished pebbles broke the tideline
between washed rocks and waterlogged wood. Ring-billed gulls and dark geese,
in singletons and pairs, worked the baylets out of the worst of the wind. An
enormous green bridge loomed overhead, spanning the expanse of cold, gray
water and whirring with morning traffic heading in and out of Astoria. So far,
so familiar. I tugged my collar higher and swiveled back into March's harsh
breath, scanning the opposite shoreline. What met my watering eyes was not
the Willapa Hills of Washington State, but the brown jumbled skyline of Harlem

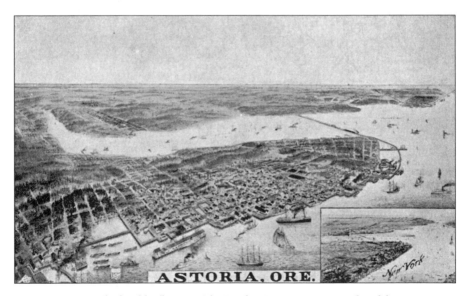

From the booklet "Astoria: The Peerless Maritime Metropolis of the
Golden Northwest" by P. Donan, ca. 1895. The Matthews-Northrup Co.
Complete Art Printing Works, Buffalo, New York. CCHS COLLECTION.

GREATER ASTORIA

COME TO THE FUTURE NEW YORK OF THE PACIFIC — WITH JACKSON

COLUMBIA HARBOR

THIS PICTURE SHOWS CONDITIONS AS PREDICTED THEY WILL BE

The Future New York of the Pacific

Astoria, the Columbia River gateway seaport, is the nearest and most economic route to the Pacific, the Orient, South America and Europe.

The future of Astoria, unless the law of gravity ceases to govern the forces of the earth, and it be cheaper to send commerce up hill than down, · · · the largest city on the Pacific Coast will ultimately be right here at the mouth of this mighty river of the West. · · ·

GOD'S HIGHWAY TO THE SEA

The future Astoria metropolis, as envisioned in 1928 by W. M. Jackson's
Columbia Harbor Development Company of Portland, Oregon.
Courtesy of Astoria Public Library. CCHS Collection.

housing projects. Far to the south, I made out not Cape Disappointment, but the pointy stump of the Empire State building. A second, graceful old bridge paralleled the first, just upstream. The pebbles were broken glass—blue, green, brown, and milky—rounded by the decades. And the geese? Atlantic brant.

I was in Astoria, all right—Astoria, Queens. Having been in New York for a lecture and research for this essay, I was about to fly home from nearby LaGuardia airport. The most intimate of the three main air terminals serving Manhattan and greater New York City, Fiorello LaGuardia International Airport sits between greater Long Island and Astoria. I wanted to glimpse a fleeting expression on the face of this town that shares its name with Oregon's oldest city. By spending my last night in a marginal airport motel I had just enough time before my flight. After a fine green pepper and onion omelet at the Airport Diner, I caught the Q19 bus opposite immense St. Michael's Cemetery and rode it along Astoria Boulevard to Astoria Park. There, sweet gums and sere grass lined the shoreline between the Triborough Bridge and smaller, trains-only Hell Gate Bridge, a span of purple iron arches and white limestone pillars named for a once-treacherous channel of the East River.

Interpretive signs along the promenade recounted tragedy in these waters. On June 15, 1904, the steamship *General Slocum* caught fire and foundered in the strong, confused current. Some 1,300 people were aboard, mostly German immigrants on their way to the Locust Grove Picnic Garden at Eatons Neck, thirty miles northeast on Long Island Sound. Many leapt into the roil, but the cork in their shoddy life vests had turned to dust, and an estimated 1,021 lives were lost—the highest death toll of any New York disaster prior to September 11, 2001. Now there were only squirrels and the hardy river birds to be seen, along with a pair of passing tugboats with big white "M"s on their black stacks.

Leaving the waterfront, I wended back through the edge of downtown Astoria. Away from the river, the similarity between this scene and its Pacific counterpart diminished. A white onion-dome topped a triangular brick building with a Chinese kitchen on its ground floor. Nearby, a famous Czech beer garden awaited summer's steamy evenings. The visual jumble of vibrant streets crowded with many small shops let me know for sure I was in an old ethnic East Coast community—largely Greek overlaid with Slavic and Asian. No surprise was the abundance of familiar Victoriana here or back home, considering that both Astorias shared much of the nineteenth century. But smells, sounds, and cultural clutter foreign to my Northwest Astoria overtook any superficial resemblance.

> *The New York suburb was named in 1836, while the West Coast fur fort that spawned Astoria, Oregon, was established in 1811.*

Not that Astoria, Queens, is any older than Astoria, Oregon. The New York suburb was named in 1836, while the West Coast fur fort that spawned Astoria, Oregon, was established in 1811. But the former, platted on old Dutch and English farms and subject to more diverse influences, developed much faster than the latter, grafted precariously into the wilderness. After all, the eastern Astoria lay just a river's-width away from the young country's major metropolis, while its western namesake was hung out to soak in the rain a continent apart from all the action. This one arose where a German immigrant, more fortunate than those aboard the *General Slocum*, set up a ferry service across the East River to the Queens side on the steamship *Pluto of Wallet's Cove*. It was here, too, at the narrows called Hell Gate, where that immigrant-made-good established his country retreat, and where his houseguest and hired scribe, Washington Irving, wrote *Astoria*—the chronicle not of Astoria, Queens, but of Astoria, Oregon.

The commonality that struck me that chilly morning transcends the Victorian facades and the vague likeness of all big rivers with bridges near estuaries. Though three thousand miles apart, the two Astorias carry the same man's name, and both owe their existence to his extraordinary reach, vision, mercantile zeal, commercial acumen, and sheer cupidity. Yet something greater than a mere continent's width sets these two cities' tales apart. While the early development of Hell Gate was inevitable, given its position near the hub of human affairs in America, no such certainty lay at the mouth of the Columbia. That distant reach could well have escaped white settlement for decades to come. As things went, it was a close call for the first city in the new Northwest. Had Astor's master plan gone just a little more wildly awry than it did, there might be no West Coast Astoria at all.

John Jacob Astor I, unlike his descendants, was not born to wealth. He came forth on July 17, 1763, in Walldorf, at the edge of the Black Forest in Baden, then one of hundreds of German city-states. His father, Johann Jakob Astor, descended of Italian Protestants, was town butcher; his mother, Maria Magdalena Volfelder, gave birth to four surviving sons and a daughter. The last son, also christened Johann Jakob, proved a quick study, good with numbers and manual skills, but also a reader. He soon learned the butcher's trade, adeptly and with neither complaint nor affection. Brothers Georg and Heinrich both emigrated and anglicized their names. George worked for an uncle making musical instruments in London, while Henry sailed to New York, where he set up his own butcher's business. Johann envied them, but his father needed him in the Walldorf butcher shop, so he remained there, cutting and selling meat.

John Jacob Astor. Engraving published in 1864 by Johnson,
Fry & Co., New York, based on a painting by Alonzo Chappel.
The painter copied the early likeness by permission from an original
painting in the possession of the family. CCHS 4981.00A.

But Johann Jr. had acquired admirers and advocates in a local schoolmaster
and pastor. They finally prevailed upon the elder Astor to allow his youngest
son to join George in England. There Johann, now John Jacob, learned flute-
making and selling at Astor & Broadwood, and in 1778 the new firm of George

and John Astor opened (Madsen 2001). But it wasn't long until he wanted to see if brother Henry was making out as well as he boasted in America. With a load of flutes in his trunk, he sailed west in November 1783; and after a sixty-six-day crossing and an ice-bound delay on Chesapeake Bay, he landed in Baltimore in late March of 1784. Three weeks later, having consigned and sold some flutes, he caught a coach for New York with his first American-made cash in his pocket.

It didn't take long in the hurly-burly of New York for John to realize that he didn't want to be a butcher there any more than at home, so he turned down his brother's offer of a job and went to work for a baker. His next job was moth-beater for a furrier called Quaker Browne. Thus began John Jacob's lifelong infatuation with fur. He also took out newspaper ads for his instruments, and found that he could sell them at a suitable gain. He invested his first intoxicating profits in more flutes from his brother George and in skins for which he bargained on the docks. In many ways, his course was set then and there.

Only a year and a half after arriving in New York, John Jacob returned to London to sell his first consignment of furs, re-stock with Henry's musical instruments, and acquire a franchise to import English pianos. Transatlantic trade proved still more intoxicating. In spring 1786, he established his own music shop. His horizon was expanding. John Jacob was never a dreamer in the artistic sense, but he was ambitious from the start. What dreams he entertained settled on business, and how business could grow, when conducted with vigor and aggressive imagination. There was money to be made in this new land. And then there was Sarah.

Sarah Todd was the daughter of Astor's landlady. When they married on September 19, 1785, he acquired an excellent business partner, friend, and mother to his children. She would bear him Magdalen, John Jacob II, William Backhouse, Dorothea, Henry, Eliza, and another son and daughter who did not survive. The couple set up housekeeping comfortably if simply in lodgings at the rear of Mrs. Todd's house, where the music store occupied the front. Then Astor booked passage on the Hudson River, in pursuit of pelts in the near north. The newlyweds plunged into the business, and as Terrell (1963, 60) put it, "furs overflowed into the woodshed and the Todd stable, and the general odor was not that of a florist's shop."

Portrait of John Jacob Astor, oil on canvas, by Gilbert Stuart, ca. 1794.

IMAGE CH198757, CHRISTIE'S IMAGES, THE BRIDGEMAN ART LIBRARY INTERNATIONAL.

To learn more about this lucrative frontier traffic then known as "peltries," and how they might be made to work for him, Astor traveled farther afield to the St. Lawrence River and west to Montreal. He befriended French and English agents and investigated the modi operandi of the rival North West and Hudson's Bay Fur Companies. Occasionally, to ingratiate himself with Indians and the ditty-loving French Canadians, he would take out a flute in village or frontier saloon. He took bales of beaver, martin, mink, and other skins back downriver, sold them for the London trade, and invested the return in his adopted city. He recognized that his greatest opportunity lay in furs, where profits might easily exceed 900 percent (Terrell 1963). Astor's plans grew with his experience. Even though the fur trade in the East and the "Old Northwest" was already spoken for, and the furbearers diminishing in those regions, it was a big country, and the sky was the limit for anyone who would push harder, farther.

The fur business vied with real estate for Astor's attention. Beginning modestly with a few small subleases and lots, he adopted a conservative and secure investment posture of letting others assume most of the risk. Instead of building on land he controlled, or owning buildings outright, he invested in vacant land or made long-term leases on properties he would then sublease. This way all capital investment, repairs and maintenance, and other responsibilities lay with the lessees; if they defaulted on payments, he could foreclose on their remaining lease, which he would then re-lease. Essentially, he was a rent-collector—and not for mansions: much of the Astor estate was covered with immigrant tenements, often of the rudest and most squalid sort.

Much of this I learned before my excursion to Astoria, Queens, when I spent a couple of days in the Astor archives at the New York Historical Society. The massive, neoclassical edifice squats just across Seventy-Ninth Street from the American Museum of Natural History, both fronting Central Park West. According to the library's summary, the contents of the ninety-five volumes and seven boxes are "primarily concerned with the family's vast interests in New York City real estate."

And so they were. Astor's rent rolls showed one hundred and seventy-four leases and tenants in November 1826; another seventy in May 1831; and thence upward. Everything he touched turned to mortgages, which he often and ruthlessly called in. His "biggest real estate killing" (Madsen 2001, 246) was worked out with Aaron Burr, back from exile after shooting Alexander Hamilton in a duel, acting as Astor's attorney. He gained control of fifty-one thousand acres, or nearly eighty square miles of farmland—nearly one-third of Putnam County—which had been confiscated during the Revolutionary War. Astor bought the rights for $100,000. Then, threatening eviction of seven hundred farmers, he relinquished the land to the state for more than half a million dollars in stock producing a $26,000 annuity for life. The maps of "Property in the City and County of New York Belonging to John Jacob Astor" as of April 1836 resemble a well-filled Monopoly board. In his decline, Astor is famously reported to have confided to an associate, "Could I begin life again, knowing what I now know, and had money to invest, I would buy every foot of land on the Island of Manhattan" (Wilson 1993, 77).

Before I came to live on the fringes of what once was Astor's far-flung empire, I had the common impression that his patrician name was a synonym for vast wealth and power, like Vanderbilt and Rockefeller. During earlier visits to Manhattan, the nearest I'd come to the name was the Waldorf-Astoria Hotel. In the spring of 1975, I attended the annual Explorers' Club banquet in the great room of the famous midtown inn, as the guest of a prominent lepidopterist friend. Roger Tory Peterson spoke at the banquet about his travels in Antarctica, along with an astronaut and a deep-sea diver. The dishes served were as zoologically varied as Astor's peltry pricelists. Cigar smoke filled the air, and the only women present, elaborately gowned, were guests and spouses, since the membership at that time was still all male.

Since that long-ago banquet, I have crossed the doormat of the Waldorf-Astoria only once. After an afternoon's work in the Nabokov archive at the New York Public Library (which arose, as it happens, out of the original Astor Library), I'd dropped into the hotel's oaky bar, still smoky, as this was before the New York ban. I ordered a beer, which came with a bill so bloated that it would have scandalized the exceedingly thrifty Astor, even adjusted for 1836 prices. But as I would later learn, the hotel has nothing to do with John Jacob Astor I, except that its thousand-room tower arose on a site his progeny had acquired at the corner of Thirty-Third Street and Fifth Avenue and bears the name of his village and his great-grandson William Waldorf, aka Willie, the first Viscount Astor, who built it in 1897 with his cousin John Jacob IV, aka Colonel Jack, who perished on the *Titanic*. It was sold out of the family altogether for $15 million, a hundred years after William Backhouse Astor had bought the site for an inflated $25,000. But in 1834 John Jacob had built the grand Manhattan hotel of its time, the Astor House, where the likes of Davy Crockett stayed when he was in town. The Astor House was the forerunner of the Waldorf-Astoria. And insofar as the Waldorf stands for an earlier era of

> *I ordered a beer, which came with a bill so bloated that it would have scandalized the exceedingly thrifty Astor.*

affluence and extravagance, it serves well as a symbol for Astor's impact on the New York skyline, and his position at its financial zenith.

The New York Historical Society's elegant reading room is less grand than that of the New York Public Library, less intimate than the leathery chamber of the Explorers' Club library, yet like both of those, it houses many a tale of heart-thumping peril and discovery. Sometimes, rather than bound in buckram editions with beguiling titles, these stories are to be found in manuscript memoirs, letters, and interviews. In the Astor papers the exciting bits are buried between the lines and figures of staid ledgers and terse letterbooks. Not much of the man himself is to be found, at least not obviously so. Astor destroyed most of his own personal papers. But just before closing time, I unwrapped an extraordinary artifact that the librarians had brought me. Dated February 16, 1838, it was the deed for property at 471 Houston Street. Written in elaborate script on a sheet of actual vellum, twenty-two inches by thirty, bearing red wax seals and a yellow ribbon, the document was signed by William Backhouse Astor, John Ward, Daniel Lord, and—finally—John Jacob Astor. This was the only manuscript signature of his that I found in the entire archive.

Property, its acquisition, speculation, management, and increase, marked the onset of Astor's millions and insured their continuation for generations to come. But real estate never fired Astor's imagination as much as furs. The peltries of the North and the West were redolent of frontier adventure. And though he was stolid and thoroughly bourgeois in his habits, Astor was not immune to the romance of the wild, at least in the abstract. He tasted it in person when he traveled to the far shores of Lake Superior, and he continued to savor it, if only vicariously. Perhaps more to the point, the potential trade in western pelage represented a vast and virgin opportunity for making money, and lots of it, which he could never resist. So while his land-office business continued to bring in the bulk of the cash, his ventures in the skin trade grew to occupy at least as much of Astor's time and enthusiasm.

His passion for pelts, like the buildings he controlled, impressed itself on the New York scene. But with the piles of pelts, trading houses, and sailing ships long gone, you have to look deeper for its evidences today. Down in the subway, for example. Entering the West Side express subway line, I passed a long montage of natural history subjects emblazoned on the ceramic tiles of the tunnel wall. The panel included several furbearers. Then, a quick and thundering trip swept me downtown for a meeting with my agent. I smiled, given the focus of the past few days, as I re-read the address of her agency: Number 10, Astor Place. It seemed the man was following me all over town. It was, after all, his town—in large measure, literally so. And when I left the train at the Astor Street station, I was met by colonies of terra cotta beavers on the platform walls. What better emblem? As much as anything other than the ground itself, the Astor fortune was built on the backs of beavers, relieved of their pelts at the pleasure of profit.

Not that Astor had much in common with the trappers, traders, and agents whose brains and experience he picked. According to Axel Madsen (2001, 258), "Except when he had roamed the woods in upstate New York to exchange trinkets for beaver skins and canoed with the Northwesters to the end of Lake Superior, he never saw the misery among the Indians or the sweat his voyageurs put into their work."

At that time, the powerful North West Company, with four thousand employees in the field, controlled much of the fur trade in Upper Missouri, and would continue to do so for a third of a century. This private British powerhouse had a formidable competitor in the royally chartered Hudson's Bay Company, which took over in Canada after the French were unseated. In 1806, attempting to break into the cartel, a group of Montreal merchants formed the Mackinac Company at the neck between Lakes Michigan and Huron. In 1810, John Astor entered as a partner. The Canadian-American alliance, to be known as the Southwest Fur Company, hoped to push the trade beyond the Rockies. Astor was now well positioned to spread his fingers through the peltries of the continent.

If I needed a reminder of Astor's eventual reach among the furbearers, it came on a recent visit to Green Bay, Wisconsin. My lodging turned out to be the Astor House Bed & Breakfast, a restored mansion south of the city center. He really was following me around! I asked my host, Greg Robinson, about the name, and he gave me a copy of "Historic Astor," an anonymously written information sheet. "The Astor District," it reads, "which was placed on the National

Register of Historic Places in 1980, includes some of Green Bay's most elegant high style homes and interesting historic sites." Comprising twenty-five acres on the east bank of the Fox River, the historic district is the southern half of a township first platted as the Town of Astor in 1837 by John Jacob Astor, at the height of his American Fur Company. Later called "Astor Heights" or simply "The Hill," it remained "the prestige neighborhood in Green Bay." If there hadn't been two of them already, would Green Bay have become yet another Astoria, giving a certain football team an entirely different image? By any name, this trading hub on the river carried the Astor empire deep into the Old Northwest, the area that later would become Ohio, Indiana, Illinois, Michigan, Wisconsin, and part of Minnesota. So how did it come to the New Northwest?

Rivalries abounded among the big fur companies, especially the North West and Hudson's Bay, but also American outfits trapping and trading out of St. Louis, including the calculating Manuel Lisa's Missouri Fur Company and William Ashley's Rocky Mountain Fur Company. The easily accessible peltries were overexploited and jealously defended. If Astor was going to make inroads into the continent's fur supply, he would have to ply new territory. Thomas Jefferson's Louisiana Purchase opened the Mississippi, but jurisdiction was far from settled, and competition along the main stem was already thick. What about the western wilderness, even the Pacific? So in 1809, with several partners and a $400,000 investment, Astor established the Pacific Fur Company.

In 1809, with several partners and a $400,000 investment, Astor established the Pacific Fur Company.

For some years, a small number of trading vessels had visited the West Coast and trafficked with the Indians. Prominent among them were Captain Robert Gray, in 1792 the first to cross the Columbia River bar in a sailing vessel, and George Vancouver, whose ship went farther upriver but a critical few weeks later. Like Gray, a number of other Boston-based merchantmen sailed around South America, up the Pacific Coast, to trade manufactured goods for sea otter pelts. These they took to China to trade for silks, spices, and teas, convertible for profit back in Boston. By this route Gray became the first American to circumnavigate the globe.

Ten years later, by the time Astor was outfitting his nascent empire with ships and cargoes bound for Canton, the feat was almost commonplace. Astor found the China trade more profitable than the continental fur trade, and he wondered if the two might be combined. This idea gave rise to the concept of a great fur fort at the mouth of the Columbia. To grasp this fundamental point, visit the Astoria Column in Astoria, Oregon, and examine the historic friezes that grace its stucco walls. Lewis and Clark are there, of course, and Astor, and other characters including the local Indians who received them all. If you look closely, near the base, you'll see the artist's portrait of the town's real *raison d'être*: beavers. They may be the funniest beavers you'll ever see, giving no great confidence that the Italian artist ever saw the animal in person. But beavers they are, and in their quiet, long-suffering way, they say *fur*, and they signify John Jacob Astor's dream: to control the peltries of the Far West, linking his Manhattan, Great Lakes, and Asian interests into one great circle of commerce and gain.

So began the ultimately disastrous chain of events leading up to the founding of Astoria, Oregon. Astor decided that the surest way to set up his outpost, along with a series of trading posts that would eventually service it, was to dispatch a two-part expedition: one by land, the other by sea. The terrestrial half was entrusted to the command of Captain Wilson Price Hunt. Along with company partner Donald McKenzie, he left Montreal with thirty men on July 5, 1810. They met partner Ramsay Crooks at Michilimackinac on the northern tip of present-day Michigan, and with hard-won reinforcements, shoved off from St. Louis on October 21 in a motley flotilla of canoes and keelboats. The party included young clerks who aspired to future partnership, seasoned hunters and trappers, and French-Canadian voyageurs. Several returning mountain men joined them, and others improbably turned up along the way, such as Kit Carson, John Colter, and four Kentuckians including the storied John Day. Hunt took along as Indian interpreter Pierre Dorian because of his experience with the much-feared Sioux. Dorian, a surly and abusive half-caste, was fleeing a whiskey debt to his previous employer, Manuel Lisa. He was accompanied by his wife, victim of his occasional beatings in transit, and their two small children. The troupe's late start and slow progress upstream obliged it to pass the first winter along the Missouri River, which ensured hard trials for the months to come.

Meanwhile, the marine component embarked from Boston aboard the ship *Tonquin* on September 8, 1811, under the captaincy of Lieutenant Jonathan Thorn. Aside from the able seamen and swabs, the crew consisted of partners Alexander McKay, Duncan McDougal, David Stuart, and Stuart's son Robert, along with twelve clerks, artisans, and voyageurs. Astor judged that Thorn, an experienced ship's master on leave from the U.S. Navy, would be the right person to guide the expedition on its perilous voyage around Cape Horn and into the mouth of the Columbia. There the crew was to rendezvous with Hunt's overland party and establish the hub of the Northwest empire.

This choice proved one of the worst in a series of fatal miscalculations. Thorn was incorruptible and expert before the mast, but also inflexible and martial to a degree the civilian crew found intolerable. The first night out of port, Thorn tried to impose an early "lights out" upon the high-spirited partners and their company. This first spark of friction nearly led to mutiny. The crew wanted to stop for sight-seeing at Cape Verde, Easter Island, and Tierra del Fuego, and lingered ashore. This so infuriated the punctilious Thorn that he left some of the truants behind and flogged others.

> @ *Astor judged that Thorn would be the right person to guide the expedition. This choice proved one of the worst in a series of fatal miscalculations.* @

The *Tonquin* reached the Pacific and the islands of Owyhee (Hawaii), where it wintered, as was common among Spanish, Russian, and British traders in the Pacific (Irving 1836). Tamaahmaah (King Kameamea), who had solidified his rule among the islands and possessed a fleet of schooners, made the visitors welcome. They enjoyed the food, women, and warmth, and took souvenirs on a side trip to the spot where Captain Cook met his fate in more hostile times. Except for Thorn, the men were loath to leave the clement, sensual islands for unknown perils on the Northwest Coast. Had they known what lay ahead, I'll bet to a man they would have jumped ship at Waititi (Waikiki) on Woahoo (Oahu), where Tamaahmaah maintained his hospitable court.

As the *Tonquin* set sail for the Columbia, the overland outfit resumed its slow row up the Missouri. Manuel Lisa set out after them, tried to get Dorian back, excited McClellan's suspicion that he meant to scuttle the competition (there was already a grudge between them), and almost came to a duel with Hunt. But cooler heads persuaded the belligerents that the strength of their combined numbers might be necessary for getting past the powerful and intimidating Sioux. Hunt and Lisa managed to avoid a fight that would almost certainly have been fatal. Their detente persisted as the rival companies exchanged boats for horses, Lisa continuing north on the river while Hunt's party turned westerly to avoid the even scarier Blackfeet.

The next months proved thrilling as well as monotonous and rigorous. Thirst and hunger alternated with sated repose as they moved in and out of well-watered buffalo country. Bison still ranged by the many thousands, and the travelers encountered passenger pigeons yet in their incredible millions. Members were lost and found, various encounters with hostile Indians turned out okay, and John Day had a close call with a grizzly bear, but they got through the Bighorn Mountains and into the western drainages. Then they crossed the shoulder of the Grand Tetons on Hoback's River (its namesake, John Hoback, was along), before hitting the water again on Henry's Fork, named for Andrew Henry of the Missouri Company. Re-embarking thrilled the voyageurs, who on foot were ducks out of water. But the easy outset turned hazardous when they entered the Snake River. Hopes of a rapid arrival at the Columbia's mouth turned to gloom as Hunt's party suffered rapids, impassable waters, and Hell's Canyon, with loss of vessels, baggage, and life.

Back onboard the *Tonquin*, crossed now from Hawaii to Cape Disappointment, things went from paradisiacal to hellish to worse. The Columbia River bar was bad, yet Captain Thorn ordered First Mate Fox to take a whaleboat with eight voyageurs, inexperienced at sea, into the wild surf to seek the channel. Fox had premonitions and remonstrated with the captain. But Thorn insisted, and the boat was lost. The captain then ordered a second boat, with five aboard, to sound across the channel, and it too capsized in the furious breakers. Not many hours later the sea subsided, and the ship crossed the bar. Of the unlucky crews, only two men, armorer Stephen Weekes and one of a dozen Hawaiians they had brought along, were later found alive near Baker Bay.

ENTRANCE OF THE COLUMBIA RIVER.
Ship Tonquin, crossing the bar, 25th March, 1811.

From a lithograph by Nathaniel Currier entitled "Ship *Tonquin* Crossing
the Bar, 1811." Frontispiece of *Voyages to the South Sea, the Pacific Ocean
and the Northwest Coast* by Edmund Fanning, New York, 1938. Fanning
was the first owner and captain of the *Tonquin*. CCHS COLLECTION.

Spirits were very low, and the party depleted. They landed on what today
is the Washington side of the river. Thorn, now paranoid as well as intolerably
impatient, began immediately to throw up a shelter; when it was done and the
men and supplies offloaded, he'd be free to sail north to trade for sea otter at last.
But McDougal and David Stuart scouted the south shore, and found it better.
Returning, they met Comcomly, chief of the Chinooks, and made friendly contact. Attempting to cross Baker Bay to return to the *Tonquin*, they capsized, and
Comcomly fished them out.

Thorn deferred to McDougal and Stuart's site survey, and sent the launch
across with sixteen men to "commence the establishment" (Irving 1836). Had
the crew relented to his first impulse, Astoria today might lie in Pacific County,
Washington. But on April 12, 1811, "the party landed, and encamped at the
bottom of a small bay within Point George," a pleasant location near today's
Kustard King Drive-In. Hearing rumors of Indian hostility, feeling vulnerable in

their depleted company with eight men lost at sea, and still lacking word from Hunt's overland party, the men built a classic log-rampart fortified post, and mounted two eight-inch cannons for its defense. Thorn couldn't wait to give this unruly lot the shake. He and a crew of twenty-three, including partner McKay, set sail northward on June 5. The feeling of good riddance was mutual.

On July 15, David Thompson, the explorer and North West Company partner, arrived from upriver by canoe. He was eager to check out the rumored American establishment. Under orders to oppose them, he worked up and down the Columbia to win over Indian support for British trade, and to plant flags and territorial claims along the way. He needn't have bothered, for the Astorians, in some ways their own worst enemies, would soon do the job for him.

If Astoria began out of misfortune among the breakers, full-scale calamity came next. On his way up the coast, Captain Thorn had picked up an Indian interpreter whom Washington Irving, in *Astoria*, called Lamazee. When the *Tonquin* reached Vancouver Island, Thorn put in to a bay, eager to begin trading. Lamazee, nervous about the bellicose reputation of the local tribes, warned him against doing so. Sail farther north, he advised, where the native people have had less contact with whites and aren't known for duplicity and violence. But Thorn insisted on trading here. And when the Indians demanded what he considered exorbitant prices for their otter pelts, he kicked the furs back in their faces.

Astor had ordered Thorn and the others always to treat the Indians with fairness and kindness. (Although capable of abstracting the effects of his actions at a remove, he was often sensitive to people's feelings face-to-face; he also understood that confrontation avoided, rather than embraced, was usually better for business). Thorn, having been if anything over-attentive to his employer's instructions and mission throughout the voyage, with this rash action might as well have kicked the pelts in Astor's face. Nor could he have doomed the *Tonquin* and its onward charge more effectively had he bored a hole in the bottom of the boat.

Deeply offended, the Indians retreated to their village. Lamazee beseeched Thorn to sail away in the night. But thinking he had taught them a lesson, and feeling secure behind his cannons, Thorn refused. At dawn the watch spotted canoes coming alongside. Apparently unarmed, the Indians offered furs to trade, and Thorn allowed them to board. Astor had also warned never to allow

ATTACK AND MASSACRE OF CREW OF SHIP TONQUIN BY THE SAVAGES OF THE N.W.COAST

From the lithograph by Nathaniel Currier entitled "Attack and Massacre of the
Crew of the *Tonquin* by the Savages." Frontispiece of *Voyages to the South Sea, the Pacific
Ocean and the Northwest Coast* by Edmund Fanning, New York, 1938. Fanning was the first
owner and captain of the *Tonquin*. CCHS COLLECTION.

trading on the deck, nor to allow more than a couple of envoys aboard. But soon
the deck swarmed with two hundred villagers holding pelts. By this time Thorn
was on deck, and began trading—mostly for knives.

A cry was given and the Indians cast their pelts aside, took out hidden
maces, and fell upon the crew. Thorn and most of the others were clubbed or
knifed and thrown overboard, where women in canoes finished them off. Only
four of the Americans escaped, later to be caught and put to death. Grievously
wounded, James Lewis hid in the hold. The next day, when the Indians again
swarmed over the ship, he set the powder magazine alight. Most of the Indians
aboard and many of those in boats in the water around were killed or maimed.
The only survivor from the shattered *Tonquin* was Lamazee, the Indian interpreter, who later escaped with the shocking story.

Hiram Chittenden, in his masterful history *The American Fur Trade of the
Far West* (1902, 179), states that "for this awful disaster Captain Thorn must
alone be held responsible." And it does seem that his obduracy in the face of
warning and opaqueness to the clear and present danger caused this catastrophe.

Yet John Jacob Astor, in placing a hard Navy man in charge of a plastic and willful band of men on adventure, may not stand blameless.

So how did Astor react when he heard the baleful report months later? He went to the theater that night. When an associate asked how he could do that, he replied, "What should I do? Would you have me stay at home and weep for what I cannot help?" (Wilson 1993, 50). He can't have been insensible to the great cost, not only to his beloved bottom line, but in human life. And Astor must have known that what happened was easily avoided if Thorn, whom he hired, had only followed his advice.

The men back in Astoria must have taken the evil tidings as hard as their patron did. They felt vulnerable to the several surrounding bands of Indians, especially if they should hear of the debacle and desire revenge. To head off such a threat, McDougal called for an audience with Comcomly and other chiefs. Then he produced a vial that he represented as containing smallpox, which had ravaged the river Indians the year before. Get out of line, he threatened, and I'll pull the stopper. The bogus biological deterrent worked, and peace prevailed. The Astorians hunkered down, and awaited knowledge of what they half expected to be an equally dismal outcome for Hunt's contingent.

Then he produced a vial that he represented as containing smallpox. Get out of line, he threatened, and I'll pull the stopper.

Through the early winter, the split-up parties of Hunt, McClellan and McDougal, and Crooks and Day, experienced heartbreaking dead-ends and detours. They suffered extreme hunger, thirst, illness, frostbite, desperate fatigue, unrelenting disappointment, despair, and what Irving called "nervous strain." At the worst, they were reduced to gnawing on old moccasin soles and boiled beaver skins. It's a good thing that their employer, with his "loathing for wide open spaces" and exasperation with hardship, had not attempted the trek himself. Both Crooks and Day, ill and spent, had to be left behind to an unpromising fate. The parties' passage of the Long Narrows and falls on the Columbia, between Wishram and The Dalles, entailed theft, threats, and violence from Indians already jaded with white contact.

Hunt's ragged band finally arrived at Astoria on February 15, 1812, eleven months after leaving St. Louis, to find McClellan's equally starved unit already there for a month. The hardy and uncomplaining Madame Dorian (as Pierre Dorian's Indian wife came to be known) survived along with her boys of four and two, though a baby she bore en route died a week after birth in the bitter cold. Still more surprising, Ramsay Crooks and John Day—robbed, naked, and miserable—were later rescued near Walla Walla and brought to Astoria by an abortive mission sent to report back to Astor. Day, the rugged early Oregon explorer, lost his reason from the severe trials and died within the year. Still, given what they endured, it is remarkable how few of the overlanders perished.

Now the tattered remnants were rejoined. But soon they split again, when David Stuart returned to the trading post he had established on the Okanogan River and his nephew Robert set out on a second attempt to report their progress to Astor in person.

A third contingent revisited Snake River country to trap and to recover a large cache of goods. The desperate travelers had been obliged to bury the cache after they had eaten their horses, their boats failed in the rapids, and they were forced to continue on foot. This time they would face the "piratical" native residents of the Long Narrows with a force of sixty well-armed men.

Before they departed, another ship hove into the mouth of the Columbia. This was the *Beaver*, owned by Astor, commanded by Captain Cornelius Sowle. It was sent from New York to resupply Astoria (if it existed), to trade up the coast, and to supply the Russian-American Fur Company's depot of New Archangel (present-day Sitka, Alaska) in exchange for cooperation in excluding freelancers who competed for furs and armed the Indians. Then the ship would backtrack to Astoria, load the accumulated furs, and head to Canton. The *Beaver's* arrival in Astoria on May 6, 1812, inflated both the population and the spirits of the embryonic village-fort. But this was short-lived, for the *Beaver* set sail for New Archangel in August, with Hunt aboard to learn the coastal trade. In his absence, Hunt left McDougal, formerly of the North West Company, and holder of Astor's proxy since McKay's ill-fated departure on the *Tonquin,* in charge of Astoria. It was another bad decision, but not as injurious as one soon to be made.

Young Robert Stuart's contingent backtracked easterly along Hunt's route until a party of Crows stole their horses. To avoid those aggressive and powerful Indians, he cut south of the Tetons and discovered the more tractable South Pass into the Missouri watershed. Winter brought privation so severe that one member suggested "drawing lots"—code words for cannibalism. When they finally found bison, built a hut, and settled in for the winter, hungry Arapaho Indians (Arapahays as Irving called them) raided their larder and drove them back into the snow. Compared to the Astorians' ordeals, coming and going, Lewis and Clark's worst trials look like a cakewalk.

Back in Astoria, the town's first residents were learning how to live in the maritime Northwest. Among them was Henry Meigs. In 1849, as a Virginia planter, he would receive seeds of cotton, sesame, linseed, lentils, and beans, bought in Alexandria, Egypt, and delivered by Lieutenant James A. Rowan aboard the USS *Constitution*. But that would be many years later and far from this wilderness outpost. For now, he kept a journal of his time in Astoria which he sent to his father in Washington, D.C., as letters. On October 18, 1811, he noted "clear, strong winds from the westward, some of the Chilwits [Indians] brought us 25 bags of wapatoes and a few fresh salmon." So things went. The first winter here, too, would be a hungry one despite abundant elk that the hunters found difficult to pursue in the thick and tangled forest. Not until the smelt, sturgeon, and especially the salmon returned in the spring would the little colony know plenty again. Yet they persisted, and they probably would have prevailed, had world, national, and local events not conspired to make the first American experiment in Astoria a brief one.

The complicated chronicle of the *Beaver* is one of frustration and miscalculation. In brief, having reached New Archangel, Hunt was delayed weeks by the obligatory alcoholic revels and extremely unhurried protocol of its "roystering" governor, Count Baranoff. Then he had to detour to St. Paul Island in the Kamchatka Sea to collect seventy-five thousand seal skins. Already late for his ordered return to Astoria to pick up the furs collected there and then sail to China, Hunt and his crew encountered heavy weather that damaged his sails and rigging. The *Beaver*'s Captain Sowle persuaded Hunt to skip Astoria for now, put into Hawaii for repairs, then send the ship on to Canton while Hunt remained in Hawaii to await the *Beaver*'s return.

Meanwhile, President James Madison had declared war on Great Britain. Donald McTavish of the North West Company arrived at Astoria and announced that a British warship was on its way to take the fort. Learning of the war when he arrived in Canton, Sowle refused to sail back until peace was established; he also badly mismanaged the sale of the Pacific Fur Company's pelts, losing most of the profit. Hunt, stranded in Hawaii and desperate, heard about the war as well and chartered the *Albatross* to get back to Astoria. Meanwhile, Astor, deeply concerned about the fate of his outpost, sent another supply ship, the *Lark*, with a letter to Hunt, saying "Had I the management of affairs, I would defy them all; but, as it is, everything depends upon you . . . our enterprise is grand, and deserves success" (Smith 1929, 173). But Hunt had already blown it. In any case, the *Lark* never reached him, foundering and nearly sinking in a Pacific storm. The survivors drifted and starved, at last making land in Hawaii, where natives plundered the wreck and the men were treated indifferently by the mercurial King Kameamea.

Given the great delay of the *Beaver*, which for all he knew had suffered the fate of the *Tonquin*, ad hoc commander McDougal welcomed McTavish, and conspired to relinquish Astoria to the North West Company. When partners Stuart and Clarke arrived from their highly successful interior trading posts, they angrily resisted McDougal's betrayal, along with many in the garrison. But the Canadians had brought further intelligence (from McDougal's uncle, a North West partner) that the coming British warship would be accompanied by a frigate and two sloops of war. The fort's seemingly precarious situation, as argued by McDougal and McKenzie, convinced the others to capitulate. On the first of July in 1813, the four partners present signed a manifesto announcing their intention to turn the enterprise over to its rivals. By the time Hunt finally reached the Columbia aboard the *Albatross* on August 20, McDougal's sellout to McTavish was a done deal. They formalized the arrangement on October 13, on very poor terms for Mr. Astor's Pacific Fur Company.

On November 30, not the expected armada, but the single sloop *Raccoon*, rounded Cape Disappointment. Had the Astorians stood up to the Royal Navy, would it have been another Alamo? With the aid of the Indians, they quite likely could have resisted successfully. But Hunt had already left again to try to make the best of a bad deal; and McDougal, to Comcomly's amazement, turned down his offered assistance and threw open the gates. On December 12, 1813, the Union Jack rose over the little settlement, which the Nor'Westers promptly rechristened Fort George.

On July 17, 1813, his fiftieth birthday, Astor contacted his indebted friend Albert Gallatin, the Secretary of the Treasury. Through Gallatin, he begged Secretary of State James Monroe to provide naval protection for Astoria. Monroe agreed to send a frigate to accompany and protect Astor's ship *Enterprise* from the British blockade, and to defend Astoria, but its crew was diverted to a hot-spot on the Great Lakes. As Axel Madsen (2001, 141) put it, "Lost, for lack of a frigate, was 614,000 square miles of the West—a domain larger than the thirteen original colonies." Lost, by the way, to a mere sloop bearing the name of one of the lesser fur-bearers. Or, you could say Astoria was lost for Thorn's arrogance on the *Tonquin*, for Sowle's timidity on the *Beaver*, or for Hunt's bad call in not returning directly from Alaska, for he surely would have vetoed the plan. Blame also lies with Madison's unnecessary War of 1812, in the absence of which "Astor's plan almost certainly would have been successful" (Porter 1931, vol. 1, 243). But the failure must trace back to Astor, too, for having entrusted his American enterprise largely to a bunch of Scots and Canadians—British citizens and veterans of the rival North West Company. McDougal sold him out, and promptly became a North West partner himself as his reward.

> *Astoria was lost for Thorn's arrogance on the* Tonquin, *for Sowle's timidity on the* Beaver, *or for Hunt's bad call in not returning directly from Alaska.*

At the end of the war in 1814, under terms of the Treaty of Ghent, Astoria again was owned by the North West Company. On October 6, 1818, at Astor's behest, Monroe sent Captain James Biddle in the sloop-of-war *Ontario* to reclaim the mouth of the Columbia, and the American flag rose there once again. In theory, Astor could reoccupy Astoria. But in practice, by then the North West Company was firmly in charge of the Columbia peltries, and for the next twenty years a treaty allowed equal access to western waters for both American and British traders. There was no one to kick the North Westers out—at least not until they merged, most unwillingly, with the Hudson's Bay Company in 1821.

McDougal, long since disowned by his father-in-law Comcomly for his craven actions, had moved back to Lake Superior and "died a miserable death" (Madsen 2001, 165). John McLoughlin took over and moved the headquarters upriver to Fort Vancouver. Hudson's Bay was a formidable presence, not easily dislodged or outcompeted. So, although he had earlier pledged that "while I breathe and so long as I have a dollar to spend I'll pursue a course to have our injuries repaired" (Terrell 1963, 239), Astor eventually let it go. All the dollars he possessed were not enough to recover the dream, or to bring back the sixty-one men lost in its pursuit, as tabulated by company clerk Alexander Ross (1855, repr. 1924, 304–305). "How vain are the pursuits of man," he wrote. "That undertaking which but yesterday promised such mighty things is today no more."

The loss of Astoria was its eponymous founder's greatest reversal, costing a fortune, his pride, and deep disappointment, not to mention all those lives. Astor wrote Hunt, "If my object was merely gain of money, I should say, think whether it is best to save what we can, and abandon the place; but the very idea is like a dagger to my heart" (Smith 1929, 173). Ever after the dagger fell, he must have wondered how things might have gone differently. Chittenden (1902, 227) wrote that "if the Astorian enterprise had succeeded the course of empire on the American continent would have been altogether different than it has been. With the valley of the Columbia and the neighboring shores of the Pacific occupied by American citizens instead of British subjects during the period of controversy over the Oregon Question, no part of the Pacific Coast line would now belong to Great Britain." And we have to wonder: would British Columbia now be the state of Astoria?

After the breakup of his Pacific Fur Company, Astor and his son, William Backhouse, beefed up the American Fur Company, chartered in New York in 1808. It would dominate the trade for decades. Ramsay Crooks, having survived his hellish walk to Astoria and back, managed the northern section from Michilimackinac, a fur-trading post on the southern side of the strait separating Lakes Huron and Michigan. Many of their affairs are summarized in three big red buckram books housed at the New York Historical Society. They comprise the *Calendar of American Fur Company Papers*—abstracts of 18,181 letters written between 1831 and 1849. An anonymous, heroic person designated simply as "the calendarer" typed them all in 1925, with multiple carbon copies on onionskin. Crooks himself either wrote or received almost half the letters. Riffling through them gives a sense of the workings of the trade that dominated so much of Astor's time, energy, and hopes:

1833. July 1, Dept. of State, Washington—Louis McLane to W. B. Astor: Has received letter from Astor to the Sec'y of War on the advantages of total abolition of the use of ardent spirits among the NW Indians, and the request that gov't cooperate with Great Britain in that object. Will submit the matter to the president.

1834. Jan. 31, from Byron Greenough to Ramsay Crooks: The season is unfavorable for the sale of buffalo robes.

1834. May 30, War Dept., Lewis Cass to WBA: discusses efforts to deal with the Indians. May have to send dragoons.

1837. Sept. 20, to C. M. Lampson, London: All Lake Superior skins have arrived. Northern returns are short in beaver, otters, and muskrats but have an excess of martins and lynxes.

The only personal Astor letters in these books are to William's cousin Sophie in Germany, written in French. I became excited when I found another big volume embossed *Journal*—but it proved to be a record of bank drafts written in New York between May 18, 1826, and January 15, 1839. Many of the checks were from Astor to his daughter Eliza Rumpff. Still another book, labeled *Ledger*, bears an entry for January 18, 1826, that explains a transaction "in consideration of a marriage which hath lately been had and solemnized between Vincent Rumpff of Hamburg Esq. and Eliza his wife late Eliza Astor Spinster the Daughter of the said John Jacob Astor and of his natural love and affection for and towards his said Daughter and for making a provision for her maintenance and support and for the Issue of the said marriage $200,000 and fifty shares of Globe Insurance." Vincent was a count, and the Rumpffs would be just fine.

William Backhouse Astor would also be fine. It was a great sadness to his father that the oldest son, John Jacob Astor II, was mentally ill and withdrawn. He lived comfortably and long, but played no role in the business. W. B. Astor was the one who carried on the work, and the fortune, and who would be John Jacob's successor. There in the historical society's library were W. B.'s *Letterbooks*—bound volumes in which copies of his correspondence were kept. I hoped they might reveal something of the father. Some were certainly of interest:

5 Aug. 1852 to J. G. [*sic*] Audubon: "Dear Sir, Referring to your circular of the 12th ult.: I would desire to have the few animals not figured but described in the 3rd volume of the *Quadrupeds of North America*, figured and of a suitable size to be bound in that volume."

15 April 1852 to Henry Clay in U.S. Senate: Acknowledges payment of an outstanding Bond of Clay's father, $5,500. "From your handwriting I trust that your health is much improved. I am my dear Sir, with great regard and esteem, your friend and servant, Wm. B. Astor."

But almost all the letters are financial, without a whiff of a curing pelt or a glimpse of personality. And there were W. B. Astor's *Daybooks, 1854–75*, five beautiful old leather-bound and ribbed volumes with marbled endpapers and facings. Promising, until opened—then all about money, and not a scrap of it personal. As inviting as they may be from the outside, I searched in vain among these tomes for anything of Astor's heart. Even the traces pertaining to his nearest and dearest are merely fiscal, as cold as stones, or ingots. More passion is to be found in the reports of the peltries, the ups and downs of deer skins and buffalo robes, beavers and martins, lynxes and mink.

Astor could see the twilight of the peltries looming. Silk was replacing felted beaver for men's top hats. Beaver were thinning out, and the mountain men were thinning on top. The buffalo herds would not last long, the passenger pigeons would no longer darken the skies, sea otters and condors were already checking in absent at the Columbia. The Indian nations themselves were unraveling under the stresses of disease, alcohol, guns, and the whites. Steamboats chugged and belched where the voyageurs once dipped their silent paddles. The wilds were getting crowded, and the profits were spread too thin. John Jacob Astor, his fur dreams done, sold the northern operations of the American Fur Company to Ramsay Crooks in 1834, and the southern branch to Choteau & Co. in St. Louis.

As I turned in the big books and packed up to leave, I took a last look around the warm reading room: long wooden tables softly lit for tapping and scribbling researchers, white pillars in pairs, tall stained-glass windows of early New York scenes, sailing ships, and Dutch settlers in silks. Looking more closely, I saw that they commemorated the arrival of Henry Hudson in the *Halve Maen* for the Dutch East Indies Company, with Indians rowing out to meet him. I chuckled at the thought of Henry Hudson and John Astor rubbing fur-clad shoulders in the New York Historical Society.

After the fur business, John Jacob enjoyed a long, comfortable denouement, filled with family and an active business life well into old age. He carried, and exercised, high influence with presidents and anyone else he desired. He subsidized the government on more than one occasion, and if he played both ends against the middle by lending money to the British as well as the Americans during the War of 1812, well, that was business. He couldn't be charged with treason because Madison owed him a personal loan. Favors, licenses, competitive advantages, and all manner of indulgences could be bought or levered, and few called it corrupt outright. Astor's image, romanized, appeared on coins for use on the frontier, to be presented like Lewis and Clark's Jefferson medals to impress Indians. Astor was the only American businessman ever commemorated in coinage, the direct result of exerting his influence with Lewis Cass, Secretary of the War Department (Madsen 2001).

But Astor suffered losses as well as victories, and not just in business. A favorite grandson drowned during a European visit. His beloved daughter Magdalen twice married badly and died too young. His greatest loss was that of his wife and lifelong partner Sarah, who died while John was returning from Europe in 1834. No wonder he broke up his million-dollar fur empire the same year. His heart wasn't in it after that. As he left more and more of the business to William, he forsook his city mansion for his country house at Hell Gate, where he indulged his old love of music and surrounded himself with literati. Two respected poets, Fitz-Greene Halleck and Joseph Green Cogswell, came often to Hell Gate, and Halleck became Astor's resident secretary.

None of this distraction effaced Astoria from his mind, and what it might have been, versus what actually happened. Though the Astoria story could be seen as Astor's greatest speculative business loss, he wanted the story told, and told to his advantage. So he prevailed upon the best-known writer of the day, Washington Irving, to come to Hell Gate and write the book that would become *Astoria, or Anecdotes of an Enterprise Beyond the Rocky Mountains*. Irving agreed, on condition that his nephew Pierre would be hired as his researcher, organizer, and assistant to help mine the corpus of materials and memories placed at his disposal, and that the book would not be a mere puff-piece for the boss. He had no desire to be Astor's flack. Still, James Fenimore Cooper, uninvited to Astor's literary soirées, was spiteful in his dismissal of Irving as Astor's animal. He predicted that Irving would present Astor as greater than Columbus.

I was disappointed to learn that Irving himself never actually visited Astoria, which I had always assumed. He did travel as far as Montreal and Missouri, where he saw the inner edges of the fur trade on the near frontier. He drew on this experience, and on journals, letters, interviews, and published and unpublished accounts of the Astor expeditions and the peltries in general. His sources included John Bradbury and Thomas Nuttall, naturalists along on the front end of Hunt's expedition; the memoirs of Astorians Gabriel Franchère and Ross Cox; Hunt's and Crooks's letters; and Robert Stuart's eyewitness account. The Irvings worked at Hell Gate through fall and winter of 1835, and *Astoria* was published in October 1836. Irving said he wrote more in a month than he had ever done before, and found the experience revivifying (Powers 1957). Astor loved the literary energy that pervaded the place and was well pleased with the outcome.

Which raises the question of whether *Astoria* is more historiography or hagiography. Irving drew very closely from certain sources, some acknowledged, others not, approaching plagiarism in places. He embellished some details, and perhaps invented others. He worried that he had hurried the job, and he certainly painted his patron in the best light and cast most of the blame on the Scots. "It was his great misfortune," Irving wrote, "that his agents were not imbued with the same spirit" (1836, 452). (Of course, Astor had hired those agents.) With greater generosity than strictly required, Irving took pains to unreel the full chain of unintended consequences—the almost Shakespearean sequence of screw-ups and bad luck—which added up to what he called, with perfect pitch, "the tissue of misadventures" that doomed the Astorian project (1836, 452). Irving's account, carefully read, implicates Astor at every turn.

Critical reactions varied. Important newspapers called it a masterpiece, and general response, wildly enthusiastic, made it an instant bestseller. Hiram Chittenden, of the Chittenden Locks in Seattle, considered Irving's work by far the best authority on "Mr. Astor's great enterprise" (1902, 907). But historian Hubert Howe Bancroft, namesake of the Bancroft Library of the University of California at Berkeley, criticized the book as propaganda. He wrote that Irving had lent "his brilliant faculties" to "base purposes" and claimed that "many of its most brilliant passages are pure fiction" (1884, 136–138).

"In his peevishness," responded Portland editor and historian Alfred Powers, Bancroft "failed to give credit to Irving's immense service in extracting the important and dramatic substance from the Astor archives . . . which are now lost," as well as in capturing the "verbal narratives" of many of the fur-trade participants. Indeed, several of the employees of the Pacific Fur Company—Franchère, Ross Cox, Alexander Ross, Robert Stuart, and others—left stirring narratives of their enterprise and times. Irving managed to capture many of their best tales and images.

When I returned from New York, I visited the Astor Library in Astoria, Oregon. This institution is a different proposition from the New York Historical Society, but it feels just as welcoming on a nippy March afternoon—cozier, if not so grand. The Astoriana alcove, maybe ten by twenty feet, is ceiled in acoustic tiles with soft-light panels, and floored with carpet. Three banks of wooden card files for newspaper articles define the seaward enclosure. The south wall bears long photographic panoramas of Astoria before and after the fire of December

9, 1922. Scanning the eastern rampart of glass-fronted oak bookcases, among the many Lewis and Clark titles, one sees *The Letters of Dr. John McLoaughlin, How Marcus Whitman Saved Oregon, The Call of the Columbia,* and *The Oregon Country Under the Union Jack.* The north end opens to the librarians' lair, and out into the local version of the great reading room: two-story, open and airy with teaky, boat-like furniture, big, bright oils by Astorian artists, and (discreetly tucked into their corner) the computers, not yet eclipsing the printed word of the periodicals and stacks.

In the middle of the alcove, I sat at the single big oak table beside the microfilm reader, school yearbooks lined up on my left, Chinook Indian documents behind me. The tiny room felt held up by great spavined leathery editions of *The Centennial History of Oregon* and the *History of the Columbia River Valley from The Dalles to the Sea.* It was here that I handled a waterstained and wavy first edition set of *Astoria,* whose whiff no webpage will ever capture. The two volumes date from 1836—just twenty-five years after the events they chronicle. The copy I actually read, however, was newer: the "Clatsop Edition" published in 1957 by the venerable Portland house of Binford & Mort.

Irving's *Astoria* is a compelling tale that I wish I had read twenty years ago. It should be required reading for anyone wishing to dwell within the city's green walls. The language and attitudes about the "savages" may seem disturbing and racist by contemporary standards, but the author was humane and often perceptive for his time. For example, after lamenting the ongoing hostilities toward whites that grew out of Lewis killing a Blackfeet and again from Kit Carson shooting a Sioux, he wrote:

> In this way outrages are frequently committed on the natives by thoughtless or mischievous white men; the Indians retaliate according to a law of their code, which requires blood for blood; their act, of what with them is pious vengeance, resounds throughout the land, and is represented as wanton and unprovoked; the neighborhood is roused to arms; a war ensues, which ends in the destruction of half the tribe, the ruin of the rest, and their expulsion from their hereditary homes. Such is too often the real history of Indian warfare, which in general is traced up only to some vindictive act of a savage;

while the outrage of the scoundrel white man that provoked it is sunk in silence" (1836, 160).

Irving can be as fine a writer to our ears today as he was considered in the days of *Knickerbocker Tales*, as in this lovely sentence, which would stand anywhere, anytime: "It is in this way that small knots of trappers and hunters are distributed about the wilderness by the fur companies, and like cranes and bitterns, haunt its solitary streams" (1836, 241). Besides tracing the essential birthing story of Astoria, this thrilling, sweeping book gives a devastating and deeply affecting portrait of the continent at the very moment of its violation, a volatile time in a violent history. Alfred Powers, in introducing that Binford & Mort edition, called it "the earliest American industrial history of importance," written by "the republic's most eminent author."

As his master-biographer Kenneth Wiggins Porter suggested, "It is curious that Astor, whose main interest throughout most of his life was making money, should have wished to be remembered for an enterprise which brought him a heavy financial loss." Jefferson had expressed his hope for a kindred state on the Pacific Coast, and Porter wondered if, through his Pacific Fur Company, Astor hadn't aspired toward just such an end. He concluded that "much as Astor loved money and the power that money gives, yet he preferred the immortality conferred on him by the pen of Washington Irving. Surely he would rather have chosen to be remembered as a dreamer of empire than as 'the Landlord of New York' " (1931, vol. 1, 242–243).

One could also conclude that, in effect, in the long run, and almost in spite of himself, Astor achieved his empire after all. When peace with Britain came, the American flag again replaced the Union Jack over the raw log fort; and today, the only place called "Fort George" is the city's best brew-pub. In any case, one of the best things John Jacob Astor ever did was to cause Washington Irving's *Astoria* to be written.

In his decrepitude, Astor's legendary grip on a dollar only grew tighter. As his biographer Howden Smith described it, "parsimoniousness turned into acquisitiveness, and acquisitiveness developed a passion for hoarding, and hoarding, once it was a confirmed habit, created the churlish penuriousness of the miser. Money! Everything was money" (1929, 76). Stories about that penuriousness abound. When he met one charity request with $50 and was told his son had given $100, he replied, "Yes, but you must remember that William has a rich father." On another occasion John James Audubon called to collect a one-thousand-dollar subscription for his planned *Birds of America* that, in a weak moment, Astor had promised. For several visits, Astor the elder had put Audubon off, pleading cash flow problems. Finally, William pointed out that his father had plenty of ready money in the bank, and Astor quietly wrote the check. John Jacob himself was fond of saying, "To give something for nothing is to weaken the giver" (Conkling 1973).

What finally weakened the indomitable Astor was not giving, but that involuntary tax levied on all life: time. Toward the end, according to several biographers, caretakers dandled Astor on a blanket to exercise his muscles, and the only nutrition he could take was breast milk from a wet nurse. This image seems all too appropriate in view of Astor's lifelong talent for suckling at any and every productive teat, government or private, foreign or domestic, legal or otherwise. When he finally expired, on March 29, 1848, ex–New York Mayor Philip Hone entered in his diary: "John Jacob Astor died this morning. . . . Bowed down with bodily infirmity for a long time, he has gone at last, and left reluctantly his unbounded wealth" (Smith 1929, 289).

Apart from the short half-million dollars he had earmarked for a library thanks to Cogswell's persistent urging, and smaller bequests for orphans, the blind, and poor in his home town, and for German immigrants, Astor left almost all the rest to the family. James Gordon Bennett of the *New York Herald* called Astor "penurious and niggardly" and described his legacy as "poor, mean, and beggarly" (1848). Horace Greeley critically contrasted Astor's meager giving with the much greater generosity of the man who was previously America's richest, Philadelphia banker Philip Girard. Astor's partner in bankrolling the U.S. Treasury during wartime (at a handsome profit), Girard had left most of his seven million–plus fortune to public purposes. However, Astor's defenders noted Girard's lack of children vs. Astor's large family. And in fact, Astor's gift, guided by Cogswell, was then the largest bequest ever made for a public library and lecture series. A codicil to his will stipulated that "To contribute to the advancement of useful knowledge and the general good of society . . . The Trustees . . . may expend such surplus in procuring public lectures, to be delivered in connection with the library, upon useful subjects of literature, philosophy, science, history and the fine arts" (anon., 10, 12). The Astor Library had 100,000 volumes, compared to Harvard's 72,000, and twice as many as the Library of Congress (Madsen 2001, 268–269); and in 1895 it evolved into the New York Public Library, one of the greatest in the world today. As Peter Baida wrote in *Forbes* (1987, 345, 348–349), public giving at the time was not commonplace. The opprobrium brought down by Astor's stinting will, leaving relatively little to the city and country from which he had sucked his wealth, meant that forever after, "no wealthy American could blithely ignore the claims of philanthropy." Perhaps this was Astor's actual, if unintended legacy.

As a boy growing up in Colorado, I gobbled old books on mountain men and trappers, gifts from my historian grandmother. I was entranced by ads in the back of *Boy's Life:* "Become a government trapper, live a life of free adventure in the great outdoors." I sent away for free pamphlets on Colorado's furbearers and instructions for trapping muskrats and skunks. And I wore out my faux coonskin cap, à la Davy Crockett. But then my sister Susan and I made a book we called *Seal Rock*, and I also fell in love with otters. At my first sight of a beaver in a mountain marsh, fascination with the animals themselves eclipsed my romantic view of trappers. I came to understand what traps actually did, and that animals' pelts more properly belonged on their own backs. Now, when we think of John Jacob Astor and his guild, we should not forget the millions of creatures killed miserably in leg-hold traps and snares on his behalf. But this haunting debt is not uniquely Astorian: furs were the currency of the time.

When I look for Astor's personal aftermath, I think of one more item I examined at the New York Historical Society, a hefty book entitled *Minutes of John Jacob Astor's Executors. Estate of John Jacob Astor, 1848–54.* The executors (W. B. Astor, J. J. Astor II, Washington Irving, James Gallatin, and Daniel Lord) found

Astor's estate to be worth $4,488,057.53. Most published estimates range from $20 million to $25 million, and some enter the next order of magnitude. Irving's signature appeared on the second volume, *Second Distribution of Residuary Personal Estate of John Jacob Astor*, along with a red sticker affixed on a gold seal, causing some excitement among the librarians. The executors' records continue another four decades, trying to sort out his tangled finances. One could be forgiven for concurring that, for Astor, it really *was* all about money.

Yet the Midas of Manhattan had, after all, other interests. Family and the work itself loomed large for him, as well as the play of politics and power. Haeger (1991, 286) believed that "no individual of his time, perhaps, better exemplified the union of capitalism and the new liberal state. In Astor's mind, the ultimate success of the new Republic depended on its commercial and geographic expansion"—not that his acts could be accused of favoring patriotism over his own pocketbook. Astor's death, Haeger wrote, "provoked disturbing questions about the glaring existence of a new American aristocracy, the presence of an urban proletariat, and the often unethical ties between business and government." He concluded that Astor was "the first businessman to epitomize the successes, the failures, indeed the character of the new republic" (286–287).

Or, as Howden Smith put it in 1929 (292), Astor was "simply the product of a period and an environment. . . . How he would have hated himself had he been able to view some of his acts objectively, as we can, through the perspective of time!"

Such regrettable acts might include Astor's lubricious maneuvers to evade Jefferson's embargo on overseas shipping; opportunism, influence trading, and coercion with Madison, Monroe, Gallatin, and other elected and appointed officials; playing both ends against the middle in the War of 1812; flying chameleon flags on his vessels; and opium running. Some of his least handsome behavior related to Native Americans, in spite of his instructions to Hunt to always treat them kindly. He wasn't overtly genocidal—far from it. Rather, as Smith (1929, 292) described, he was "prey to a moral blindness which was instinctive rather than reasoned." So as Madsen charged, Astor was "never happier than when surrounded by his grandchildren," but "was also a slumlord, a war profiteer, and a ruthless jobber who shipped opium to China, and sold liquor to Indians knowing the devastating consequences" (2001, 4).

Native Americans devastated by alcohol, firearms, and disease might be enough. Yet another legacy that does not appear in the executors' minutes books, but can be readily found in the business ledgers, includes countless other lives: 390,000 bison and 375,000 beavers just from 1815 to 1830. Astor's mining of the peltries caused boundless cruelty to furbearers while devastating populations. Astor alone was not responsible; he was just doing what everyone else was doing, which was his oft-stated rationale. But he did much more of it, and more energetically, than anyone else.

Astor was the first great American preview of the baleful consequences of rapacious power mixed with unlimited capital expansion for its own sake: a worthy instrument of Manifest Destiny, the grand conceit of his benefactor, James Monroe. He was a suitable precursor for all the takers—the Buffalo Bills, the Carnegies and Rockefellers (minus their conspicuous philanthropy), all the Kennecotts and Halliburtons to come. By the measure of a country in love with *laissez faire* and the self-made man on the make or the take, Astor was indeed "a most excellent man," as Thomas Jefferson once called him. But by any modern standards we might want to emulate—humanitarianism, mercy, sustainability, restraint, wanting less and conserving more—maybe not.

Not that the man was without modern merit. As Howden Smith wrote, "In his features you might trace meditation, courage, and masterful resolve—and coldness, indifference, and acquisitiveness. But never brutality, intolerance, or stupidity. . . . And add this for him: at his most detestable, he was no hypocrite" (1929, 472). An astonishing array of the notable people of his era had truck with him or his people: Jefferson, Madison, Monroe, Gallatin, Hamilton, Burr, various Napoleons, Kameamea, Comcomly, Daniel Boone, John Colter, John Day, Kit Carson, Thomas Nuttall, Audubon, Irving, and on and on. No one can say that Astor, apart from being the first major plutocrat in the country, failed to touch its people, and sometimes for the good.

※ ※ ※

In *Furs by Astor*, John Terrell suggested that Astor never forgave McDougal for selling out Astoria. Yet he retained pride over his project on the Pacific. "When everything else he had accomplished was long forgotten," Terrell wrote,

"Astoria would stand as an indestructible monument to his memory" (1963, 472). In various ways, his impact extends beyond the city's founding. When John Jacob Astor V, Baron Astor of Hever, came to Astoria with Lady Violet and their son Gavin in 1961 for the town's sesquicentennial, he left behind a check for $100,000 for the city's betterment. It broke the fundraising log-jam for that fine little library that bears his family name. Though this gift was one-fifth of what his ancestor left for the other Astor Library, and the facility it helped to build is not a hundredth part of the massive one on Forty-Seventh Street, it enriches the lives of all Astorians no less than the edifice behind the lions uplifts New Yorkers.

John Jacob Astor I was arguably the most eminent Astorian of all, though he never beheld the city, and though Astoria arose in spite of his overreaching grasp and ultimately violent failure. Does the city deserve his name? The word "Astoria" falls pleasantly on the ear. And like its unofficial sister city in Queens, this Astoria is an amenable, stimulating, and lively place. But as a town known for its strong communitarian, conservationist, and traditional working- and middle-class values, its nomenclatural debt to the founder of the Astor dynasty might be seen as ironic, even embarrassing.

Today, if you perch on any available dock or waterside bench, the town you see is very much more than it was when Astor died in 1848, but less than he might have imagined or what some still picture as possible. On an Indian summer pre-sunset eve on the veranda of the Wet Dog Saloon, I watched cormorants and gulls bobbing off a still-open stretch of shore between a fish market and a gentrified pier with restaurants below a dental office with the best view ever. Across the three miles of river, past two ruby-hulled freighters at anchor, lay the subtle hills of Willapa in Washington, where I live. Upriver, sea lions honked on the mooring basin slips. A school of small boats testified to the strong run of summer Chinooks. Toward the sun, beyond the steak house, the crab plant, and the boomer couple mounting their classic Harley, stretched the longest bridge on the West Coast. Its traffic was RVs and show-bound hot rods, instead of commuters.

Most of the Astoria–Megler Bridge is flat like something out of the Florida Keys. The part I could see was the elevated south end over the shipping channel: a green steel fretwork of triangles, other angles, and curves. It too has pebbled shores beneath, but of siltstone instead of the glassy burden of the other Astoria;

and brant in winter, but the black brant of the Pacific. The only tug in sight was the little green-and-white pilot boat returning from a freighter loaded with the carcasses of a couple of thousand local trees, bound for Japan. The eve was still mellow and warm, a rarity at the mouth of the river. It felt a million miles from the high green bridge of Astoria, Queens, in the stiff March wind; light-years from the veranda at Hell Gate, where Irving penned *Astoria*. Yet the elements are much the same: river, bridge, and waterbirds, and a name that sounds like a flower, but rhymes with a dollar sign.

If the nature of this place changes wholesale in ways that presently threaten— with big money crowding out affordable housing, high-rise condos erasing the public shoreline, and dangerous, profit-chasing big industry eroding the river's health and security—then the provenance of the city's moniker could become all too suitable.

In another vision this estuarine enclave, where beavers again thrive, and where the air and water and room to move are the envy of a crowded nation, could choose to embrace its vicarious founder's name in a different way: as a reminder of what we have, how it could be lost to greed and hubris, and how it should be cherished.

Acknowledgments

I wish to express my large appreciation to the Astor Library in Astoria, Oregon, and its staff including Jane Tucker, Library Director, Patty Skinner, Megan, Amy, and Lindsay; Liisa Penner and Marsha Elliott of the Clatsop County Historical Society and Heritage Museum; the Timberland Regional Library and Appelo Archives in Naselle, Washington; Marilyn Gudmundsen; and the New York Historical Society, particularly librarians Loraine Baratti and Anna Djordjeve, for their kind assistance in researching this essay. Michael Bales, Karen Kirtley, and Steve Beckham are kindly acknowledged for their careful reading and comments. Steve Forrester's vision and support for the whole project made it possible.

Works Cited

Anonymous. 1850. "Annual Report of the Trustees of the Astor Library of the City of

New York: Made to the Legislature, January 29, 1850" (Albany).

Anonymous. 1925. *Calendar of American Fur Company Papers,* vol. 1, 1831–1839 (nos. 1–7294); vol. 2, 1840–1844 (nos. 7295–14,629); vol. 3, 1845–1849 (nos. 14,630–18,181). Bound typescript in New York Historical Society.

Baida, Peter. 1987. "Poor Jacob!" *Forbes* 400 (26 October).

Bancroft, Hubert Howe. 1884. *History of the Northwest Coast,* vol. 2, 1800–1846. San Francisco: A. L. Bancroft.

Bennett, James Gordon. 1848. *New York Herald*, 5 April.

Chittenden, Hiram Martin. 1902, reprint 1935. *The American Fur Trade of the Far West,* 2 vols. New York: The Press of the Pioneers.

Conkling, Gary. 1973. "John Jacob Astor: From Rags to Riches." *Oregonian,* 1, 3, 7 July.

Haeger, John Denis. 1991. *John Jacob Astor: Business and Finance in the Early Republic.* Detroit: Great Lakes Books, Wayne State University Press.

Irving, Washington. 1836. *Astoria, or Anecdotes of an Enterprise Beyond the Rocky Mountains.* Philadelphia: Carey, Lea and Blanchard. 1957 reprint, "Clatsop Edition." Portland: Binford & Mort.

Madsen, Axel. 2001. *John Jacob Astor: America's First Multimillionaire.* New York: John Wiley.

Meigs, Henry. 1811–1812. Transcript of a journal kept at Astoria from March 1811 to June 1812, sent to his father Josiah Meigs in Washington, D.C., as letters.

Porter, Kenneth Wiggins. 1931. *John Jacob Astor: Businessman,* 2 vols. Cambridge: Harvard University Press.

Powers, Alfred. Undated. "Irving's Writing of *Astoria*." Introduction to 1957 reprint, "Clatsop Edition" of Washington Irving's 1836 *Astoria*. Portland, OR: Binford & Mort.

Ross, Alexander. 1855. *Fur Traders of the Far West.* 1924 reprint, Chicago: R. R. Donnelly.

Smith, Arthur D. Howden. 1929. *John Jacob Astor: Landlord of New York.* Philadelphia: Lippincott.

Terrell, John Upton. 1963. *Furs by Astor: The Full Story of the Founding of a Great American Fortune.* New York: William Morrow.

Wilson, Derek. 1993. *The Astors, 1763–1992: Landscape with Millionaires.* London: Weidenfeld & Nicolson.

George Gibbs

BY STEPHEN DOW BECKHAM

A man almost entirely unknown in accounts of the history of Astoria, Oregon, George Gibbs was, for a time, the town's most prominent and best-educated resident. Born in 1815 at Sunswick Farms in Astoria, New York, he was an heir to one of America's richest families of the early nineteenth century. Gibbs received a remarkable education, earned a college degree, and made a European grand tour. He practiced law and wrote books, but by the late 1840s

George Gibbs, ca.1860. COURTESY OF THE OREGON HISTORICAL SOCIETY. CN666058.

George Gibbs, ca. 1870. Courtesy of the Washington State Historical Society. 2005.0.129.

he was restless and unfulfilled. Throwing aside social connections and his career in New York City, he cast his lot with tens of thousands of adventurers who emigrated to the Pacific Northwest. Gibbs dropped anchor in Astoria, where he launched a new life. This community was where he began to do linguistic and ethnographic research with the Indians of the Pacific Coast, an activity that shaped his life from 1849 to 1873.

❧ ❧ ❧

George Gibbs was the eldest of eight children born to Colonel George Gibbs and Laura Wolcott Gibbs. His grandfather George Gibbs (1735–1803), the "merchant prince" of Newport, Rhode Island, lived in one of the town's great eighteenth-century mansions overlooking the "stone mill" in a square he owned in the heart of the city. Grandfather Gibbs made his fortune shipping Madeira wines, slaves, sugar, flaxseed, barrel staves, silk, tea, and other Asian commodities. The elder Gibbs had married Mary Channing. Walter Channing, her brother, was a partner in the shipping enterprise. By 1800 more than seventy of their vessels plied the world seas, traveling from Europe to Africa, to the West Indies, to the seaboard colonies in North America, and to China.

Born to great wealth but having little interest in business, Colonel George Gibbs (1766–1833) became a gentleman farmer and scholar. His wife Laura was the daughter of Oliver Wolcott, who succeeded Alexander Hamilton as Secretary of the Treasury in the administrations of George Washington and John Adams. The young couple—Laura was fifteen when they married—settled in 1813 in what is now Queens on Long Island. The colonel hired workmen to drain swamps, build fences, construct barns and outbuildings, and outfit his estate, Sunswick Farms, purchased for $40,000. His energies were primarily spent, however, in studying mineralogy and amassing the largest "cabinet" of geological specimens in the Western Hemisphere. An active member in the American Philosophical Society, the Linnean Society of New England, and the American Geological Society, Gibbs published in journals and used his wealth to purchase minerals from European collectors. In time he gave more than 22,000 specimens to Yale University to become part of the teaching collections in the Sheffield School of Science.

The home in which George Gibbs grew up on Long Island was handsomely furnished. His father, a friend of Gilbert Stuart, commissioned portraits of Washington, Adams, Jefferson, Madison, and Monroe. These images, including the Washington portrait later used on the U.S. dollar bill, hung in the family's formal dining room. Stuart also painted portraits of Colonel George Gibbs and Laura Gibbs. The colonel owned artworks by Washington Allston—painter, sculptor, and a cousin from Rhode Island. Many of the furnishings came from the finest craftsmen in Newport and New York City.

When he was seven, George Gibbs left Sunswick Farms to attend one of America's most interesting experimental institutions, Round Hill School at Northampton, Massachusetts. The school was founded by Joseph Green Cogswell and George Bancroft (later Secretary of State in the Jackson administration and author of the six-volume *History of the United States* published between 1848 and 1888), who had studied and traveled in Europe after graduating from Harvard. In Switzerland, they encountered the educational philosophies of Johan H. Pestalozzi and Philipp E. von Fellenberg. They carried those ideas to New England and founded a school stressing outdoor education, modern languages, and physical activity. George Gibbs studied French, Italian, German, Spanish, and Latin. He had extensive instruction in natural history and went on lengthy camping trips with his classmates and instructors during the summers. Gibbs also studied composition, dancing, mathematics, gymnastics, and drawing at Round Hill.

In 1833 Gibbs entered Harvard College. The situation in Cambridge was convenient. In 1823, his widowed grandmother, Mary Channing Gibbs, purchased the Harrison Gray Otis mansion on Mount Vernon Street in the Beacon Hill neighborhood of Boston. His aunts Miss Sarah Gibbs and Ruth (Gibbs) Channing, who had married her first cousin, William Ellery Channing, resided there. (William E. Channing was a major figure in American religion in the 1830s and the 1840s and preached Unitarian tenets each Sunday in the Arlington Street Church.) Gibbs's brother Wolcott was enrolled in preparatory school and lived in the family home in Boston. Gibbs took rooms at Mr. Willard's in Cambridge and boarded at the University Commons.

Gibbs studied at Harvard's Dane Law College with distinguished mentors and jurists Joseph Story, John Hooker Ashmun, and Simon Greenleaf. More than law, however, occupied Gibbs's interests. In March 1833, he visited the Boston Athenaeum to see an exhibit of paintings by John Audubon. "They are superb, of full size on elephant paper [over-sized, hand-colored plates produced between 1827 and 1839]," he wrote to his sister Eliza (Gibbs 1833).

Ruth Channing arranged for him to meet Audubon. Gibbs declared him "a complete original" and "a remarkable man" (Gibbs 1832). Gibbs also met and became a close friend of an older classmate, Charles Sumner, who subsequently became a senator from Massachusetts during the Civil War. The two worked together to develop a catalog of the more than 3,300 volumes in the law library.

In 1834 Gibbs published *The Judicial Chronicle*, a volume summarizing nearly eight hundred years of English judges, reports, and chancery officers, with alphabetical indexes. Joseph Story, fabled American jurist, wrote the preface for the young man's book and hailed it as "a highly valuable present to the profession" (Gibbs 1834, iii–iv). Worn down by these labors, Gibbs then left Harvard to spend two years traveling in Europe with his unmarried aunt Sarah Gibbs, her friend Harriet Hare, and John Hare, who was a year younger than Gibbs and a recent graduate of the University of Pennsylvania.

Gibbs received his law degree from Harvard in 1838. For the next eleven years, he lived with his mother and younger siblings at 261 Greene Street in New York City, a property his mother purchased following his father's death in 1833 and the sale of the Long Island property. Gibbs's father's estate was invested in real estate in New York City. By 1838 its value was $112,863, and it provided annual income to the widow and the children in proportionate shares. Gibbs and his mother spent a month each summer at Sharon Springs, Lake Saratoga, or other rustic retreats in New York. Gibbs became a member of the New York Bar and opened a practice with offices on Wall Street.

He found law boring and repetitive and increasingly turned his interests to the New York Historical Society. In 1839 Gibbs became the society's curator of manuscripts. He cemented friendships with John Russell Bartlett, later in charge of the Mexican boundary survey; Albert Gallatin, former treasury secretary in Jefferson's cabinet and student of Indian languages; and John Lloyd Stephens, explorer of Mayan ruins in Yucatan. In 1843 Gibbs gained appointment as librarian of the New York Historical Society and launched an ambitious program to develop a catalog of all its holdings: artifacts, books, manuscripts, maps, coins, and newspapers.

In 1845 Gibbs published a massive two-volume work, *Memoirs of the History of the Administrations of Washington and Adams*. He drew heavily from the personal papers and library of his grandfather, Oliver Wolcott, to construct a chronicle of the Federalist Party. The work was partisan. Gibbs phrased his role as "the avenger of a by-gone party and buried race." He also lashed out at John Adams for inconsistency, "morbid irritability," and "egregious vanity and egotism" (Gibbs 1845, vol. 1, ix; vol. 2, 508).

When the history was published, Gibbs was at loose ends. He connected with wilderness places again in 1845 during two weeks of hiking and sketching at Lake George and Lake Champlain and in the Connecticut Valley. More importantly, Gallatin and Stephens fostered his interest in Indian languages and place names. Lewis Henry Morgan, a fellow attorney engaged in Indian kinship studies and terminologies, further fostered his interests. Gibbs joined the new American Ethnological Society, but he hungered for adventure.

A desire to head into the wilds of the American West was kindled in 1848 by the return of Gibbs's brother Wolcott Gibbs from a geological expedition to

Michigan with Louis Agassiz and by the arrival of geological and ethnographic collections from Mexico sent by his brother Alfred Gibbs, who served in the Mexican War. His brothers' adventures in the "field" quickened Gibbs's hunger to flee New York City and get on with life.

News of the discovery of gold in California swept through New York City in December 1848. In January 1849, Gibbs's friend George Templeton Strong wrote: "It seems as if the Atlantic Coast was to be depopulated, such swarms of people are leaving it for the new Eldorado" (Strong 1952, 55). Gibbs was among those who caught the enthusiasm.

On March 20, 1849, Gibbs abandoned everything familiar and struck out to build a new life. He left behind his desultory law practice, the historical society, his mother and siblings, and New York City. Traveling to Fort Leavenworth, Kansas, he attached himself, as a civilian, to five companies of Mounted Riflemen outfitted to travel the Oregon Trail on a five-month, two-thousand-mile march to Fort Vancouver. Their mission was to establish an American military presence in the Oregon Territory, organized under the Organic Act of 1848. A number of old friends, including Philip Kearny and John Ruggles, were part of the expedition. At departure from Kansas Territory in May 1849, the Overland Riflemen was a contingent of 31 officers, 600 enlisted men, several women and children, agents, guides, teamsters, 160 wagons, 1,200 mules, and 700 horses. As the expedition moved west, it diminished with the assignment of men to the new military posts along the Oregon Trail (Bushnell 1838, 2).

During the overland journey, Gibbs wrote a descriptive diary of the route and his adventures. He sent installments back, as he could, to New York City, and his account of the overland passage began to appear in the fall of 1849 in the *Journal of Commerce*. He also worked as an artist, making many sketches. Gibbs thrilled at landscape features, trail scenes, and persons encountered during his travels. Literally everything along the Oregon Trail attracted his interest and vivid commentary. For example:

> **May 18, 1849:** "There are odd characters and odd vehicles among
> them too. Every profession and every class in society are represented,
> and every mode of conveyance from the Conestoga wagon and its
> lumbering oxen, and the light draft mule-team, to the saddle horse.

We even saw a doctor's buggy with a bell fastened to the hinder axle"
(Settle 1940, 286–287).

May 18, 1849: "The birds particularly noticed today were the turkey
buzzard, common crow, buffalo bird (the cow bunting of the east),
doves, small woodpeckers, and a number of the sylviae, upon which
I could not waste shot. The yellow-throated blackbird was also
constantly seen in the flocks of the buffalo bird" (Settle 1940, 287).

May 19, 1849: "The evening we again passed round the campfire of
an officer, and the scene that our party exhibited was one not to be
forgotten. The night was blackness itself; a wind such as blows only
on the prairie or on the sea roared around us, a blazing fire was built
under an enormous mass of red quartz rock, and around it lay on
their blankets some twenty men in the rude costume of the march—
our old guide among them. On its top stood some half dozen others
leading the chorus which thundered from beneath to the good old
song of 'Benny Havens, O!' As the firelight danced on their faces I
could not but recall the pictures of [Salvator] Rosa and regret that the
inspiration of such a pencil was wanting here" (Settle 1940, 289).

June 19, 1849: [Platte River] "Everywhere objects of interest gave way
to more interesting country. The bluffs for the first time are covered
with red cedar, heretofore found only in ravines, and the valley
throughout its whole extent is covered with dry branches and trunks,
evidently driftwood. Mr. [John C.] Frémont's theory is these must
have been washed down from the Black Hills, but their distance is so
great that I should have been disposed to question it, thinking that
they either grew on the spot or came from the adjacent bluffs, were it
not that they are everywhere, intermingled with cones of the pine tree
which nowhere occurs in this region" (Settle 1940, 320).

June 20, 1849: [Platte River] "Mr. T[appan] and myself again
remained behind to sketch the bluffs" (Settle 1940, 322).

Astoria, Oregon, in 1845. Watercolor by Sir Henry James Warre, courtesy of the University of Washington. WSU553. In 1816, Fort George, surrounded by fifteen-foot pickets, covered almost an acre. When Warre visited almost thirty years later, only a few of the fort's original structures remained.

William Henry Tappan, the Boston engraver who executed the frontispiece for Gibbs's 1845 book, had joined the expedition at Fort Kearny. It is highly probable that the handsome plates published in 1850 in the Congressional Serial Set with the journals of Major Osborne Cross and the report of Colonel William Wing Loring (the commanding officers of the Mounted Riflemen) were executed by Gibbs and Tappan during their overland journey.*

Gibbs was delighted with his sketches and made side trips to record features he believed previously undocumented. On August 15, 1849, for instance, he traveled ten miles off the Oregon Trail to sketch the Canadian Falls, on the upper Snake River. He and his travel compatriots decided to change the name to Great Shoshone Falls, today Shoshone Falls (Settle 1940, 184–185). Gibbs's illustrations provided significant primary documentation of notable features along the Oregon Trail.

---

*Osborne Cross's *A Report in the Form of a Journal, of the Regiment of Mounted Riflemen to Oregon, May 20–October 5, 1849* was published in the Congressional Serial Set, Senate Executive Document No. 1, 31st Congress, 2nd Session, with thirty-five lithographic plates, Washington, DC, 1850.

The Mounted Riflemen reached the Cascades and took the Barlow Road south of Mount Hood. Their heavily loaded wagons bogged down in the swamps and mud of the volcano's southern slopes. While the soldiers dug cache pits in which to leave many of their supplies over the winter (at a site subsequently known as Government Camp), Gibbs sketched the south face of Mount Hood and Crater Rock.

The Mounted Riflemen established camps at Oregon City, Vancouver, and Astoria. Ruggles hurried off to the diggings in California, contracted dysentery, and died in May 1850 off the coast of Mexico while trying to return by sea. Tappan moved to Milton City, which subsequently became St. Helens, Oregon.

In December 1849, Gibbs cast his lot with Astoria, a small settlement of log cabins, a few frame buildings, old Fort George, and stumps and mud. On January 10, 1850, the Oregon City newspaper *Oregon Spectator* carried his business card:

George Gibbs
Councellor at Law

SHIPPING AND COMMERCIAL AGENT
CUSTOM HOUSE BUILDINGS, ASTORIA

Will attend to all business confided to him in the
preparation of legal papers, the loading and discharge of
vessels, receiving consignments for sales or storage, &c.

At age thirty-five, Gibbs estimated his personal estate at $5,000. He and three other bachelors took room and board with the Adam Van Dusen family in Astoria.

Colonel Loring, one of the expedition leaders, gave Gibbs a good recommendation. His law degree and background were impressive. Thus John Adair, the first collector of customs, hired Gibbs as his deputy and offered the new resident of Astoria a salary of $2,000 a year.

The prospect of the job and his valuation of the town's setting persuaded Gibbs in June of 1850 to join Adair and James Frost in purchasing a mile of

Adam and Caroline Van Dusen with their children, ca. 1857. CCHS 14953.00V.

Unfinished pencil sketch by George Gibbs depicting Astoria as seen from the
end of a pier, ca. 1851. Courtesy of the Peabody Museum of Archaeology and Ethnology,
Harvard University. Peabody-Harvard Digital File Number 98630096, Peabody-Harvard Images.

shoreline. The men envisioned selling lots and transforming Astoria into a
major city at the mouth of the great river of the West. Gibbs also invested $1,000
in a steamboat, the *Columbia*, to provide passenger and freight service between
Astoria, Portland, and Oregon City. He described his new hometown in a letter
to his mother. "There is as you might imagine," he wrote, "a general recklessness

of character pervading all men. Money is of but little consideration to any but those who look forward to a return to civilized life." Gambling and drinking, he observed, were the "every day vices of the country" (Carstensen 1954, 1213).

Adair traveled frequently, leaving Gibbs a lot of time to himself at the customs house. He read New York newspapers, wrote letters, and took on the Hudson's Bay Company. In March 1850, during one of Adair's absences, Gibbs challenged the British company when it shipped goods directly from Fort Victoria in British Columbia to Fort Nisqually on Puget Sound, bypassing the customs duties. In August, the new territorial governor John Gaines and territorial judge William Strong arrived by ship from California. Peter Skene Ogden, head of operations at Fort Vancouver, offered the officials and their families, along with their baggage, passage up the Columbia on the *Prince of Wales*. Gibbs intervened and vetoed the opportunity. He pointed out to all concerned that the ship was under bond to do no business other than convey freight for the Hudson's Bay Company.

Governor Gaines acquiesced and put his family on board the *Columbia*, the steamboat in which Gibbs was an investor. Judge Strong refused, missed passage, and waited a month for a means to go upstream from Astoria. Finally, in a fury, he departed by canoe to paddle a hundred miles against the current and

The old customs house in Upper Astoria where George Gibbs had an office.
The building was burned in 1918. CCHS 152.713.

tides to Portland. Gibbs had enraged and humiliated Judge Strong, a man with political preference and patronage. The reverberations of Gibbs's intervention compelled Gibbs to write to the Treasury Department: "If any one is more than another to blame, it is myself." To preserve harmony and protect his patron, Adair, he resigned his position (Gibbs 1850).

Gibbs plunged into other affairs at the mouth of the Columbia. He became an agent for the *Oregon Spectator*, seeking subscriptions and probably forwarding news items from Astoria to the publishing office in Oregon City. He appeared before the Territorial Court and gained admittance to the Oregon Bar, and in 1850 he was named one of three commissioners for Clatsop County. Along with William H. Gray and George W. Coffenberg, he also became a school examiner, reviewing teachers' credentials and certifying their eligibility to enter the classroom. On January 21, 1851, the territorial legislature elected Gibbs—on the first ballot—prosecuting attorney for Oregon's Third District, which then embraced the northwest coast of the Oregon Territory.

Following his departure from the customs house, Gibbs quickly secured another federal appointment. In June 1850, Congress authorized creation of the Willamette Valley Treaty Commission to secure cession of Indian lands in western Oregon.* When the three commissioners began work in April 1851, they hired Gibbs as commissary. He also worked as a topographer with Edward A. Starling to develop perhaps the first detailed map of the Willamette Valley, showing settlements, roads, trails, and tribal distribution. Because of his growing fluency in Chinook Jargon, Gibbs also worked as secretary to the commission and recorded its proceedings. The appointment afforded the opportunity to collect Indian vocabularies.

In 1803, Albert Gallatin, working with Thomas Jefferson and Benjamin Smith Barton, had developed a word list given to Meriwether Lewis, who was to interview the various tribes the Corps of Discovery encountered and record the basic vocabulary. The plan was to use the comparative word lists to ascertain the origins of the Indian tribes: were they descendants of Welsh or Basque fishermen, Phoenicians, the "lost tribes of Israel," survivors from Atlantis?

---

*The term "cession" is a legal one. Indian tribes engaged in treaties of land cession. They gave up major parts of their homelands and retained "reservations," small tracts of "Indian country" exempt from taxation.

In the 1840s, Gallatin was president of the New York Historical Society, where Gibbs served as chair of the executive committee as well as librarian. By that decade Gallatin had a 180-word basic list for use in gathering linguistic data from scattered tribes. This was the word list Gibbs used from 1849 to 1861. For the Chinook and Nisqually Tribes he was more ambitious in the words enumerated and compiled dictionaries.

Gibbs wrapped up work with the commission at Oregon City in June 1851. He used his time also to sketch portraits of "Slacum," chief of the Willamette Falls band; Alquema, or "Joe," chief of the Santiam; views of the Indian fishery at Willamette Falls; and the new town of Milwaukie at the mouth of Johnson Creek. When his youngest brother, Francis "Frank" Sarason Gibbs, arrived in Oregon City in transit to the family trading house in Canton, China, Gibbs decided the two should sail to California to visit their brother Alfred, who was stationed at Sonoma Barracks with the U.S. Army. Alfred, a West Point graduate, was a veteran of the Mexican War. In California on frontier duty, he had purchased a ranch near Sonoma.

Within two weeks of arriving in California, Gibbs secured appointment as secretary and topographer to assist Redick McKee, one of three members of the California Indian Commission, in negotiating treaties of land cession with the Indians from the Russian River Valley north to the Klamath River and east to Mount Shasta. For the next five months, Gibbs had an expense-paid research trip among the tribes of northwestern California.

Gibbs documented McKee's travels and negotiations. In an expedition diary much more expansive than that penned on the Oregon Trail, he described the Indians they encountered, made population estimates, recorded word lists, executed numerous sketches, and traded for bows, arrows, baskets, and Indian clothing, which he shipped as curios to his family in the East. His diary was published in 1853 in the third volume of Henry R. Schoolcraft's *Information Respecting the History, Condition and Prospects of the Indian Tribes of the United States*. In time Gibbs wrote other contributions for this multi-volume set.

Completing his duties with the California Indian Commission in San Francisco in March 1852, Gibbs succumbed to the lure of gold. He sailed to Humboldt Bay and took up a placer claim at Orleans in the canyon of the Klamath River. Unlike fellow miners, Gibbs hired Karuk Indians to work his claim. He paid them with counterfeit dentalium shells made of white porcelain in China and shipped by his brother Frank from Canton. Gibbs ordered 5,000 fathoms of counterfeit "Indian money." It is unlikely that anyone realized the deception.*

During his two years in northwestern California, Gibbs greatly expanded his Indian vocabularies and notes. With the onset of winter rains and rising water levels, he left his claim and walked to the coast. He had no choice: there were no roads and little or no feed for horses. On September 4, 1852, Gibbs wrote about travel conditions from the Salmon River, a tributary of the Klamath, to John Austin Stevens in New York City:

> Our party consisted of four, all thoroughly armed & we took with us
> two mules, one carrying blankets, mining tools, a few cooking uten[s]ils,
> and such provisions as our rifles would not supply us with; the other
> intended to pack game or to ride in case of need. Our first days [sic]
> travel was directly up a long steep spur of a mountain between two
> creeks, lying in deep ravines, or gulches as they are called here, the
> object being to attain at once the crest of one of the high ridges. Upon
> these crests it is necessary to travel altogether, for the smaller streams
> lie always in deep & broken beds, very narrow & filled with dense
> forest and underbrush. From eight to ten miles a day was a good
> journey & the very severe march only enabled us to reach a level flat
> near the summit in which we found water & grass for the animals
> (Carstensen 1954, 21).

Gibbs sailed from Humboldt Bay to San Francisco and took passage for Astoria, this time to serve the Millard Fillmore administration as collector of customs. He wrote to his mother, "The idea of going back to Astoria at the old pay of a collector, as I supposed it still to remain, did not please me, but I was of course ignorant how far I might be committed, was pretty near broke again, and had every prospect of present starvation" (Carstensen 1954, 28).

---

*To this day none of the porcelain dentalium shells has been reported, though Gibbs's correspondence confirms that he infused the counterfeits into the Indian trade network of the Klamath River canyon.

He found Astoria little changed, except for snow, freezing rain, and chill winds. Actona—the subdivision he and Adair had ardently promoted—had no residents. Upper Astoria (Adairsville), where Adair had settled, was likewise abandoned. Even the U.S. Army had pulled out and removed its token troop garrison from old Fort George. Gibbs found a room with Herman Leonard and J. Green, two former New Yorkers who ran a mercantile store in Astoria. Reluctant but in need of the $3,000 annual stipend, Gibbs assumed his post at the customs house. The original building, erected by Adair, had burned in 1852. Gibbs rented an office, painted it, outfitted the interior in "white domestic cloth" (probably canvas, a common wall-covering before the advent of wallpaper), and with security bond in hand, went to work (Carstensen 1954, 39).

Gibbs wrote to his brother Alfred: "I mean to go seriously to work at a book on Oregon intended to be of a permanent character. I ought to have done this before, but had no settled quarters of my own since I have been in the country" (Carstensen 1954, 36). In spite of his intentions to write a book, however, Gibbs instead revised his California journal for publication and carried on with work at the customs house. Customs revenues picked up in February 1853 with the arrival of a British vessel carrying a cargo valued at £20,000, on which Gibbs collected duties.

Gibbs continued to explore the region. In April 1853 he wrote to his mother:

> I took a run the other day up the Lewis & Clark's river as it is called to
> the place of the W[inter] encampment [Fort Clatsop], which long as
> I have been here I never visited before. The site of their log hut is still
> visible, the foundation logs rotting where they lay. Their old trail to
> the coast is just visible being much overgrown with brush. Their camp
> was about 4 miles from the beach. Indians are still living who knew
> them, though the numerous tribes of that day are almost all gone &
> the small pox has again swept them this winter (Carstensen 1954, 43).

With the 1853 turnover of administrations in Washington, D.C., when Franklin Pierce succeeded Millard Fillmore, John Adair was reappointed collector and Gibbs lost his position. When Adair returned to Astoria in June, Gibbs was again adrift. In a matter of days, he signed on as a civilian with the Pacific Railroad Surveys, another expense-paid research expedition. Gibbs found employment as geologist, linguist, and ethnologist with the Western Division team headed by George B. McClellan (later the Union general who declined to advance against the Confederate Army in northern Virginia and was fired by Abraham Lincoln for his temerity). During the summer and fall of 1853, Gibbs traveled with this party via the Lewis River to the Columbia Plateau and east along the flank of the Cascade Range, as documented in his diaries and formal reports.

McClellan timidly examined potential passes, but concluded there was no feasible route for a railroad through the mountains—a conclusion that soon put him in head-on confrontation with Isaac Ingalls Stevens, the first governor of Washington Territory and director of national railroad survey explorations from St. Paul, Minnesota, to Puget Sound on the Pacific Coast. Stevens wanted a railroad over the Cascades. He surveyed a long route from St. Paul to the eastern margin of the Cascades and was furious when he discovered that his western party, headed by McClellan, had only once crossed the mountains, in a half-hearted exploration. Stevens was hell-bent on his agenda and was compelled to do further explorations himself and with officers other than McClellan. Gibbs, serving under McClellan, was caught in the conflict.

Gibbs continued his work on the surveys and returned to Astoria in December 1853 to mount a "Reconnaissance of the Country Lying Upon Shoalwater Bay and Puget Sound." He crossed to the north shore of the Columbia, explored Cape Disappointment and the Long Beach Peninsula, and worked his way to the head of Willapa Bay. He found few settlers. "The principal trade, so far," he noted, "has been in oysters, which abound on the flats. They are taken up, during the low tides of summer, from their natural beds, separated, and replanted, as in the States. They sell alongside the vessel at $1.50 per bushel, and in San Francisco are worth $7" (Gibbs 1855a, vol. 1, 465).

Gibbs's primary assignment under McClellan was to scout a route from Willapa Bay to the trail running from the south end of Puget Sound via the Cowlitz to the Columbia. With three local residents, he paddled fifteen miles up the Willapa River by canoe, fighting his way through swamps, brush, prairie grasses, and vine-maple thickets to a small range of hills. Gibbs estimated the cost of a wagon road, bridges excluded, at $15 per mile to connect the tidal part of the bay with the trail via the Cowlitz River.

McClellan liked Gibbs and admired his labors. On February 25, 1854, McClellan wrote: "I have no hesitation in saying that no one could have been found who could have made so complete and excellent a report upon Indian matters as that of Mr. Gibbs. His report upon the geology will show the care with which he pursued this portion of his duty; in addition to this, he has more than once conducted important reconnaissances with great benefit to the survey" (McClellan 1854, 202).

Gibbs then settled in Olympia to work closely with Governor Isaac Stevens in writing up the railroad survey reports. These projects consumed the first half of 1854. His contributions, in addition to the Shoalwater Bay narrative, included an assessment of the geology of the Columbia Plateau, a study of the region's mammals co-authored with Dr. George Suckley, and an ambitious overview of the Indian tribes and cultures of Washington Territory.

Perhaps most important were Gibbs's recommendations on Indian policy, subsequently incorporated into the template treaty that Stevens used throughout Washington Territory. Gibbs wrote:

> To remove the Indians altogether into any one district is
> impracticable, for the western verge has been reached. To throw
> the fishing tribes of the coast back upon the interior, even were the
> measure possible, would destroy them; nor is there any suitable
> region east of the Cascades where all the tribes now living could be
> concentrated and find food. They must, therefore, remain as they
> are, adopting such a plan only as will remedy, so far as may be, the
> inconvenience of the contact (Gibbs 1855b, vol. 1, 422).

Governor Stevens needed to clear Indian title to Washington Territory because of increasing settlement and proposed railroad projects to link the east and the west of the transcontinental United States. In December 1854, he turned to Gibbs, the Harvard-educated lawyer, to draft a treaty template. After nearly five years of studying the Indians of the Pacific Coast, Gibbs had concluded that the survival of the tribes required protecting their access to traditional natural resources. His life in Astoria and observation of the annual frenzy of fishing by the Clatsop, Chinook, and Wahkiakum Indians helped fix his commitment to rights of access to subsistence. Thus he wrote into the treaty language that preserved both hunting and fishing rights "at usual and accustomed places," a matter of importance to this day.

Gibbs worked with Stevens as secretary to the Western Washington Treaty Commission in 1854 and 1855 in councils at Medicine Creek, Point Elliott, Point-No-Point, and Neah Bay, and in the abortive council at Cosmopolis on the Chehalis River. Gibbs's language of reserved rights was eventually incorporated into ten ratified Pacific Northwest treaties. By ceding their lands to the United States, the western Washington tribes reserved small, scattered tracts of land held in federal trust (non-taxed) status. Some of the treaties compelled bands, often former enemies, to live together. The agreements—at the insistence of Gibbs—reserved to the tribes their aboriginal rights of fishing, hunting, and gathering at usual and accustomed places both on the reservations and within the larger treaty cession areas. The treaty-reserved rights extended beyond the boundaries of the reservations. Gibbs worked as surveyor of the new reservations as well as secretary. He kept detailed and sometimes verbatim notes on council proceedings.

Having completed these labors, Gibbs went to Fort Vancouver to join Lt. George Horatio Derby, of the U.S. Army Corps of Topographical Engineers, in road surveys. They laid out a route and hired crews to clear brush for a wagon road from Astoria to Salem. This ambitious trace crossed the Coast Range through immense forests and downed snags, the legacy of numerous fires. A "Military Wagon Road" funded by Congress, the route was supposed to provide wagon access to Astoria. Because of poor grading and limited improvements, however, it was not transformed from a muddy trail into a useful highway. Gibbs next worked with Derby to survey the Fort Vancouver–Fort Steilacoom Military Wagon Road connecting the Columbia River to Puget Sound. Much of that route became the Pacific Highway and, later, Interstate 5. Gibbs produced a large map showing the route and principal features of the geography.

Between 1855 and 1857, Gibbs sojourned intermittently at his farm, Chetlah, a donation land claim near Steilacoom on Puget Sound. He used his time there to work on Indian languages while hired men cleared and tilled the property. At Chetlah, he pursued several major projects that eventually led to publication in New York City in 1862 and 1863:

Alphabetical Vocabularies of the Clallam and Lummi
Alphabetical Vocabulary of the Chinook Language
A Dictionary of the Chinook Jargon, or Trade Language of Oregon
Grammar and Dictionary of the Yakima Language

Gibbs actively corresponded with scientists Spencer F. Baird and Joseph Henry at the Smithsonian.* He shipped kegs of fish preserved in alcohol, bird eggs, mineral specimens, fossils, and other "curiosities" to the national museum. He preserved fish for Louis Agassiz and botany specimens for Asa Gray, both friends of Charles Darwin. He solicited the assistance of military officers stationed at forts from Arizona to Puget Sound to fill out lists of Indian words to expand his mastery of comparative linguistics. In February 1855, the Washington Territorial Legislature selected Gibbs as brigadier general of the territorial militia. Although he helped to organize and arm several companies, he led no troops into conflict.

In 1858 Gibbs began three years of service as geologist and ethnographer for the Northwest Boundary Survey. Teams from the United States and Great Britain went into the wilds along the American–Canadian boundary to survey the precise location of its route from Puget Sound to Lake of the Woods, Minnesota. The American team, directed by Alexander Campbell, surveyed, cut, and erected monuments of stone cairns and wooden posts along the forty-ninth parallel west from Semiahmoo Bay near present Blaine, Washington. The work was hard, with exposure to bitter weather, rugged mountains, unfordable rivers, and

> *He shipped kegs of fish preserved in alcohol, bird eggs, mineral specimens, fossils, and other "curiosities" to the national museum.*

---

*Spencer F. Baird was an ornithologist who expanded his publications to cover mineralogy, botany, and anthropology. Joseph Henry was an experimental physicist working especially in electricity and meteorology. Both men were dedicated to the development of the Smithsonian Institution and its embrace of multiple disciplines of inquiry.

grueling elevation changes. Yet the assignment provided yet another expense-paid research adventure, and Gibbs thrived. The crews retreated only in winter to a base camp near Blaine, where they worked on maps and reports. The seasonal breaks enabled Gibbs to expand dramatically his collection of vocabularies and notes on Indian oral literature, or myth tales, of the region. He also wrote an account of Indian mythologies in Washington Territory (Gibbs 1955–1956, posthumously published) and the "Physical Geography of the North-Western Boundary of the United States" (Gibbs 1872–1873).

With the outbreak of the Civil War in 1861, Gibbs decided to return to the East Coast to visit family and friends and to see the boundary survey reports through to publication. He set out via Panama for his first homecoming in a dozen years. He never returned to his land claim on Puget Sound, nor did he again walk the shore in Astoria, where he initially cast his fortunes in the West. Instead, Gibbs took up quarters in one of the towers at the Smithsonian castle. Here, over the next decade, he laid the foundations for the Bureau of American Ethnology and continued to publish his research. From time to time, he was called on because of his extensive knowledge of the Pacific Coast. Gibbs became the conduit of information to Charles Sumner, his classmate from Harvard, when in 1867 the senator delivered a six-hour oration endorsing the purchase of Alaska from Russia.

During the 1860s, Gibbs also served as secretary for the American staff of the Hudson's Bay Company Claims Commission. He was responsible for gathering and organizing evidence of the values of the company's investments in the Pacific Northwest. These materials became multi-volume sets of documents:

Evidence for the United States in the Matter of the Claim of the Hudson's Bay Company (1867)
Evidence for the United States in the Matter of the Claim of the Puget's Sound Agricultural Company (1867)

In 1871, at the age of fifty-six, Gibbs married for the first time. Mary Kane Gibbs, his first cousin, was his bride. She was a contemporary, probably born in the 1810s, and had never married. She had spent years caring for her father, the former governor of Rhode Island. Although both had long considered marriage, they waited until the death of Gibbs's mother, Laura Wolcott Gibbs, in December 1870, and the death of Mary's father, William Channing Gibbs, in February 1871. George and Mary married on April 11, 1871. He was a timid groom, writing to Spencer Baird that he had his brother Wolcott Gibbs at the ceremony "ready with some smelling salts & nitro glycerine lest I should faint (Gibbs to Baird, 1871). The couple removed to New Haven, Connecticut, and settled at 77 Wall Street, as Gibbs noted, "where under the shadow, almost, of the Sheffield Scientific School, I have pitched my camp" (Gibbs to Baird, 1871).

Gibbs was eager for a married life. "I have a very pretty place, and have bought the furniture that was in it, so that the only additions will be, my wife, my books & pictures & papers. I hope now to do some work in earnest, the more especially since I have no pecuniary cares" (Gibbs to Baird, 1871). His parents' estate had resolved any financial concerns. On February 3, 1872, Gibbs wrote to Joseph Henry: "I now look back on many years wasted in bachelorhood with great regret" (Gibbs to Henry, 1872).

Beleaguered by gout and the ravages of exposure to wilderness conditions on the West Coast of North America, Gibbs died on April 9, 1873, at the age of fifty-eight. He was buried beside many of his family at Miss Sarah Gibbs's stone chapel, Oakland, on Newport Island.

The measures of George Gibbs are many. He expressed faith in the future of Astoria and, for a time, invested his resources and energies in the community, where he speculated in waterfront real estate. Living in Astoria opened the opportunity to engage in linguistic and ethnographic studies, a commitment that became a compelling activity in the next two decades of his life. He was the first member of the Oregon bar to practice law in Astoria, and he served as one of Clatsop County's first commissioners and the second collector of customs. His work with the Chinookans of the Lower Columbia led to two books in 1863.

Gibbs was also a cartographer, field geologist, naturalist, and ethnographer, and singularly the architect of the "reserved rights" causes in Pacific Northwest

Indian treaties. His commitment to traditional subsistence of the tribes was fostered, in part, by observing the annual salmon fishery at the mouth of the Columbia.

A century and a half after his residency in Astoria, scholars still quote his letters, diaries, and publications. His Indian word lists—more than a hundred manuscripts—are among the treasured holdings of the Office of Anthropological Archives of the Smithsonian Institution. Today Gibbs's collections, including numerous Indian artifacts retrieved from his mother's home in New York City, are preserved at the Smithsonian.

Gibbs was also a documentary artist. While many of his images of the West remain unpublished in libraries in Wisconsin and Massachusetts, a number of his pencil sketches and watercolors illustrated his published works and those of others. For most of his eleven years on the West Coast, he penned daily observations in his journals, made extensive field notes on the Indians, and wrote dozens of informative letters. His tracing of Jedediah Smith's manuscript map of the American West, which he saw at Fort Vancouver, preserved the only documentary record of that famed explorer's far-flung travels to the Pacific Coast (Morgan and Wheat, 1954).

A man drawn to the West by opportunity, George Gibbs found his greatest riches not in real estate, a steamboat, or law practice, but in his encounters with the diverse languages and cultures of the native peoples of the Pacific Northwest. He had a profound sense of history and an intense curiosity about the world around him. The life of the mind quickened for George Gibbs among the mud and stumps of Astoria. From the customs house, he propelled himself to a succession of remarkable adventures that nurtured his publications and his respected position in Washington, D.C., for the last decade of his life.

Works Cited

Bushnell, David Ives, Jr. 1838. Drawings by George Gibbs in the Far Northwest, 1849–1851. *Smithsonian Miscellaneous Collections,* nos. 8 and 10.

Carstensen, Vernon, ed. 1954. *Pacific Northwest Letters of George Gibbs.* Portland, OR: Oregon Historical Society Press.

Gibbs, George. 1832. Letter of March 27. Gibbs Family Papers, 1796–1903. The State Historical Society of Wisconsin, Madison, WI.

———. 1833. Letter of March 17 to Eliza Gibbs. Gibbs Family Papers, 1796–1903. The State Historical Society of Wisconsin, Madison, WI.

———. 1834. *The Judicial Chronicle, Being a List of the Judges of the Courts of Common Law and Chancery, in England and America, and of the Contemporary Reports, from the Earliest Period . . . to the Present Time.* Cambridge, MA: J. Munroe & Co.

———. 1845. *Memoirs of the History of the Administrations of Washington and Adams,* Edited from *the Papers of Oliver Wolcott, Secretary of the Treasury,* 2 vols. New York: W. Van Norden, Printer.

———. 1850. Letter to Treasury Department. Letters from Collectors, C-O, II (1850). RG 56: General Records of the Department of the Treasury, National Archives, Washington, DC.

———. 1855a. Report of George Gibbs on a Reconnaissance of the Country Lying Upon Shoalwater Bay and Puget Sound. *Pacific Railroad Reports,* vol. 1. Washington, DC: Beverly Tucker, Printer.

———. 1855b. Report of Mr. George Gibbs to Captain Mc'Clellan on the Indian Tribes of the Territory of Washington. *Pacific Railroad Reports,* vol. 1. Washington, DC: Beverly Tucker, Printer.

———. 1871. Letter of April 2 to Spencer F. Baird. Smithsonian Incoming Correspondence, 1871–1874, vol. 4. Washington, DC: Smithsonian Archives.

———. 1872. Letter of February 3 to Joseph Henry. Smithsonian Incoming Correspondence, 1871–1874, vol. 112. Washington, DC: Smithsonian Archives.

———. 1872–1873. Physical Geography of the North-Western Boundary of the United States. *Journal of the American Geographical Society of New York,* vol. 3, 134–157; vol. 4, 298–392.

———. 1955–1956. George Gibbs's Account of Indian Mythology in Oregon and Washington Territories. Ella E. Clark, ed. *Oregon Historical Quarterly,* 56, 293–325; 57, 125–167.

Gibbs, George, and George Suckley. 1860. Report Upon the Mammals Collected on the Survey. *Pacific Railroad Reports,* vol. 12, part 2, 107–139. Washington, DC: Thomas H. Ford, Printer.

McClellan, George B. 1855. "General Report of Captain George B. McClellan," *Pacific Railroad Reports,* vol. 1. Washington, DC: Beverly Tucker, Printer.

Morgan, Dale L., and Carl I. Wheat. 1954. *Jedediah Smith and His Maps of the American West*. San Francisco, CA: California Historical Society.

Schoolcraft, Henry R. 1853. *Historical and Statistical Information Respecting the History, Condition, and Prospects of the Indian Tribes of the United States*, vol. 3. Philadelphia: Lippincott.

Settle, Raymond, ed. 1940. *The March of the Mounted Riflemen: First United States Military Expedition to Travel the Full Length of the Oregon Trail from Fort Leavenworth to Fort Vancouver May to October, 1849, as Recorded in the Journals of Major Osborne Cross and George Gibbs*. Glendale, CA: Arthur H. Clark Company.

Strong, George Templeton. 1952. *The Diary of George Templeton Strong: The Turbulent Years, 1850–1859*. Allen Nevins and Milton H. Thomas, eds. New York: The Macmillan Company.

Ranald MacDonald and Astoria

By Frederik L. Schodt

The Astoria Column towers one hundred and twenty-five feet above Coxcomb Hill, overlooking the Columbia River. Built in 1926, this imposing landmark commemorates European settlement of the Pacific Northwest. A replica of a Chinook burial canoe, erected at the same site thirty-five years later, commemorates Comcomly, the Chinook chief who greatly aided the first Europeans in the area. Several blocks below these memorials, at the corner of Fifteenth and Exchange Streets, is a little park with a partial reconstruction of Fort Astoria, depicting part of a blockhouse and a palisade. And in a corner of the park is a granite stone memorial to Comcomly's grandson, Ranald MacDonald. Like the person it commemorates, MacDonald's memorial is often overlooked. Dedicated on May 21, 1988, with funding from the Portland Japanese Chamber of Commerce as well as generous individuals, the monument has an English inscription on one side and a Japanese inscription on the other. The English version reads:

> Birthplace of RANALD MacDONALD, 1824–1894. First teacher
> of English in Japan. The son of the Hudson's Bay Co. manager of
> Fort George and Chinook chief Comcomly's daughter, MacDonald
> theorized that a racial link existed between Indians and Japanese.
> He determined to enter Japan although it was closed to foreigners
> for over two hundred years. Sailing in 1848 as a deckhand on an
> American whaler, he marooned himself on Rishiri Island near
> Hokkaido. While awaiting his deportation, he was allowed to teach
> English to 14 Japanese scholars, some of whom became leaders
> in the modernization of Japan. He spent his active life in Europe,
> Canada and Australia. He is buried in an Indian cemetery near
> Curlew, Washington.

The Japanese on the reverse side is a loose, abbreviated translation of the English, except it specifically mentions that MacDonald was imprisoned while in Japan.

Given the spatial limitations on the monument, the inscriptions are an accurate representation of MacDonald and his best-known accomplishment. Yet neither in English nor in Japanese do they convey the extraordinary nature of his adventure. He was one of the better-documented ordinary citizens of his era. But regardless of the many articles and books written about him in the last century, it remains difficult to recreate with precision what MacDonald did and explain exactly why it was important.

Inevitably, mention of MacDonald's name today evokes Big Macs, golden arches, and a similarly named red-haired clown. Yet to those who know the story of the real Ranald MacDonald, he is a classic example of an individual

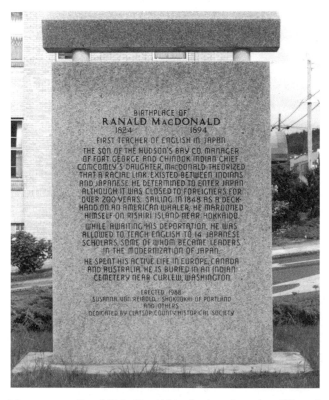

Monument to Ranald MacDonald in the Astoria park at Fifteenth and Exchange Streets. Friends of MacDonald Collection, CCHS.

Ranald MacDonald, July 5, 1891. Courtesy of the Washington State

University Library. Manuscript, Archives and Special Collections, Negative No. 97-004.

who, overcoming great odds, did something heroic then fell through the cracks of history. He should be far better known than he is.

What was so extraordinary about MacDonald?

In 1848, Japan still enforced a strict and unyielding isolationist policy, as it had since the beginning of the seventeenth century. For an ordinary North American to go to Japan was like an individual today, with no connections to NASA, deciding to go to the moon and somehow doing so.

It was a policy initiated out of fear of European encroachment, particularly fear of Christianity, for at the end of the sixteenth century, Portuguese and Spanish Catholic missionaries had succeeded in converting large swaths of the population in the south of Japan. The frightened Shogunate's response had been to expel missionaries and to force converts to Christianity to revert to native religions, go underground, or be exterminated. With the exception of a handful of Protestant Dutch and relatively irreligious Chinese traders allowed to live in prison-like conditions in the southern port of Nagasaki, foreigners were thereafter forbidden to enter Japan, and Japanese were not allowed to leave. Occasionally the policy was modified, but it continued in relatively draconian form until 1853, when Commodore Matthew Perry and the U.S. Navy forced Japan to end its isolation. To most North Americans in the 1840s, Japan was a mysterious, unknown land. Those who knew anything about Japan commonly believed that foreigners caught on Japanese soil would be promptly executed.

MacDonald's surviving writings, as well as those of his contemporaries, hint that he had many and sometimes conflicting motivations for attempting to enter Japan. He was twenty-four years old and may have been on a pure quest for adventure. A devout young man, he may have had a religious impulse; perhaps he hoped to spread the word about Christianity. He may also have wanted to demonstrate to his powerful father, Archibald MacDonald of the Hudson's Bay Company, that he was capable of doing something dramatic on his own terms. Most certainly, he hoped to make his fortune by serving as an intermediary— probably by learning the language and becoming an interpreter—between the Western world and Japan when the latter finally opened to trade.

Ranald MacDonald knew of Japan through his father and his father's contemporaries, and he believed that one day it would be open to the outside world. The son of the Chief Factor of the Hudson's Bay Company, Archibald MacDonald, and Princess Raven (after her Chinookan name Koale'xoa) or "Princess Sunday," one of Chinook chief Comcomly's daughters, he was one of many mixed-race children sired by the company's men and raised in a rich, multi-lingual, multi-racial, and multi-cultural environment unique to Hudson's Bay Company forts. He had, moreover, also been raised with romantic stories of Japanese shipwrecked in Hawaii and the Pacific Northwest. In fact, in 1834 at Fort Vancouver where he attended elementary school in what is today's Washington State, he just missed meeting three Japanese sailors—Otokichi, Kyukichi, and Iwakichi—brought there after being shipwrecked in what today is Northeast Washington. Among the officers of the Hudson's Bay Company, this news was similar to hearing that Martians had landed on earth.

The same year, in 1834, the ten-year-old MacDonald was sent to the Red River Settlement, in today's Winnipeg, Canada, where he attended schools for the children of the Hudson's Bay Company officers. In 1839, he was sent farther east to St.

Thomas, Canada, and apprenticed to a local businessman. His father hoped that in this largely European environment, his son would learn the ways of the civilized world and prepare himself for a respectable career. But the half-Indian boy from the frontier did not fare well. To his father's dismay, MacDonald dropped out—abandoned the career path chosen for him—and made his way to Sag Harbor, New York. There, in 1842, he signed on as an ordinary sailor on a whaling ship.

MacDonald left no written record of his activities in this period, but it is worth noting that interest in Japan was particularly high in the Sag Harbor area. In the 1840s, the seas near Japan were a popular hunting ground for the U.S. whaling fleet because the Atlantic had largely been fished out. Ships from New England ports regularly plied Japan's coast, occasionally landing illegally to pick up water and firewood. In 1845, Mercator Cooper, a famous Sag Harbor captain, picked up several Japanese castaways and—to the astonishment of the international community—sailed into Tokyo Bay and negotiated their return with Japanese authorities. Around that time, John Manjiro, another castaway and the only Japanese national in all of North America, was living in Fairhaven, a short distance from Sag Harbor. There is no record that MacDonald ever met Manjiro, but it is well within the realm of possibility. It is hard to imagine that MacDonald had not heard of the famous castaway.

In those days, New England ships regularly reprovisioned in Hawaii, the Pacific hub of the whaling industry known then as the Sandwich Islands. Here interest in Japan was at a fever pitch. The record of Ranald MacDonald's movements during this period suffers from large gaps. But it is well known that he was in the Hawaiian Islands, in Lahaina, on Maui, in 1847, where he made a bargain with the captain of the whaling ship *Plymouth*, exchanging his wages for a small boat and the opportunity to be left off the coast of Japan.

The captain of the *Plymouth* held to his bargain and left MacDonald adrift near the Japanese coast. He chose to land in June 1848, on the tiny island of Rishiri, so far north that it was on Japan's frontier. He had with him a large number of books, including a Bible, which was strictly forbidden in Japan; some food; navigation equipment; and two pistols. On the optimistic assumption that the Japanese would take pity on and aid him instead of putting him to death, MacDonald feigned being shipwrecked and presented himself as helpless.

But instead of meeting the Japanese he had expected to find on Rishiri, he was rescued by the indigenous people of Japan's north, the Ainu. At that time the Ainu were under the control of the more organized and technologically advanced *wajin*, or Japanese. They were required to report any foreigners to their masters, and they did so. Within days MacDonald was placed under custody of Japanese samurai who arrived from the main island of Hokkaido. From that point on, MacDonald saw very little of Japan, because he was either in jail or being transported under guard by ship or palanquin to other parts of the country. As the Japanese text on the monument in today's Astoria suggests, MacDonald spent nearly his entire time in Japan, a total of ten months, as a prisoner.

> *From that point on, MacDonald saw very little of Japan. He was either in jail or being transported by ship or palanquin to other parts of the country.*

From Rishiri Island, MacDonald was taken by boat to a Japanese military base in Soya, at the northern tip of Hokkaido, where he was briefly incarcerated and interrogated. From there he was transported by ship to the castle town of Matsumae, in southern Hokkaido, where he was again briefly incarcerated. From Matsumae, MacDonald was transported by ship all the way down the western coast of Japan to the southern port of Nagasaki, where the law said all foreigners had to be taken and eventually deported. He spent over six months in Nagasaki at a refurbished temple, confined to a tiny room. It was here that he made his contribution to Japanese history, leaving the room only to travel to the harbor on the day he was finally deported, April 26, 1849.

Other American whalers who wound up on Japanese soil in those days were also confined in Nagasaki, and their sometimes rough treatment became one reason the United States later sent Commodore Perry with an armed fleet to force Japan to end its isolation.

American sailors of the nineteenth century tended to be an unruly bunch. Around the time of MacDonald's arrival, the Japanese had been struggling to control one group of men who, although feigning shipwreck, had actually deserted from their whaling ship. Since shipwrecked Americans and even deserters of the era generally had no desire to be in Japan (the deserters usually hoped to reach the Asian mainland), escape attempts were not uncommon. MacDonald, however, was different. He was not a deserter, nor was he the shipwrecked sailor he claimed to be. He had entered Japan of his own volition, and he was in no hurry to leave.

Because of its two-century-long policy of seclusion, the Japanese government was in an awkward position. Japan had expelled all foreigners in the early 1600s. As a result, by 1848, almost no foreign traders could communicate with the Japanese except through sign language. To maintain occasional contact with the Dutch and the Chinese allowed to carry on limited trade in Nagasaki, the government maintained a cadre of professional Dutch- and Chinese-speaking interpreters. These men not only helped to control trade, but lent their aid when European and American ships were in trouble off the coast or when ships tried to visit (with no success) to obtain trading rights.

By the mid-nineteenth century, the outside world had changed drastically since the seclusion laws were enacted. Instead of Portuguese, Spanish, Dutch, or Chinese ships, most foreign vessels now sailing near Japan were British or American. The British had become so powerful that they had folded large parts of the world into their empire. With their huge navy, they threatened the sovereignty of Asian nations, including once-powerful China. The Americans, too, were in an expansionist mode in the Pacific. In addition to warships, a vast armada of their whaling vessels were hunting near the Japanese islands.

In contacts with the British or the Americans (or the occasional French or Russians), Dutch- or Chinese-speaking interpreters were of little use. With this in mind, early in the nineteenth century the Japanese Shogunate had ordered the interpreters in Nagasaki to study English. But there were no native speakers to learn from—until Ranald MacDonald arrived.

MacDonald was brought to Nagasaki around October 1848. Shortly after authorities initially questioned him, they decided to have him teach English conversation to fourteen of the professional Dutch-speaking interpreters. To the delight of modern historians, this period of his stay in Japan can be verified from three sources: Japanese records of MacDonald's interrogation, the journal of a Dutch trader who visited him in jail, and MacDonald's own surviving notes and recollections.

While he was in jail, MacDonald maintained a glossary of Japanese words and expressions which, along with other handwritten materials, can be seen today in the British Columbia Archives in Victoria, Canada. In 1848, however, it was illegal for foreigners in Japan to learn Japanese, so this glossary therefore reveals not only MacDonald's linguistic abilities, but his bold attempts to understand the language of his captors. The glossary, furthermore, has been the object of intense study by Japanese linguists, who find it a gold mine of information. It reveals the types of subjects MacDonald discussed with his pupils and guards, and even how the Japanese language has changed over the last century and a half. And included with the glossary is a list of MacDonald's interpreter pupils.

After Ranald MacDonald died in 1894, several North American researchers who did not know Japanese and had trouble deciphering his handwriting drew erroneous conclusions from his glossary. As a result, the wrong interpreters have occasionally been identified from his list. One recent biography devotes an entire chapter to an interpreter, Gohachirô Namura, who apparently had nothing to do with MacDonald.

Due to the diligent recent work of Japanese historians such as Chisato Ishihara, the pupils' identities have now been firmly fixed, and their later careers can be tracked with considerable accuracy. Many, it turns out, played an active role in interpreting for the Japanese government after 1853, when Japan was finally opened to the outside world. In particular, MacDonald's favorite pupil, Moriyama Einosuke, played a starring role during the tense negotiations with Commodore Perry in 1853. Although the official languages were Dutch and Chinese, Moriyama's command of English greatly impressed the foreign visitors and helped to smooth over frictions.

Today it is hard to understand how tense these negotiations must have been. For the Japanese officials, the fate of their nation was at stake, and one false step could have meant personal and national disaster. For Commodore Perry and the men of the fleet he commanded, failure could have meant slaughter on the shores of Tokyo Bay. Because MacDonald taught English to government interpreters at such a critical juncture in Japanese history, he therefore indirectly helped to preserve the country's independence and contributed to its modernization.

Most popular histories of U.S.–Japan relations emphasize that they began with Commodore Perry's visit in 1853. Yet MacDonald preceded Perry to Japan by five years. After such an adventure, why is he not better known today?

Had MacDonald immediately returned to North America after his deportation in April 1849, he might have claimed a more prominent place in history. Ever the adventurer, however, he remained in Asia; later he sought his fortune in the Australian Gold Rush. By the time he returned to North America in 1853, news of Commodore Perry's expedition to Japan had captured the nation's attention, and MacDonald's account was easily overlooked.

Although MacDonald kept a journal during his months in Japan, most of it was lost during a shipwreck in Asia after he left Nagasaki. Upon returning to North America, he visited St. Andrew's in Canada, near Montreal, where his stepmother and several half-siblings had relocated from the wilderness. His father had died shortly before his return. While in the area, MacDonald stayed briefly with a lawyer, Malcolm McLeod, who, like MacDonald, was of mixed race.

McLeod was captivated by MacDonald's story and wrote most of it down. With MacDonald's permission, over the years he tried many times to have the account published in both Canada and the United States, with no success. In effect, he became the editor, even the ghostwriter, of MacDonald's autobiography. Unfortunately, he also introduced a florid and hard-to-read style, along with many errors of fact and interpretation, into the text. Not until 1923, nearly thirty years after MacDonald's death, was the work committed to print, and then only through the heroic efforts of editors William S. Lewis and Naojiro Murakami, who supplied copious footnotes and appendices to make the work comprehensible to contemporary readers and to explain errors and contradictions in the original text. By that time, MacDonald's story of adventure, and his entry into a once-closed Japan, had lost its currency.

Although it is easy for us in our multicultural modern world to forget, a "half breed" such as MacDonald faced many obstacles in mainstream society in the late nineteenth century. This alone made it difficult for him to get his story published, and it may have affected where he chose to spend the rest of his life. After returning from Japan, he lived on the frontier, far from any publishers, working as an explorer, entrepreneur, and rancher in what are now British Columbia and Washington State. Here MacDonald found others like himself, frequently of mixed race, with connections to the land and often to the old Hudson's Bay Company.

In the twentieth century, interest in MacDonald tended to come in waves, often triggered by people who rediscovered his story and became enthusiasts. Only recently, in both Japan and the United States, has MacDonald's story achieved enough critical mass to ensure his place in history.

Bruce Berney, head of the Astoria City Library from 1967 until 1997, initiated the project to build the city's monument to MacDonald. Berney had once taught English in Japan and was interested in Japanese language and culture. Like most Americans, he had never heard of Ranald MacDonald.

Around 1970, weeding out some old books in the library, he came across the 1923 edition of MacDonald's book *Ranald MacDonald: The Narrative of His Life 1824–1894,* published posthumously by the Eastern Washington State Historical Society. Berney found the story of MacDonald's Japanese adventure almost too amazing to believe. By coincidence, he and MacDonald shared a birthday, February 3. To celebrate the connection, Berney held a "birthday party" for MacDonald in 1974, and created a four-page program outlining the MacDonald story for the occasion.

The program made its way around the country, and one copy was read by Torao Tomita, then a Japanese Fulbright student studying American history at Yale University. Tomita, who knew of MacDonald and was already interested in him, traveled to meet Berney in Astoria. There, he was given an original copy of the 1923 book, which he later translated into Japanese, thus rekindling interest in MacDonald in Japan.

In an interview with the author on August 13, 1994, Berney explained what happened next:

After the "birthday party," I realized not only that MacDonald's
story was authentic, but that people really were interested in him. As

library director in Astoria, I also thought the book helped show that literature is important to the community. There were many sailors then coming to Astoria from all over, walking around town without knowing anything about Ranald MacDonald and the fact that he was born here. So I decided there ought to be a monument to him, both in English and in Japanese.

With help from individual donors and the local Japanese head of the Epson Company in Portland, Mas Tomita, money was raised for the stone memorial. University of Oregon Japan scholar Steve Kohl and Mas Tomita helped to organize a Friends of MacDonald Society as a committee of the Clatsop County Historical Society. Under the auspices of the Friends Society, a formal dedication ceremony was held. Those attending included local notables, representatives of the British and Japanese consulates, descendants of the great Indian leader Comcomly, and relatives of MacDonald from Washington and Montana.

There were many sailors then coming to Astoria without knowing Ranald MacDonald was born here.

Today MacDonald's story is far better known than it was even ten years ago. In the United States, in addition to his own autobiography, at least four biographies of MacDonald have appeared. In Japan, his autobiography has been published in translation. He also features prominently in a famous historical novel about the period by Akira Yoshimura, titled *Umi no Sairei* ("Festival of the Sea"), and his story is included in several English-language textbooks. Thanks to the efforts of the Friends of MacDonald Societies in both Japan and the United States, moreover, both countries now have at least two permanent monuments to Ranald MacDonald.

In 1994 a stone memorial to Ranald MacDonald was erected in Nagasaki at the site of his former prison. It features a bas-relief image based on a surviving daguerreotype of MacDonald as a young man. The inscription on the monument reads (in translation by the author) as follows: "Fascinated by Japan, Ranald MacDonald landed on Rishiri Island in 1848 and was sent under escort to Nagasaki. On this site he became the first person to teach English conversation

Monument to MacDonald in modern Nagasaki. A detail shows his portrait,
sculpted by Kazukuni Yamazaki. Photo by Frederik L. Schodt, 1998.

to Japanese, and thus laid the foundation for the dramatic progress in English
studies later made in Japan."

There would never have been any monuments to MacDonald if, around the
time he was born, the Hudson's Bay Company had not significantly changed
policy regarding the relationship between its employees and the native people.
After 1813, when the British took control of Astoria, the company shifted its
policy on marriage to local Indians in favor of such unions, at least in the Pacific
Northwest. George Simpson, in particular, realized that the highly organized
Indian societies at the mouth of the Columbia were different from those inland.
In 1821 he wrote, "Connubial alliances are the best security we can have of the
goodwill of the Natives, I have therefore recommended the Gentlemen to form
connections with the principal Families immediately on their arrival, which is
no difficult matter as the offer of their Wives & Daughters is the first token of
their Friendship & Hospitality" (Galbraith 1976, 63).

Ranald MacDonald's father, Archibald McDonald, took Simpson's recommendation to heart. He married Comcomly's daughter, who was variously
known as Princess Raven or Princess Sunday, and he was at least the third white
man to marry one of the chief's daughters. Many whites were critical of what
they saw as the loose morals of single Chinook women, but thought highly of

them as wives. As one usually acerbic Astorian wrote, "Many of these women, who have followed a depraved course of life before marriage, become excellent and faithful wives afterwards" (Cox 1957, 172).

About six months later, on or about February 3, 1824, Ranald was born. His mother died shortly after his birth. Ranald was entrusted to the care of her Chinook sister, Car-cumcum, who lived in a lodge next to the fort. He became, according to his own account, "the favorite, the 'Toll, Toll' (Chinook for 'The Boy! The Boy') of Gran'pa" (MacDonald 1923, 93).

In the same year, under Simpson's direction, the company's Columbia River operations were relocated some eighty miles up the river, on the north bank. More convenient for fur collection, this became Fort Vancouver. About a year later, in his travels Archibald MacDonald met and fell in love with Jane Klyne, the métis daughter (said of persons with one French-Canadian parent and one American Indian parent) of an HBC employee who worked in the Rocky Mountains.

Jane Klyne took in and raised Ranald as her own child. In his autobiographical *Narrative,* he implies that until much later in life, he did not know his birth mother was a Chinook princess, the daughter of Comcomly, or even that he was part Chinook. This is highly unlikely. Yet MacDonald (or his editor) goes on to say that when he learned the real history of his birth, "the disillusionment pained me beyond expression" (MacDonald 1923, 98). Exactly what Ranald MacDonald knew about his ancestry, and how soon he knew it, remains a mystery.

The fusion of Chinook and Scottish blood that MacDonald represented helped him in several ways during his later adventure. His features had a slight Asian cast. This may not have been an aid when he first landed in Japan, as even returning Japanese castaways were treated harshly. But to his guards, he may have seemed less threatening than other foreigners. In support of this theory, one of his cousins wrote in 1916 that "Ranald's mother, was the daughter of an Indian chief on

> *The fusion of Chinook and Scottish blood helped him in Japan in several ways. To his guards, he may have seemed less threatening than other foreigners.*

the Pacific Coast, hence, his complexion was that of Japanese only unusually larger, which I think [was] the true salvation of all the prisoners. No doubt the Japanese Governor, who employed Ranald, possibly thought that Ranald was of his tribe, etc." (Donald MacDonald to N. B. Wheeler, March 30, 1916).

While the hereditary aspects of personality may be argued, in MacDonald the end result was a gregarious man of extraordinary intelligence and absolute courage, who possessed a phenomenal memory. Like his father and his Chinook grandfather, he genuinely enjoyed people. In his surviving letters, he displays a wonderful sense of humor. The letters of those who knew him, and even Japanese government records, make it clear that he had a rare ability to attract people from broad walks of life, put them at ease, and endear himself to them.

Even more than his lineage, the geographic location of MacDonald's birth helped to explain his adventure in Japan. Born into a polyglot environment, he had an easy familiarity with languages. The Hudson's Bay Company employees around the Columbia River spoke a myriad of languages, including French, Cree, Hawaiian, and Iroquois. Even before the whites arrived, the area had been a complex linguistic environment, because the Chinooks were used to communicating with other tribes who spoke different languages.

Living with his father and stepmother, the young MacDonald was exposed to a variety of languages. His father's native tongue was Gaelic, while his stepmother's was presumably French, mixed with some Chinook. Given that one of MacDonald's stated reasons for going to Japan was to become an interpreter, it is worth noting that his father was acutely aware of the importance of interpreters. In a letter of August 8, 1842, to a company superior, Archibald noted that hostile Indians had recently rained arrows on him and on his men, mainly because they had no interpreters with them and a misunderstanding arose. Condemning the company's recent cutbacks in interpreters, he warned of the long-term consequences and stated flatly: "Interpreters are a necessary evil" (Cole 2001, 222).

Most important to understanding MacDonald's adventure in Japan is the uniquely global perspective shared by the people at the mouth of the Columbia River. The Astorians traded with China and dreamed of Japan. The Hudson's Bay Company traded with the Russians in Alaska, the Spanish in California, and the independent Kingdom of Hawaii. In an age when most people spent their entire lives within a radius of a hundred miles, company officers such as MacDonald's father regularly traveled vast distances across the North American continent and back and forth to Europe. Some, such as Governor George Simpson, were constantly on the move and even circled the globe. To these company men, Japan was a place of intense interest. As MacDonald writes in his *Narrative*, "Japan was our next neighbor across the way—only the placid sea, the Pacific, between us" (MacDonald 1923, 120).

Given that MacDonald lived in Astoria / Fort George only a couple of years, what, later in life, were his connections to his birthplace?

In his surviving writings, he does not mention returning to the area after he left it at the age of ten. Yet he may well have revisited his birthplace, while he was a sailor or after his return from Japan. It is clear that he identified with Astoria in a deeply personal way.

In his writings, MacDonald rarely refers to his birthplace as "Fort George," though this was its name when he was born in 1824. The name "Astoria" had gained a mythic quality after the publication in 1836 of Washington Irving's best-selling book *Astoria,* which represented the Americans' expansionist dreams and gave the first hint of a nation that eventually spanned a continent. By contrast, the British "Fort George" interlude lasted only a few years and had little long-range impact.

MacDonald was born under a British flag to a British father and a Chinook mother and raised until the age of ten in a wilderness ostensibly controlled by both Britain and the United States and loosely managed by the Hudson's Bay Company, a British corporation. Astoria did not officially fall under United States jurisdiction until the mid-1840s.

Later in life, however, MacDonald seems to have felt considerable pride that he was born in the famous Astoria. In his writings, he describes making a journey in 1839, at age fifteen, from the Red River Settlement to the town of St. Thomas, in Ontario. While crossing Lake Huron by steamship on the way to Detroit, he notes that the American passengers were impressed to learn he was from Astoria. Near the end of his life, in a letter to Eva Emery Dye (who wrote her 1906 book *McDonald of Oregon: A Tale of Two Shores* at MacDonald's request), he mentions having visited San Francisco around 1842 and comments that he "never thought it would outstride Astoria. It had some 20 or 25 adobe dwellings besides the HBCo post" (Ranald MacDonald to Mrs. C. H. Dye, July 24, 1892).

In depositions the Japanese took of MacDonald in 1848, he merely claims to be from "Oregon." (He may have blurred responses to questions about his native country in order to claim multiple nationalities.) But in depositions taken by the Americans aboard the U.S.S. *Preble*, which retrieved him from Nagasaki in 1849, he said he was from Astoria. The same year, a report by an official in the British Consulate in Hong Kong (where the *Preble* let MacDonald off) describes MacDonald as being from "Fort George" (Charles Gutzlaff to J. G. Bonham, May 23, 1849).

Toward the end of his life, after spending many years in British Columbia, MacDonald lived in the northeast corner of the modern state of Washington. After a lifetime of confusion about his racial identity, he had begun to identify with Native American culture, specifically with that of the Chinook Tribe in the Astoria area. With the encouragement of the editor of his autobiography, he had asserted a claim to the entire Pacific Northwest as the descendant of Chinook chief Comcomly. This may have been a ploy to help market the book he sought to publish, but it no doubt helped him to re-identify with Astoria and its history.

In early February, 1891, the *Astorian* newspaper ran an article entitled "The Oldest Native Astorian: A Brief Sketch of the Life of the Grandson of King Kumkumly, the Old Indian Chief." Copies of the newspaper and any correspondence MacDonald may have had with the publisher were lost in a fire that later swept through the city, but reprints that appeared in other newspapers were preserved. In entertaining and somewhat exaggerated fashion, the writer described MacDonald's life, his adventure in Japan, and how his Chinook grandfather had been "in command of all the tribes from the mouth of the Columbia River to the Flathead country, and was the only chief recognized by the Hudson's Bay Company, on account of his great influence with all the tribes." MacDonald, it said, was "the only lineal descendant of King Kumkumly, and is still looked upon by all the Indian tribes, particularly down this way, as their only chief, although he cannot speak any of the Indian dialects with fluency." Comcomly, or "Kumkumly," the author added, "lives in the songs and chronicles of dusky descendants, and . . . had a street in Astoria named after him till the summer of 1888, when the *Astorian* changed the name to First Street." Throughout the article, MacDonald is proudly described as an Astorian (*Morning Oregonian,* February 12, 1891*)*.

MacDonald died in 1894 and was buried in an Indian cemetery in Toroda, Washington, about seventy-five miles northwest of Colville and near the Canadian border. His gravestone was erected in 1951. Like the modern monument in Astoria, it valiantly attempts to sum up an extraordinary life.

RANALD MACDONALD

1824–1894

SON OF PRINCESS RAVEN

AND

ARCHIBALD MACDONALD

HIS WAS A LIFE OF ADVENTURE

SAILING THE SEVEN SEAS

WANDERING IN FAR COUNTRIES

BUT RETURNING AT LAST

TO REST IN HIS HOMELAND

"SAYONARA"—FAREWELL

ASTORIA   EUROPE

JAPAN   THE CARIBOO

AUSTRALIA FT. COLVILLE

Acknowledgments

Scores of people helped me in writing my book, *Native American in the Land of the Shogun: Ranald MacDonald and the Opening of Japan* (Berkeley: Stone Bridge Press, 2003), but for making this contribution to *Eminent Astorians* possible, I should particularly like to thank Bruce Berney, Steve Forrester, Karen Kirtley, and the Friends of MacDonald Society.

Works Cited

Bancroft, Hubert Howe. 1886. *The Works: The Native Races.* Vol. 1, *The Wild Tribes.* San Francisco: History Company. Copyright 1882.

Bishop, Charles. 1967. *The Journal and Letters of Captain Charles Bishop on the North-West Coast of America, in the Pacific and in New South Wales, 1794–1799.* Ed. Michael Roe. Published for the Hakluyt Society. Cambridge: The University Press.

Cole, Jean Murray, ed. 2001. *This Blessed Wilderness: Archibald McDonald's letters from the Columbia, 1822–1844.* Vancouver: University of British Columbia Press. Archibald McDonald to John McLeod, August 8, 1842.

Cox, Ross. 1957. *The Columbia River, or scenes and adventures during a residence of six years on the western side of the Rocky Mountains among various tribes of Indians hitherto unknown; together with "A Journey across the American Continent."* Ed. Edgar I. Stewart and Jane R. Stewart. Norman: University of Oklahoma Press.

Franchère, Gabriel. 1967. *Adventure at Astoria, 1810–1814.* Trans. and ed. Hoyt C. Franchère. Norman: University of Oklahoma Press.

Galbraith, John S. 1976. *The Little Emperor: Governor Simpson of the Hudson's Bay Company.* Toronto: Macmillan of Canada. (Quoting from E. E. Rich, *Journal of Occurrences in the Athabasca Department*, p. 392.)

Gutzlaff, Charles. Letter to J. G. Bonham, May 23, 1849. "Letters Received by the Secretary of the Navy from Commanding Officers of Squadrons ('Squadron Letters'), 1841–1886, Roll 4, East India Squadron, vol. 4, 12 February 1848–19 June 1850, "The Deposition of Ranald MacDonald, 30 April 1848"; British Foreign Office, China Correspondence, F.O. 17/155, "Visit of U.S. Ship 'Preble' at Nagasaki."

MacDonald, Donald. Letter to N. B. Wheeler, March 30, 1916. "Donald Macdonald Letters," Eastern Washington State Historical Society.

MacDonald, Ranald. 1923. *Ranald MacDonald: The Narrative of His Life 1824–1894.* Ed. William S. Lewis and Naojiro Murakami. Spokane: Eastern Washington State Historical Society.

_____. Letter to Eva Emery Dye, July 24, 1892. "MacDonald, Ranald 1824–1894, 'Correspondence Outward—Letters to Mrs. C. H. Dye,' MS-1249, box 9, folder 11, British Columbia Archives.

Walker, Alexander. 1982. *An Account of a Voyage to the North West Coast of America in 1785 and 1786, by Alexander Walker.* Ed. Robin Fisher and J. M. Bumsted. Seattle: University of Washington Press.

Captain George Flavel
and the Building of Astoria

By William F. Willingham

After sailing the brig *John Petty* through the mouth of the Columbia River in February 1850, Captain George Flavel observed the ramshackle hamlet of Astoria a few miles upstream on the south shore. Flavel was bound for Oregon City and had no way of knowing that his future and that of Astoria would intertwine, making him wealthy and transforming the city into a vital and robust port.

John Jacob Astor founded Astoria in 1811 more than a decade before Flavel's birth, as another outpost in his vast fur-trading network. But in the intervening years, Astoria had shown none of its promise, passing into British ownership between 1813 and 1846, first under the North West Company and then under the Hudson's Bay Company. When the United States gained sole control of the Northwest in 1846, the Hudson's Bay Company closed its operation at Astoria. Until Methodist missionaries and emigrants from the eastern United States began arriving in 1840, the hamlet barely survived.

While settlement of the Willamette Valley had begun in earnest by the early 1840s, development along the Oregon coast lagged. Those who pushed to the coastal area began farming, joining the missionaries who had become the first permanent inhabitants near Astoria. In 1841, Lieutenant Charles Wilkes of the United States Exploring Expedition entered the Columbia River and noted Astoria's run-down appearance: "In the morning we had a view of the somewhat famous Astoria, which is anything but what I should wish to describe. Half a dozen log houses, with as many sheds and a pig-sty or two, are all that it can boast of, and even these appear to be rapidly going to decay" (Wilkes 1845, vol. 4, 320). As late as 1860, one early settler wrote that "the entire peninsula on which Astoria stands was one solid forest of tall hemlock and spruce timber" except for a few acres on Astor Hill and along the shore of the Columbia River (Gillette's Diary, Clatsop County Historical Society, 360).

While Astoria languished, Portland—as head of navigation for ocean-going vessels on the lower Willamette River—boomed. To supply Willamette Valley settlers with finished goods and to ship their surplus agricultural produce to outside markets, several shipping firms started regular connections between San Francisco and Portland. This economic activity brought seamen such as George Flavel to Oregon.

In fall 1849, the twenty-five-year-old captain arrived in San Francisco after sailing the *John Petty* from Norfolk, Virginia. Unable to sell all his cargo in San Francisco, Flavel took the remainder to Portland, then rapidly becoming the chief trading point of the fast-settling Willamette Valley, where he successfully disposed of it. He repeated this type of venture successfully during the next few years, returning to Oregon as master of three ships, the *John Petty, Goliath*, and *Goldhunter*. These voyages to and from the Columbia River's treacherous mouth later proved invaluable.

Almost nothing is known about Flavel's life before his arrival in San Francisco. The best available evidence suggests he was born in New Jersey on November 17, 1823. He joined the Odd Fellows Lodge in Norfolk in January 1849, just before he sailed for San Francisco. Flavel maintained an air of mystery throughout his life, choosing not to reveal much about his past. Flavel's friend, Dr. Bethenia Owens-Adair, a prominent pioneer Oregonian, may have best captured his elusive nature:

> He was of a proud and reticent nature, which repelled any inquiry
> into his private affairs; not that there was, presumably, anything to
> conceal, for during the whole of his long life in Astoria, which was
> open to all, his honor was unquestioned, and he invariably showed the
> greatest scorn for hypocrisy or meanness of any description. But there

was a dignity and reserve in his demeanor which even those nearest him did not venture to attempt to break through (Owens-Adair 1906, 257–258).

As Flavel sailed back and forth between San Francisco and Portland, he learned the treacherous intricacies of the river's ever-changing mouth. Ocean tides and currents combined with the river current to constantly alter the entrance. Navigation charts noted a shifting sandbar and two channels. Given the volume of commerce and the size of ships, neither channel provided a passage of sufficient depth and dependability. At best, a channel of seventeen to twenty-one feet over the bar left little room to spare for ships of the day. Bad weather and huge waves on the bar frequently detained sailing vessels for weeks and steamers for days. The largest ships could enter only during a smooth sea and high tide. Only desperate or foolish captains attempted the entrance without the aid of a pilot or tug.

With his knowledge of bar conditions at the mouth of the Columbia, Flavel saw a promising financial opportunity and seized it. In December 1850, the Oregon territorial government approved his application for one of the early branch piloting licenses granted for guiding ships from the Pacific upstream through the Columbia to the Willamette River. Flavel quickly gained a reputation

Captain Flavel's Tug, oil painting by Cleveland Rockwell, 1884. CCHS 152.

as a fearless bar pilot and a shrewd businessman. Within eight years, he and several partners or associates had secured a virtual monopoly on bar piloting and ship towing on the Columbia. Other pilots challenged his hold on the business, but none succeeded for long.

Stories abound of Flavel's bravery and tenacity in guiding ships across the bar under adverse conditions. One of the most memorable episodes took place January 29, 1852, during a blinding snowstorm and unusually rough seas. A steam-powered sailing ship, the *General Warren*, was carrying eight hundred live hogs, tons of wheat, and sixty passengers as it tried to enter the Columbia. The ship lost its foretopmast and sprang a leak that pumps could not control. Flavel valiantly tried to guide the ship across the bar, but the weather and currents thwarted him.

Taking on water at an alarming rate, the ship could not raise enough steam and made no headway. Flavel, realizing that the ship would sink, concentrated on trying to save the passengers. He ordered the ship beached on Clatsop Spit. As the ship began to break up, waves carried away all but one lifeboat. The *Warren*'s captain persuaded Flavel and a carefully picked crew of oarsmen to make for Astoria, hoping they could return with help for the remaining passengers and crew. As he set off in the breakers and darkness, Flavel promised the captain, "I'll come back if I am alive."

Flavel made it to Astoria, but on his return to the *General Warren*, he found the ship destroyed and no survivors. For his efforts to save the passengers, Flavel received much praise. A surviving oarsman succinctly captured Flavel's dramatic role in the tragedy: "He was the bravest seaman I ever saw. It was only his pluck saved us in the boat and brought us to land safe" (*Oregonian*, Flavel obituary, July 9, 1893, 6).

While developing his piloting operation in the 1850s, Flavel invested its profits in ventures around Astoria and in other shipping opportunities. Some proved successful, others did not. In 1852, for instance, Flavel purchased an interest in an Astoria sawmill. At first the business made a profit in the San Francisco market, but it failed when lumber prices collapsed. Flavel later recouped his losses by focusing on the piloting business and forging a productive thirty-year partnership with Captain Asa Meade Simpson, who had a sawmill and shipyards at North Bend on Coos Bay in Oregon. (Simpson lived in

LEFT: Mary Christina Flavel, ca. 1854. FLAVEL COLLECTION, CCHS 532.00F.

RIGHT: Captain Flavel, ca. 1855. FLAVEL COLLECTION, CCHS 531.00F.

San Francisco, where he oversaw his retail lumber yards and sawmills and ship-yards in California, Oregon, and Washington until his death in 1914.) In the late 1850s, Flavel successfully operated various ships in the coasting trade between Astoria and California.

As his business affairs prospered, Flavel decided to marry. He chose for his wife Mary Christina Boelling, the daughter of the proprietor of the boarding house where he stayed while in Astoria. They were married March 26, 1854. The captain was thirty and Mary only fourteen. When not in San Francisco, the couple lived in a simple, two-story clapboard house at Eighth and Duane Streets. They had three children, one son and two daughters, born between 1855 and 1864. The daughters, Nellie and Katie, earned reputations as accomplished musicians; the son, George C. Flavel, followed in his father's footsteps with a career as sailor, bar pilot, and businessman.

In 1860, Flavel invested in the fast-sailing barkentine *Jane A. Falkenberg* and resumed regular shipping voyages between San Francisco, Astoria, and Portland. Flavel also had a large contract supplying lumber to the Hawaiian Islands in the early 1870s. During the time he commanded the *Falkenberg*, Flavel and his family spent several months each year in San Francisco. They found the cosmopolitan social and cultural life an alluring contrast to the limited opportunities in frontier Astoria.

As Flavel's shipping and piloting businesses grew, he began expanding his docks at Astoria and constructed a new warehouse on the waterfront. In 1869, he and his partners built the steam tug *Astoria* for use as a pilot boat. The state of Oregon had offered a subsidy for constructing and operating a steam tug on the Columbia River bar. The *Astoria* became the key to Flavel's continuing dominance of the piloting business. In 1869, to take advantage of the large number of ship passengers traveling through Astoria, he constructed the Occident Hotel at Tenth and Bond Streets, considered the finest in the area. Flavel also operated a ship chandlery and built a fine block of brick buildings across the street from his hotel. Over time, he also constructed a number of commercial brick buildings in downtown Astoria.

While actively engaged in various business enterprises, he also found time for public service during the 1870s. Voters elected him to serve five years on the Astoria Board of Trustees (city council). As a trustee, he focused on developing the town's infrastructure, such as streets and fire protection. Through his East Coast business connections, he bought a fire engine and 250 feet of hose for the Astoria volunteer fire department. He contributed generously toward a fire bell

The *Jane A. Falkenberg,* oil painting by Cleveland Rockwell, 1884. CCHS 465.001.

Captain Flavel, ca. 1870. FLAVEL COLLECTION, CCHS 530.00F.

tower for the town. Flavel also served as the Clatsop County treasurer in 1872 and as a school board director for three years in the 1870s.

Flavel faced many challengers to his dominance of the piloting business on the Columbia River. Not only did various Astoria seamen attempt to enter the business, but others outside the community challenged his methods of operation. In 1875, William Reid—lawyer, railroad financier, and secretary of the Portland Board of Trade—alleged in the press that Flavel charged monopoly rates for towing and piloting vessels across the bar and vowed that the board would take him to federal court over the matter. In his defense, Flavel responded in a local newspaper that he had "never at any time . . . had the exclusive monopoly of the business of pilotage and towage on the bar" and had "never failed to carry out, intact, to the strict letter, the laws of the State of Oregon relating to business of pilotage and towage on the Columbia River bar." In this exchange with Reid, Flavel revealed his injured pride when he stated that "no gentleman has ever questioned my integrity hitherto." He further asserted that he could "conceive of no more degraded and humiliating spectacle than that of a man professing to be a gentleman, to fly into print with the purpose of injuring the business and reputation of another, without a statement of the facts" (*Oregon's Seaport: Astoria,* 1875, 47). Reid's vow to sue Flavel proved to be an empty threat.

Flavel also took the offensive in defending his business interests. In 1878, he used his political clout to kill a bill in the Oregon Legislature (pushed by Portland interests) that would have undercut his business. Among other provisions, the bill required bar pilots to board Oregon-bound ships before they left San Francisco.

An attack on Flavel was an attack on Astoria, for their economic well-being seemed inseparable.

None of these attacks reduced Flavel's popularity in Astoria, where people saw the character and political assaults as thinly veiled attempts to malign Astoria's reputation as a port. An attack on Flavel was an attack on Astoria, for their economic well-being seemed inseparable. Reminiscing about Flavel and his role in developing Astoria, Dr. Bethenia Owens-Adair wrote that "he was loyal to the little city of his adoption, and made his interest largely hers. Her finest buildings were erected by him, and much of the money he made was put into the place where it was amassed" (Owens-Adair 1906, 260).

In the years of Flavel's peak activity, Astoria boomed economically. Between 1870 and 1890, its population grew more than 1,000 percent, from 639 to 7,127. Part of the growth stemmed from Astoria's serving as the main intermediate transfer point on regular steamer service between Portland and San Francisco. Steamers bound for California customarily made the trip from Portland to Astoria during the day and tied up at Astoria overnight before crossing the bar the next morning. Geographically isolated from the rest of Oregon, Astoria depended upon water transportation to foster economic growth. Unfortunately, the city's location also had drawbacks. Access to the Washington side of the river was difficult because the estuary was so wide and the north shore lacked good landing spots. The high, rough terrain south of the city cut it off from parts of Oregon. In addition, the city, sandwiched on a narrow shelf of land between the river and Coxcomb Hill, had little room for expansion. Finally, the hinterland of Astoria was not productive for agricultural purposes.

Also during the 1870s, Flavel and other Astoria leaders battled with Portland to control the future flow of trade between Oregon and outside markets. This struggle involved not only statewide politics, but also an attempt to gain federal money to improve navigation at the mouth of the Columbia.

Astoria attempted to take over Portland's wheat export trade in the mid-1870s. Claiming that Astoria could handle deeper-draft vessels than Portland, Flavel and other promoters urged farmers and shippers to save on towage or piloting between Portland and Astoria by sending their wheat and flour directly to Astoria for overseas shipment. Astoria attempted to develop its wharf and warehouse facilities, but it lacked the capital and expertise to compete with Portland's extensive shipping facilities and entrenched merchants. Despite the city's best efforts, Astoria's experiment never developed into a major activity. The value of exports from Astoria and Portland dramatically revealed the former's inability to supplant the latter as the region's chief port. For example, in 1876, Astoria exported goods valued at $1.5 million, while Portland shipped $2.4 million of commodities. From 1876 to 1886, Portland's exports equaled $5.7 million and Astoria's only $1.3 million.

Although Astoria failed to supplant Portland as Oregon's leading port, it developed a thriving salmon canning industry. In 1866, pioneer canner George Hunt put up 4,000 cases; by 1873, eight canners operated on the Lower Columbia. The industry peaked in 1883 when thirty-nine Lower Columbia processors packed a record catch of 42.8 million pounds of salmon (629,400 cases). Thereafter the industry gradually waned from over-fishing. As the salmon enterprise began to contract in the late 1880s, Astoria's dominance of the industry increased. Of the thirty-nine canneries operating in 1887, twenty-two were in Astoria. They managed to produce an annual average of 412,000 cases of salmon between 1891 and 1940.

Astoria lacked the capital and expertise to compete with Portland's extensive shipping facilities and entrenched merchants.

Along with canning, Astoria developed a lumber industry. In the 1880s, four mills and box factories operated along the waterfront. The lumber mills served local and California markets. Over time, the lumber industry waxed and waned as nearby timber disappeared and logging companies had to build rail access to more distant wood sources. To fully develop its economic potential, Astoria needed rail connections with Portland and the Willamette Valley and an improved navigation channel. While Astoria did not achieve a railroad until after Flavel died, it did get crucial navigation improvements at the mouth of the Columbia and elsewhere in the river while he was running his piloting operation.

During the 1870s, Astoria interests lobbied Congress for surveys by the U.S. Army Corps of Engineers to determine the best way to improve channel conditions at the Columbia's mouth. The Corps' initial studies downplayed existing navigational problems. In 1875, Major Nathaniel Michler, the engineer officer in charge of the Corps' Portland office, declared that the bar was no more dangerous than the entrance to San Francisco Bay. He confidently asserted that channel markings and reliance on "pilots, and avoidance of storm crossings could overcome the bar's difficulties" (*Annual Reports of the Chief of Engineers, 1875*, 747). Many who used the river rejected the opinion as unrealistic. They believed that the steady increase in river traffic and size of vessels severely taxed the existing, largely unimproved channel. As another Portland engineer officer, Major George Gillespie, noted in 1880, "The citizens of Astoria are anxious that some extensive work of improvement should be taken in hand to increase the depth of water over the bar" (*Annual Reports of the Chief of Engineers, 1880*, 2315).

After extensive study, the Corps recommended a plan for stabilizing the sands at the entrance of the Columbia and forcing the river to scour one permanent, deep channel across the bar. The improvement called for a 4.5-mile low-tide jetty, extending from near Fort Stevens on the south cape to a point about three miles south of Cape Disappointment on the north. The Corps had concluded that the stone jetty would provide a thirty-foot-deep channel depth at low water. Congress funded the jetty project in 1884. Completing the south jetty required ten years and $2 million, but the benefits accrued quickly. Within two years, the value of tonnage passing over the bar more than doubled the average for the previous decade.

George Flavel died before the Corps of Engineers improved river navigation. In the 1880s, however, he continued to dominate Astoria's business and social scene. Before retiring from the bar-piloting business in 1887, Flavel added to his fleet of pilot- and tugboats and carried out several lucrative ship-salvage operations. In awarding him a salvage judgment, a federal judge noted that Flavel's conduct was "highly meritorious and deserved the special recognition of the award" and that his displays of "enterprise and gallantry . . . would reflect great credit on a much younger and abler man than himself" (quoted in *Cumtux*, vol. 11, no. 3, 15). Flavel's contemporaries generally agreed with the authors of *Lewis and Dryden's Marine History of the Pacific Northwest* (Wright 1895) that his success in piloting—even though he charged high rates—stemmed from the fact that "his service could not be excelled" (26–27).

As Flavel became less active in his pilot business, he branched into other ventures such as real estate and banking. In 1882, he bought forty head of cattle and three hundred acres, including Tansy Point. On the property he developed a gentleman's farm for raising race horses and fine cattle. He and other investors established the First National Bank of Astoria in 1886, and Flavel presided as president until his death. In 1892, Flavel sold his Tansy Point land (now two thousand acres) for $350,000 to a development company, which had grand plans to develop a major seaport at the location. The speculative undertaking, named Flavel, boomed twice but ultimately failed.

In 1887, at age sixty-four, Flavel sold his interest in the bar-piloting business to his longtime partner, Asa Simpson, and retired. A measure of the respect Captain Flavel had earned for his career in bar piloting and helping to develop his hometown was recorded in *Lewis and Dryden's Marine History of the Pacific Northwest* (Wright 1895, 26–27):

> No man whose name had been so prominently before the people was more roundly abused by both press and public for many years than Capt. George Flavel; and yet in less than a year after his retirement, desires were expressed for a restoration of the Flavel management. Captain Flavel's success was due in large measure to a thorough, practical knowledge of the business in which he was engaged. He never sent a man where he would not go himself, and coupled with absolute fearlessness he possessed rare good judgment.

As a reflection of his wealth and standing in the community, Flavel commissioned a grand, Victorian Queen Anne–styled mansion one block south of the Astoria courthouse. Designed by Astoria architect Carl Leick, the wood-framed, two-and-a-half-story house with a brick foundation contained 11,600 square feet of space. The asymmetrical volume had a façade displaying elements

The Flavel House at Eighth and Duane Streets, Astoria, ca. 1885.

SEPIA PRINT. FLAVEL COLLECTION, CCHS 30189.965.

of the stick style; a hipped roof with lower cross gables; decorative imbricated shingles; and a one-story, wrap-around front porch. Added exterior touches included cast-iron cresting, stained-glass windows, and decorative window molding. The house's most dramatic element was a three-story octagonal tower with conical roof on the northeast corner of the house. The interior rooms were finely finished, with rich hardwood floors and moldings, decorative plaster ceiling and cornice moldings, brass ornamental hardware, and six fireplaces with unique mantels. The house had indoor plumbing, gas lighting fixtures, and central heating supplied by a wood furnace in the cellar. At its completion in 1886, Flavel's ornate mansion was reputed to have cost $36,000—at a time when a typical upper-middle-class home cost $10,000 to build. The house clearly reflected Flavel's worldly sophistication and personal sense of success.

After a period of feeble health, Captain George Flavel died at his home on July 3, 1893. He was sixty-nine years old. The *Astorian Daily Budget* said his passing "cast a gloom over his entire community, where he was known to almost every man, woman, and child, and highly esteemed and beloved by all. Astoria will miss Capt. Flavel" (July 5, 1893, 1).

Perhaps Dr. Bethenia Owens-Adair best summed up his character when she noted that "Captain Flavel had a will of iron, with which he did not fail to control himself, as well as others. He was a born commander, but a magnanimous one, and working men were eager to be employed by him, for, if he exacted the best of service, so also, did he pay the best wages, with most gratifying promptness, adding generous commendation when deserved" (Owens-Adair 1906, 260).

Flavel left an estate valued in probate at nearly $500,000 and provided generously in his will for several charities. His wealth probably exceeded the probate value, because prior to his death he had distributed property to family members. Out of great respect for Flavel, streets in both Astoria and Portland were named in his honor.

In 1936, his descendants donated the family mansion to Clatsop County as a memorial to the captain and his achievements in helping to develop Astoria's economic potential. Today the restored and well-maintained Flavel House in Astoria's downtown continues to remind all visitors of the captain's commanding role in the community's history.

Acknowledgments

I especially want to thank Liisa Penner, Archivist at the Clatsop County Historical Society, for her assistance in researching this essay. I also appreciated the careful reading and editing of my essay by Karen Kirtley and Mike Bales. Finally, my involvement in this project resulted from Steve Forrester's farsighted commitment to preserving the history of Astoria.

Works Cited

Dennon, Jim. 1991. "The Flavel House Special Issue." *Cumtux.* Clatsop County
    Historical Society Quarterly, vol. 11, no. 3, Astoria, OR.
Gillette, P. W. Diary. Collections of the Clatsop County Historical Society, Astoria, OR.
Lockley, Fred. 1928. *History of the Columbia River Valley from The Dalles to the Sea,* 3
    vols. Chicago: S. J. Clarke Publishing Company.

Oregon's Seaport: Astoria. 1875. Astoria, OR: *The Astorian.*

Owens-Adair, Bethenia Angelina. 1906. *Dr. Owens-Adair: Some of Her Life Experiences.* Portland, OR: Mann & Beach, Printers.

Portrait and Biographical Record of Western Oregon. 1904. Chicago: Chapman Publishing Company.

Schmitter, Michelle, and Lisa Studts. 2001. *The Flavel House and Family.* Astoria, OR: Clatsop County Historical Society.

U.S. Army Corps of Engineers. 1880. *Annual Reports of the Chief of Engineers.* Washington, DC: Government Printing Office.

Willingham, William. 1983. *Army Engineers and the Development of Oregon: A History of the Portland District, U.S. Army Corps of Engineers.* Washington, DC: Government Printing Office.

Wright, E. W., ed. 1895. *Lewis and Dryden's Maritime History of the Northwest.* Portland, OR: Lewis and Dryden Printing Co.

Bethenia Angelina Owens-Adair

By Jean M. Ward

Alittle girl with dark curls and flashing black eyes perched on the shoulders of a tall and lanky man, facing westward toward the Pacific. Three years old and small for her age, she had tired of walking barefoot, breathing the heavy dust kicked up by the wagons and livestock, and riding in her parents' rolling wagon. The child was Bethenia Angelina Owens (1840–1926), who became a leading social reformer and one of the first women to practice medicine on the Pacific Coast. The man was Jesse Applegate (1811–1888), a leader of the Great 1843 Migration to Oregon Country. Bethenia wrote in her 1906 autobiography that she considered Jesse Applegate her second father: "He nursed me as a babe, and carried me on his brawny shoulders for many miles over those rough, almost endless emigrant trails" (Owens-Adair 1906, 283). Through the years that followed, the two formed a lasting friendship.

Bethenia's life was marked by the pluck Applegate saw in her as a child. She left an abusive early marriage, provided for herself and her son, gained an education, earned two medical degrees, and became a pioneering doctor. Pluck helped her endure the criticism she received, not only as a woman doctor, but as a reformer involved in the woman's rights, temperance, and eugenics movements.

Bethenia wrote that her father, Thomas Owens, the tall, handsome, Virginia-born son of a wealthy Kentucky planter, was a courageous man with the reputation of knowing "neither danger nor fear." While serving as sheriff of Pike County, Kentucky, he married violet-eyed Sarah Damron, a petite and capable Kentucky girl of sixteen, and they soon settled on a farm near Piketon and began a family. In an attempt to avoid the chills and fever of "continuous affliction with the ague," the family made moves in Kentucky and Missouri until "Oregon

147

fever" touched them with its promise of better health and economic opportunity (Owens-Adair 1906, 143, 144).

When the Owens family began the six-month journey to Oregon Country, Sarah Owens, then twenty-five, had buried her first-born, who died as an infant in Kentucky, and given birth to three living children. Diana was born in 1838 in Kentucky; Bethenia was born February 8, 1840, in Van Buren County, Missouri; and James W. F. "Flem" was born two years later, at Platte Purchase, Missouri. Seven more children, two sons and five daughters, were born to Thomas and Sarah Owens in Oregon.

In the spring of 1843, the Owens family joined a gathering of men, women, and children at Independence, Missouri, and set forth under the leadership of Peter H. Burnett on the overland trek of two thousand miles. In "A Day with the Cow Column in 1843," Jesse Applegate wrote that this first major wagon train migration to Oregon was "strictly an experiment; not only in respect to the members, but to the outfit of the migrating party." Could "over one thousand souls, with about one hundred and twenty wagons, drawn by six-ox teams, averaging about six yokes to the team, and several thousand loose horses and cattle" make it through such rugged country (Applegate 1868, 489, 490)? Could covered wagons cross the Northern Rocky Mountains into Oregon? Would they find safe passage through Sioux country?

> *Could over one thousand souls, with about one hundred and twenty wagons, make it through such rugged country?*

Traveling as a single body proved too cumbersome, and the emigrants divided into two columns. Those with wagons, teams, and only a few loose cattle joined the "light column," which moved at a fast pace under Burnett's guidance. Those with more than four or five cows joined "the heavy or cow column," which was larger and required more discipline (Applegate 1868, 490, 491). Applegate, then in his early thirties, was chosen captain of the cow column, overseeing about five thousand cattle, oxen, and horses, and about sixty wagons.

In sagebrush country, the wagons divided into fifteen platoons of four wagons each, taking turns breaking through sagebrush that stood two to six feet high.

Despite hardships and dangers, Sarah Owens recalled Applegate's cow column as "a jolly train. We had music, singing and dancing nearly every night. In the evening, while the men were attending to the cattle and horses, their wives and daughters would be carrying buffalo 'chips' in their aprons, making fires and preparing supper, which was eaten and relished with appetites that only out-of-door life can give" (Owens 1906, 145–146).

When they reached buffalo country in present-day Wyoming, near the Sweetwater River, Tom Owens was made captain of the buffalo hunters, and Sarah took over driving the oxen. The hunters were successful and reported that buffalo were plentiful. For their crossing at the turbulent Platte River, they tacked buffalo hides on the bottoms of several wagon beds, and these "novel boats" were filled with portable goods and pulled across the river with ropes held by strong swimmers (Owens 1906, 146).

As the travelers neared their destination, Tom Owens was instrumental in negotiating the long, steep descent to the Grand Ronde Valley. Sarah Owens recalled, "Mr. Owens drove almost every wagon from the top to the valley," where all camped "by a beautiful stream of water, with plenty of luxurious grass for the stock" (Owens 1906, 149).

The next day, the emigrants reached the Waiilatpu mission of Dr. Marcus Whitman, near present-day Walla Walla, Washington. Whitman and his wife,

View of Waiilatpu before 1847, from *Historic Sketches: Walla Walla, Whitman, Columbia and Garfield Counties, Washington Territory,* by Frank T. Gilbert, Portland, Oregon: A. G. Walling, 1882. CCHS COLLECTION.

Narcissa, had come to Oregon County in 1836. Eager to welcome the emigrants of 1843, Whitman had met them at the Platte and journeyed with the wagon train to the Blue Mountains. He moved ahead to blaze a route, then sent back critical supplies of wheat, corn, and peas.*

Leaving their stock and wagons at the Whitman Mission, the emigrants used small boats, canoes, and Indian guides to travel the dangerous waters of the Columbia River to Fort Vancouver, where Dr. John McLoughlin, Chief Factor of the Hudson's Bay Company, would assist them with provisions and seed for crops. The journey was heartbreaking for Jesse Applegate and his wife, Cynthia, who lost their first-born son in the fast waters of the river. As others watched, a boat carrying three adult men and three Applegate boys overturned in the whirling waters, and two were drowned: Edward Bates Applegate, age nine, and a man of seventy who tried to save the boy.

After arriving at the small settlement of Astoria on Christmas Day of 1843, the Owens family crossed the bay to Clatsop Plains, a sandy coastal prairie about ten miles long and one and a half miles wide, located midway between the mouth of the Columbia River and Tillamook Head to the south. They landed at Tansy Point, later called Flavel.

Solomon Smith, the first white man to come to Clatsop Plains, had settled here in 1840 and later established a store at Skipanon with his Indian wife Celiast (Helen), daughter of Chief Coboway of the Clatsops. Smith was followed to Tansy Point by Calvin Tibbets and his Indian wife, and by Eldridge Trask, W. T. Perry, and the Rev. J. L. Parrish with their white wives and families. Sarah Owens recalled that her family was welcomed into this small community and taken to the Trask and Perry farm, where they stayed until their own cabin was completed on a nearby claim.

Bethenia watched as her father built the cabin and her mother chinked the logs with a mixture of dried ferns and clay. No nails were available, and to hold

---

*In 1847, a band of Cayuse and Umatilla Indians killed the Whitmans and thirteen others at the mission, in what became known as the "Whitman Massacre."

the clapboard roof in place, poles were laid across the roof and tied down at the ends. A large fireplace and chimney were built of sod. Here Sarah cooked salmon and potatoes for her growing family.

During the ten years the Owens family lived on the Clatsop claim, Bethenia witnessed not only the courage, but the hard labor and enterprise of her parents in a trade and barter economy. Her father cut and split rails to fence their land, planted their fields with wheat and potatoes, and gradually acquired livestock. He split rails for neighbors in exchange for provisions, and the family's first young pig was received in trade for three hundred split rails. A trade for a herd of about sixty spirited Spanish cattle brought milk and butter to the family table as well as profit, with butter bringing 50 cents to $1.50 a pound. Their small flock of sheep, the first in Clatsop, also proved profitable, with wool selling for 50 to 60 cents a pound. "From this time on," said Sarah Owens, "we made money easily" (Owens 1906, 158).

Commercial ventures often took Tom Owens away from home. In the summer and fall of 1845, working with neighbors Trask, Perry, and Tibbets, Owens constructed Clatsop's first gristmill near the mouth of Ohanna Creek. In the spring of 1848, the same group went to Skipanon to build a small two-masted schooner, which they named the *Pioneer*. The chief carpenter, Robert S. McEwan, was selected captain, and the farmers became the crew. The schooner was filled with "dried and salt salmon, potatoes, butter, cabbage, carrots, cranberries, and a few skins." The men sailed for California, where their "vessel and cargo were sold at a great profit" (Owens 1906, 159).

In time, Tom Owens had a valuable claim of 640 acres, thriving herds, and the "largest and best" house at Clatsop Plains. The 1850 Manuscript Census Record for Clatsop County shows the value of the Owens farm at $10,000. John Hobson, who became Bethenia's brother-in-law, once told her: "Your father could make money faster than any man I ever saw. He came here in 1843, with fifty cents in his pocket, and I do not think there was one hundred dollars in the whole county [Clatsop], and in less than ten years he was worth over twenty thousand dollars" (Owens-Adair 1906, 27).

Bethenia's resourceful mother supplemented the family income and food supplies. Treasured flax seeds Sarah Owens brought to Oregon produced a fiber Indians coveted for their fishnets, and she was soon trading flax for salmon.

As a capable seamstress, she could turn out five to six shirts a day to sell at 25 cents each to fishermen, who then traded the shirts to the Indians for salmon. "With this income," she recalled, "I was able to procure shoes and clothing for the children, and assist in getting food for our rapidly growing family" (Owens 1906, 158). Berries, particularly cranberries, were abundant and could be dried without sugar and saved in barrels. According to Sarah, the berries proved to be quite profitable: "After 1845 cranberries brought $10 to $12 a barrel in San Francisco, and I gathered from ten to twelve barrels for market yearly for several years" (Owens 1906, 152).

Childcare often fell to young Bethenia. "I was the family nurse," she recalled. "Where there is a baby every two years, there is always no end of nursing to be done; especially when the mother's time is occupied as it was then, every moment, from early morning till late at night, with much outdoor as well as indoor work. She seldom found time to devote to the baby, except to give it the breast" (Owens-Adair 1906, 89). Bethenia added that her mother's "idea of raising children could not be improved upon—simply to give them sufficient wholesome food, keep them clean and happy, and let them live out of door as much as possible" (Owens-Adair 1906, 52).

"The regret of my life up to the age of thirty-five was, that I had not been born a boy."

Bethenia loved the freedom of the outdoors. In fair weather, she hauled the youngest baby "in its rude little sled, or cart, . . . with a two-year-old on one hip, and a four-year-old hanging to my skirts, in order to keep up" (Owens-Adair 1906, 9).

Tom Owens bought Bethenia a cayuse pony when she was nine, and she loved to ride horses, climb trees, and explore the world around her. Her mother sometimes lamented, "[S]he is such a tomboy I can never make a girl of her" (Owens-Adair 1906, 14). It is not surprising that Bethenia resisted gender prescriptions. In her autobiography, she wrote: "The regret of my life up to the age of thirty-five was, that I had not been born a boy, for I realized very early in life that a girl was hampered and hemmed in on all sides simply by the accident of sex" (Owens-Adair 1906, 8).

The same accident of sex made Bethenia the target of unwanted sexual advances. One morning when she was "just past thirteen," as she was doing the family wash in the storeroom, stirring down the clothes in the huge pot with a long broom-handle, an Englishman who worked for her father came up behind her. "[C]atching me around the waist," she recalled, "[he] hugged, and tried to kiss me, and then he jumped back and laughed triumphantly." Bethenia turned "like a tiger" and gave the lothario "such a whack with the broom-handle that he staggered, and rushed under the stairs, and plunged his head into the cranberry barrel." She continued to beat him until her mother came and pulled her off. But Bethenia had the last word: "You little skunk, if you ever dare to come near me again, I'll kill you!" (Owens-Adair 1906, 20, 21).

Not all men were "skunks" to young Bethenia. She had great affection for her father and sturdy brothers, and she "simply worshiped" Mr. Beaufort, a young teacher who boarded with the Owens family while he taught a three-month school at Clatsop in the summer of 1851. Bethenia, not yet twelve, had a school-girl crush on Mr. Beaufort, who "held himself aloof from the young people of his age, and kept his person so clean, neat and trim that the country young men disliked him" (Owens-Adair 1906, 10, 11). When challenged to a potato-digging contest by the Clatsop boys, including Legrand Hill, one of Tom Owens' farm-hands and Bethenia's future husband, the clever teacher bested them all by using a special hoe he had cut short for easier digging, and he raked in their money, watches, rings, and scarf pins.

Beaufort was Bethenia's first and only teacher prior to her marriage. Although she learned little in the three-month school and could barely read or write, he taught her how to run, jump, lasso, and spring up on a horse's back. "He was," she wrote, "in my young, crude, and it might be called barren life, a green, flower-strewn oasis, with a fountain of cool water in its midst." For Bethenia, "it was a sad, sad day" when he left for unknown places, and she fervently wished Beaufort had taken her with him (Owens-Adair 1906, 13, 14).

In 1853, Tom Owens decided he needed more range for his growing herds and moved his family and livestock to the Umpqua Valley of southern Oregon. Under the Donation Land Act of 1850, he settled on a 640-acre section of land on Deer Creek, Douglas County, across the South Umpqua River and about a mile from the town later named Roseburg. He soon established a profitable river ferry and built the home his family would occupy for about fourteen years. According to Sarah Owens, her husband "accumulated wealth [in Douglas County] as rapidly as he had in Clatsop County," and these were generally years of "peace and plenty" (Owens 1906, 160–161).

In 1851, Bethenia's tall and fair older sister, Diana, known as "the Beauty of Clatsop," had married John Hobson, the twenty-seven-year-old son of William Hobson, an English immigrant to Clatsop. Diana was thirteen years old.

Early marriages of young girls were common in the Pacific Northwest, particularly in remote areas. The 1850 Federal Census for Oregon Territory showed that men outnumbered women about three to one. Moreover, the female population was quite young. Bowen (1978, 185) reported a median female age of 12.9 years, which dropped to 12.3 years in rural areas.

While she was still thirteen, Bethenia became engaged to Legrand Henderson Hill, almost twice her age and a former employee on her father's Clatsop farm. Bethenia briefly recorded Hill's stay in Douglas County: "During the winter, Mr. Hill came to visit us," she wrote. "It was now arranged that we should be married the next spring, when father's house was far enough completed to move in" (Owens-Adair 1906, 24).

Hill returned to Douglas County in April, helped the Owens family move into their new home, and took Bethenia as his bride. They were married on May 4, 1854, at the Owens' home. Bethenia had not yet reached her full height of five feet four inches and recalled that her husband "was five feet eleven inches in height, and I could stand under his outstretched arm" (Owens-Adair 1906, 25).

Bethenia came to her marriage with "high hopes and great expectations" (Owens-Adair 1906, 27). She had used the months following her engagement to prepare her trousseau—carding wool, quilting, and sewing. With her mother's help, Bethenia completed four quilts she had pieced earlier, and she used her mother's gift of muslin to make four sheets, two pairs of pillowcases, two tablecloths, and four towels. She cut and sewed two calico dresses for everyday wear and, with her mother's assistance, completed her wedding dress of "a pretty, sky-blue figured lawn" (Owens-Adair 1906, 24).

Although Hill's possessions were limited to "a horse and saddle, a gun, and less than twenty dollars," Bethenia thought this "a most excellent start in life."

She knew that her parents had begun life together with little, and she believed that her husband "was the equal of any man living." Hill was strong and healthy, and she, "practical and methodical" from childhood, "had been trained to work, and bred to thrift and economy." Without a doubt, Bethenia was in love: "My soul overflowed with love and hope, and I could sing the dear old home-songs from morning to night" (Owens-Adair 1906, 27, 28).

The day after they were wed, Bethenia and Hill moved to a 320-acre farm Hill had bought for $600, on credit, to be paid in two years. Bethenia was eager to plant a garden, settle their livestock and chickens, and set up housekeeping. The farm, about four miles from her parents' home, had few improvements. Just twelve acres were fenced, and an open shed could hold only six to eight head of stock. The small, unfinished cabin measured twelve by fourteen feet and was constructed of round logs that had never been properly chinked. Until Bethenia filled the wide cracks with grass and ferns mixed with mud, the openings "admitted both draughts and vermin," including snakes and lizards. The cabin had a low door and a crude window of two panes of glass, and there was neither floor nor chimney, which meant all cooking had to be done outside. Bethenia was not dismayed: "My happy buoyant nature enabled me to enjoy anything—even cooking out of doors, over a smoky fire, without a covering over my head" (Owens-Adair 1906, 26, 28).

The cabin was furnished with a one-legged bed, supported by rails set into the logs of a corner wall; a table made from a rough shelf fastened to the wall; and three wall shelves that held Bethenia's tin-ware dishes, which she kept "scrupulously bright and shining." From her own meager savings, Bethenia had bought her prized "sugar-bowl, cream jug, steel knives and forks (two-tined) and one set of German silver teaspoons" (Owens-Adair 1906, 27).

To help the couple set up housekeeping, Tom Owens told his daughter to purchase what she wanted at the store. Many years later, Bethenia remembered that she bought "a full supply of groceries" on her wedding day, plus "a pot, tea-kettle and bake-oven (all of iron), a frying-pan and coffee pot, a churn, six milk pans, a washtub and board, a large twenty or thirty-gallon iron pot for washing purposes, etc., and a water bucket and tin dipper." Her father also gave Bethenia a fine thoroughbred mare named Queen, a fresh cow and heifer calf of her choice, a second cow to be fresh in the fall, and a wagon and harness.

(Bethenia, a skilled rider, had her own saddle.) Her mother provided "a good feather bed, and pillow, a good straw bed, a pair of blankets and two extra quilts" (Owens-Adair 1906, 27).

Tom Owens advised Hill to fell timber from his farm, and to use his carpentry skills to replace the ramshackle cabin with a new house. But Hill "was never in any hurry to get down to work" and "managed to idle away the summer going to camp meetings, reading novels, and hunting." Bethenia, who usually accompanied Hill when he hunted, remembered him as a good marksman who kept their larder filled with wild game; she wrote, however, that "Mr. Hill was always ready to go hunting, no matter what work was pressing to be done" (Owens-Adair 1906, 30, 28).

In the late fall, construction of a new cabin began in earnest with a house-raising by family and friends under Tom Owens' direction. Hill had finally felled and finished the logs, and Bethenia's father provided two doors, two windows, shingles, nails, and rough lumber for the floor. After the house-raising, Bethenia was thrilled when Hill followed her father's advice and worked for several days, putting on the roof. But Hill smashed his left thumb while hanging a door and claimed he could no longer work. Bethenia later wrote, "I did not then know . . . that a man with a perfect right hand and a quick and willing wife to help him, could have gone right ahead and finished the work" (Owens-Adair 1906, 32).

> ⊚ *The couple had "not a dollar" with which to make their April payment for the farm.* ☙

One crisis led to another. With help from Tom Owens, the new house was finally put in order. But the couple had "not a dollar" with which to make their April payment of three hundred dollars for the farm. When the former owner offered sixty dollars for return of the property, the Hills accepted. They left Douglas County and traveled south to join Hill's parents, immigrants from Tennessee, who had established a dairy farm in Jackson County.

After spending several months with his family, Hill determined that he and Bethenia should follow the "gold excitement" to Yreka, California. There they lived with his Aunt Kelly, who had recently lost her only child—a son—in a conflict with the Rogue River Indians.

In early spring of 1855, at Aunt Kelly's suggestion, the Hills invested in a one-room house with a lean-to kitchen. The cost was $450, and the down payment of $300 was all that was left from the sale of Bethenia's two cows and heifer, and the wagon and horses. Hill wanted Bethenia to sell her prize mare Queen, but she refused.

> *"No," insisted Bethenia, for her baby was "too precious to give to anyone."*

At the age of sixteen, within a month of moving into their Yreka house, Bethenia gave birth to a son, George Hill, on April 17, 1856. Aunt Kelly promptly begged Bethenia to give the child to her, pledging to make him her heir. "I will give him all I have," she promised, "and that is more than his father will ever do for him. I know very well that Legrand will just fool around all his life, and never accomplish anything."

"No," insisted Bethenia, for her baby was "too precious to give to anyone" (Owens-Adair 1906, 45).

Almost a year and a half later, in September of 1857, Bethenia was overjoyed when her parents arrived for a visit. They had come to see their new grandson, but it did not take long to confirm what they had heard: the Hills were living from hand to mouth, with most of the work falling on Bethenia. Tom Owens proposed that Bethenia and Hill move back to Roseburg, and they happily accepted his offer of an acre of land and material to build a house.

Bethenia selected the property for their new home in Roseburg, and her father told Hill he could use the Owens team to haul the lumber for building. But Hill's sights were set on a different enterprise: a partnership in brickmaking, with Bethenia to do the cooking for the men who burned the bricks. Tom Owens told Hill that the venture was doomed to failure, but he was not dissuaded. He put the little money from the sale of the Yreka house into the business and moved Bethenia and little George "into a tent in a low, damp valley, near the river" (Owens-Adair 1906, 48). Heavy, constant November rains put a stop to any brickmaking, and Bethenia fell seriously ill with typhoid fever.

Once more, Bethenia's parents came to the rescue. They took the Hills into their home, where Bethenia could convalesce. But when Tom Owens urged Hill to start building a house, Hill insisted on having a deed to the acre of land before he began construction. Bethenia's parents refused. They had decided to deed the property to Bethenia and little George.

Hill sulked for a while and then purchased two lots for $75 each, apparently with a loan from his father-in-law, who also paid for building supplies. When the roof was on and the kitchen partly finished, Bethenia moved in but was besieged by unwanted visitors. Skunks "rattled around among the pots and pans, even jumping on the table, and devouring the food, if I did not keep everything securely covered, while I often lay and listened to their nocturnal antics, not daring to get up to drive them out, as the dire consequences of disturbing them suddenly were well known, and dreaded" (Owens-Adair 1906, 49).

Bethenia had never fully recovered from childbirth and typhoid fever, Baby George was "ill and fretful, much of the time," and Hill was not providing for his family. Moreover, his bad temper, which he had begun to exhibit within the first six months of marriage, was apparent whenever Bethenia "objected to any of his plans or suggestions" (Owens-Adair 1906, 49, 32). No longer could she put him in a good humor with girlish charm or the playfulness of their honeymoon period, such as waking him by skipping into the bedroom and tickling his feet.

Bethenia confessed to her parents that she did not think she could bear her marriage any longer. Her mother wanted Bethenia to leave Hill immediately: "[A]ny man that could not make a living with the good starts and help he has had, never will make one; and with his temper, he is liable to kill you at any time." But her father wept and begged Bethenia to stay with Hill: "Oh, Bethenia, there has never been a divorce in my family, and I hope there never will be. I want you to go back, and try again, and do your best. After that, if you *cannot possibly* get along, come home" (Owens-Adair 1906, 50). Bethenia agreed to try one more time.

The couple's relationship did not improve. The breaking point concerned the care and discipline of their son. George, then about twenty-two months old, was "a sickly, tiny mite, with an abnormal, voracious appetite, but his father thought him old enough to be trained and disciplined, and would spank him unmercifully because he cried" (Owens-Adair 1906, 50). Bethenia could not endure this. At one supper, against Bethenia's objections, Hill fed the child six hard-boiled eggs, and she feared little George would have convulsions.

One morning in the late winter of 1858, following "a tempestuous scene," Hill "threw the baby on the bed" and rushed out. Once her husband was out of sight, Bethenia gathered a few necessities and fled with the baby in her arms. She ran about three-quarters of a mile to the ferry and, "almost in a state of collapse," crossed the river. Her brother Flem, "always ready to smooth out the wrinkles," took the baby in one arm, supported Bethenia with the other, and guided her up the hill to their parents' home (Owens-Adair 1906, 50). Later, in divorce papers, Bethenia was more specific about the incident, testifying that she was "beaten and driven" from the house by Hill on February 28, 1858, and told never to return.

Hill asked Bethenia several times to forgive him and return. But Bethenia stood firm: "Legrand, I have told you many times that if we ever did separate, I would never go back, and I never will" (Owens-Adair 1906, 51).

Separating from Hill, filing for divorce, and waiting many months for the divorce decree were overwhelming for eighteen-year-old Bethenia. "I was, indeed, surrounded with difficulties seemingly insurmountable," she recalled, "a husband for whom I had lost all love and respect, a divorce, the stigma of which would cling to me all my future life, and a sickly babe of two years in my arms, all rose darkly before me" (Owens-Adair 1906, 52). Short of dependence on her parents, she did not know how she would support herself and baby George.

The first step toward divorce was legal division of the couple's property. In March 1858, Bethenia turned over the house and land to Hill, assigned the live-stock—two horses, a heifer, and a steer—to her father, and scrawled: "I assine the writhin bilasile [I assign the written bill of sale] to Thomas Owens for value received this third day of March 1858. Beatheany Hill" (Exhibit A in Divorce, Hill vs. Hill, Probate Records, Douglas County, Roseburg, Oregon).

Once the documents were signed in the office of attorney Addison Crandall Gibbs, Hill gave a package to Bethenia, which appeared to be a bundle of cloth-ing, and then hurried away. Bethenia untied the bundle. There, to her shock, were her wedding clothes: a "blue-flowered dress" and a dark-figured mantilla she had probably worn as a veil. According to the attorney's later deposition, yellowish stains marred the clothing, and in some places the dress had been torn or rotted away, as if "strong acid" had been flung on it (Deposition of Addison C. Gibbs, October 8, 1859, Douglas County, Roseburg, Oregon). Gibbs raced after Hill and asked him to explain the ruined dress, but Hill hotly denied any knowledge of the matter. The garment was still damp from Hill's final rage of temper and insult to Bethenia: apparently he had urinated on her wedding dress of "pretty sky-blue figured lawn" (McFarland 1984, 75, n. 8; Owens-Adair 1906, 24).

In late January of 1859, at her father's urging and almost a year after leaving her husband, Bethenia filed for a divorce from Legrand Hill. She would wait some nine months for a divorce decree.

Her suit was strongly contested, as Hill sought to secure custody of his son by proving Bethenia an unfit mother. His mother, now widowed, lived alone near Ashland and hoped Hill would settle down and come with her grandson George to live with her, thereby allowing her to remain in her home. Through her attorney, Stephen Fowler Chadwick, Bethenia asked the court to restore her maiden name, to grant her custody of George, and to provide support for her and her son.

> @ *"After the decree . . . was rendered giving me custody of my child, and my father's name, . . . I felt like a free woman."* ☙

After hearing lengthy testimony, the Honorable Paine Page Prim handed down his decision on October 18, 1859. Bethenia had won: "After the decree of the court was rendered giving me custody of my child, and my father's name, which I have never since discarded, and never will, I felt like a free woman" (Owens-Adair 1906, 56).

☙ ☙ ☙

During her long convalescence at her father's home before she filed for divorce, Bethenia had determined that she must obtain an education. Sarah Owens, who at age forty was pregnant for the eleventh and last time, encouraged Bethenia to attend the Roseburg school called the Academy and said it would be no trouble for the other Owens children to take care of little George.

To help her parents, Bethenia was up early to assist with milking and housework until 8:30, when she went to school with her younger brothers and sisters. On Saturdays, she and the children did the family's washing and ironing, and she worked on her studies. After four months, Bethenia proudly "finished the third reader, and made good progress with . . . other studies of spelling, writing, geography and arithmetic" (Owens-Adair 1906, 53).

When Diana and John Hobson visited Roseburg in the fall of 1858, they invited Bethenia to return home with them for a visit at Clatsop. With George in hand, Bethenia accepted, perhaps hoping to leave behind the stigma of deserting her husband. But the scandal accompanied her to the Hobsons' farm. A longtime neighbor and friend to the Owens family, Mrs. Nancy Irwin Morrison, asked Bethenia why she had left her husband. "Because he whipped my baby unmercifully, and struck and choked me, and I was never born to be struck by mortal man," Bethenia replied. "But did he commit adultery?" asked Mrs. Morrison. "No," said Bethenia. "Then, my dear child," said Mrs. Morrison, "take my advice, and go back, and beg him on your knees to receive you—for the scriptures forbid the separation of man and wife for any other cause than adultery" (Owens-Adair 1906, 53).

Years later, one of Mrs. Morrison's daughters fled from the beatings of a brutal husband. Mrs. Morrison begged Bethenia's forgiveness and explained: "When I saw my own child bruised and mutilated, I realized that there are things as bad as adultery" (Owens-Adair 1906, 54).

✤ ✤ ✤

After Bethenia returned to Roseburg and received her divorce, she resolved to create a better future for herself and her son. She commenced a daunting regimen of work, soon combined with study. She sought work, including the profitable but menial job of taking in washing.

"Why can't you be contented to stay at home with us?" Tom Owens asked. "I am able to support you and your child" (Owens-Adair 1906, 57). But Bethenia was determined to earn her own livelihood.

Bethenia had learned about practical nursing and midwifery in the homes of her parents and neighbors. According to her mother, even as a child, Bethenia

The Astoria Public School, ca. 1861–1862, was erected in 1859 at the corner of
Ninth and Exchange Streets and was Astoria's first building intended specifically
for a school. The teacher, Mr. Deardorff, stands at far left. Bethenia is identified as
the tenth female from the left; her small son George Hill stands twelfth in the line of
boys, holding his hat. George Conrad Flavel, son of Captain George Flavel,
is thirteenth in the line of boys, standing next to George Hill. CCHS 137.513.

was nurturing, always feeding pretend food and medicine to her rag dolls with
a spoon (Gaston 1912, vol. 4, 592). Bethenia noted that she "always had a fond-
ness for nursing" and early on proved to have "a great natural ability to care for
the sick" (Owens-Adair 1906, 79, 305). When her father presented her with a
sewing machine, the first in the area, she also took up sewing.

In 1860, after a year of work in Roseburg, Bethenia received a plea from her
sister Diana, who needed help on the large Hobson farm. Once again, Bethenia
and George headed north to Clatsop. Still sparsely populated, Clatsop County
had but 498 residents in 1860, most of whom lived in Astoria. At Clatsop,
Bethenia found the independence she was seeking, and she did not return to
live in Roseburg for about seven years.

Late in the fall of 1860, the sisters crossed the Columbia to visit Bethenia's
friend Sarah Kimball Munson at Oysterville, in Washington Territory, and
Bethenia admitted her "great anxiety for an education." Mrs. Munson, who was
pregnant, invited Bethenia to stay in her home. Bethenia eagerly accepted and

arranged to take in washing to pay room and board for herself and George. Once she was attending the Oysterville school, her "desire for knowledge grew daily stronger," and this was "one of the most pleasant and profitable winters" of her life (Owens-Adair 1906, 57, 58).

When she returned to the Hobson farm in the spring of 1861, Bethenia told Diana that she was "determined to get at least a common school education" (Owens-Adair 1906, 58). The Hobsons made arrangements for Bethenia to enroll in school at Astoria in the fall, after she helped Diana with farm and household chores through the summer.

Prior to her move to Astoria, the student became a teacher. Bethenia organized and taught a three-month subscription school at Clatsop Plains, with sixteen students at two dollars each. She rose at four in the morning to do the milking and other chores before teaching, and she did the Hobson family's washing on evenings and Saturdays. Because three of Bethenia's students were beyond her level, John Hobson helped her in the evenings to work through the lessons in advance. "[T]hey never suspected my incompetency," she wrote (Owens-Adair 1906, 59).

The nine-month school term began in Astoria in the fall of 1861. Bethenia, with her son George, age five and a half, and her nephew Frank Hobson, age seven, lodged together in a small room in the old Boelling Hotel, and all three attended school. Although she was deeply humiliated to be placed in the school's primary class for mental arithmetic, Bethenia soon advanced to the third and highest class. At the end of the term, Bethenia had passed into most of the advanced classes. "[N]ot that I was an apt scholar," she wrote in her autobiography, "for my knowledge has always been acquired by the hardest labor" (Owens-Adair 1906, 59).

In the fall of 1862, Bethenia and George returned to Astoria for a second nine-month term. This time Bethenia took three small rooms on the second floor of the "Old Gray House," the former residence of the late historian Dr. William H. Gray and his family. Bethenia picked berries and did laundry for three families, which gave her five dollars a week for living expenses.

One evening, as Bethenia stood ironing with a schoolbook propped in front of her, she was visited by Captain A. C. Farnsworth, a successful middle-aged Columbia River pilot and a good friend of the Hobsons. The captain, who admired Bethenia's accomplishments and diligence, explained that he had no family but more money than he needed. He offered to pay all expenses for Bethenia and her son so that she could attend the school of her choice, for as long as she wished, anywhere in the United States. The gift entailed no obligation.

Although moved to tears by the captain's generosity, Bethenia refused the offer, saying she could not "incur such an obligation, from even so good a friend." The captain was direct: "[Y]ou are a great deal too independent for your own good," he said, and although they would remain friends until his death in 1874, Captain Farnsworth was "clearly disgusted" with her "obstinacy" (Owens-Adair 1906, 64, 63).

She later observed, "[M]y self-will, independence, and inexperience decided me to refuse." This was a decision Bethenia Owens came to regret: "[M]any were the times during my after years of struggles and hardships, in my supreme effort to get ahead, in which I bitterly repented my hasty decision, feeling that it was the mistake of my life. The acceptance of that offer would have far earlier opened the doors of science, and saved me many long years of bitter experience, and irretrievably lost opportunities" (Owens-Adair 1906, 64).

While still attending school at Astoria in 1862–1863, Bethenia was asked to teach the three-month remainder of the term in the primary department. To complement her salary of $25 a month, she earned room and board by cleaning nine rooms in a private boarding house. Before the Astoria term was completed, she was offered another three-month school, at $25 a month, this time in Bruceport, Washington Territory, on Shoalwater Bay.

Shortly after she began at Bruceport, subscriptions were raised for another three months. Before the Bruceport school was completed, Bethenia was asked to teach at Oysterville, where she had been a student a few years earlier. Although the Oysterville school had "the undesirable reputation of being ungovernable" (Owens-Adair 1906, 66), the little teacher from Clatsop restored discipline and order.

In the spring of 1864, Bethenia returned to Clatsop Plains for her last teaching position, a four-month school at $40 a month. Bethenia and George lived free of charge in the old parsonage at Skipanon, where she was "happy as a lark" (Owens-Adair 1906, 68). Bethenia sewed and crocheted to cover their living expenses and add to savings.

When her term ended at Clatsop, Bethenia retired from teaching and moved with her son into a new house in Astoria, the first home she ever owned. With four hundred dollars she had saved from teaching, she bought a half lot in Astoria and "contracted with a carpenter for a small, three-roomed cottage, with a cosy little porch." Five years had passed since her divorce, and she was "proud as a queen" of the home she had earned entirely by herself. For the next three years, until she returned to Roseburg, Bethenia enjoyed her independence in Astoria. "I had won the respect of all," she wrote, "and now work came to me from all directions. As I could 'turn my hand' to almost anything, and was anxious to accumulate, I was never idle" (Owens-Adair 1906, 68, 69).

Even a surprise visit from Legrand Hill could not dampen Bethenia's spirits. Following their divorce in 1859, Hill had gone to Ashland, where he appeared in the 1860 Federal Census as a carpenter, though he had not provided any financial support for his son or Bethenia. He had written a number of times, asking Bethenia to remarry him, but she had refused. Apparently Hill thought an unexpected, face-to-face meeting with his former wife might overcome her opposition. Bethenia wrote later: "But alas for him! He found not the young, ignorant, inexperienced child-mother whom he had neglected and misused, but a full-grown, self-reliant, self-supporting woman, who could look upon him only with pity. He soon realized that there was now a gulf between us which he could never hope to cross" (Owens-Adair 1906, 69). In future years, Hill and his son spent time together on occasion. But the gulf between Hill and Bethenia remained until his death in Ashland in 1886.

In the fall of 1867, Bethenia rented out her Astoria house and traveled with George for an extended visit with her family in Roseburg, where she was eventually persuaded to remain as a dressmaker and milliner. With the assistance of Hyman Abraham, her sister Jane's husband and a successful dry goods merchant, Bethenia secured the stock she needed and soon had a profitable business and the respectable occupation of shopkeeper. After two years of success, she purchased her Roseburg home, which was soon surrounded by the flowers and gardens she loved so dearly.

Visitors to Bethenia's shop would find a stock of cloaks and shawls and a variety of hats, as well as hosiery, hairnets, false hair, assorted fabric trims, and fancy goods, such as jewelry, ornaments, and toys. Before long, Bethenia was making her own hat-blocks, creating new hats out of old, and professionally cleaning, stiffening, fitting, bleaching, pressing, and trimming them. In November of 1869, to increase her knowledge and purchase stock, she borrowed money to travel to San Francisco and spent three months learning the trade from the city's best milliner, Madame Fouts. At the end of 1869, Bethenia had cleared a profit of $1,500, and the following year she enrolled George in the University of California at Berkeley.

With George away at school and money from her business coming easily, Bethenia gave more thought to her secret, growing desire for a medical education. Neighbors and friends often called her to aid the sick, and one night she found herself standing next to a Dr. Palmer, at the side of a friend's sick daughter. Dr. Palmer had lacerated the child in unsuccessful attempts to insert a catheter. When he briefly paused, Bethenia picked up the instrument "and passed it instantly, with perfect ease, bringing immediate relief to the tortured child" (Owens-Adair 1906, 79). The mother was overjoyed, but the doctor was emphatically displeased. This incident, Bethenia wrote, determined her future: she would study medicine and become a doctor.

To avoid anticipated opposition from family and friends, as well as public ridicule, Bethenia confided only in three older men who were friends and mentors. When she explained her ambitions to Dr. Salathiel Hamilton, he was supportive and agreed to lend her his medical books in secret, beginning with *Gray's Anatomy*. As she walked out of Dr. Hamilton's private office in Roseburg, she encountered Stephen F. Chadwick, the attorney who had won her divorce case. Chadwick had overheard the conversation and shook her hand warmly: "Go ahead. It is in you; let it come out. You will win" (Owens-Adair 1906, 79).

Support also came from Jesse Applegate, "[my] dear and revered friend" and the "one other person who ever gave me a single word of encouragement to study medicine" (Owens-Adair 1906, 79–80). The father of thirteen children, Applegate reserved a special place in his heart for Bethenia and her son. In her autobiography, Bethenia included correspondence with Applegate, evidence of what he called "the mystic cord of affection" that brought and held them

Bethenia Owens. Photograph taken by Buchtel and Stolte in Portland, Oregon, probably in the early 1870s before Bethenia left for medical school in the East in December 1873.

<small>COURTESY OF THE DOUGLAS COUNTY HISTORICAL SOCIETY, ROSEBURG, OREGON. N5925.</small>

together. After Bethenia shared her plan for medical school, the sixty-two-year-old Applegate replied in November of 1873: "If you had the means (and if I had them you should have them) your plan is just such a one as I would form for you, as your inclinations lead you in that direction" (Owens-Adair 1906, 287).

Bethenia gave herself one year to study anatomy and arrange her business and personal affairs before informing her family that she was leaving Roseburg to study medicine. She confided her plan to Abigail Scott Duniway of Portland, a friend and coworker in Oregon's temperance and woman's rights movements of the early 1870s. Duniway, editor and owner of the *New Northwest,* the weekly human rights newspaper she established in 1871, had published a number of Bethenia's writings, and Bethenia was a subscription agent for the newspaper. Supportive of Bethenia's aspirations, Duniway agreed that George should live with the Duniway family in Portland and work in the printing office of the *New Northwest* while his mother was away.

Next Bethenia wrote to Mrs. Frances Goodell Adams, the mother of her life-long friend Inez Adams Parker. She asked Mrs. Adams, then living in Portland, to join the Duniways in looking after George's welfare. Mrs. Adams encouraged Bethenia to study medicine in Philadelphia, at the Eclectic Medical College of Pennsylvania, where her husband, William Lysander Adams, had gone, "partly for study, and partly for his health" (Owens-Adair 1906, 80).

In December of 1873, two weeks before her departure from Roseburg, Bethenia Owens informed family and the public of her decision to study medicine in Philadelphia. An announcement in the *Tri-Weekly Astorian* read: "Miss B. A. Owens, a well-known lady of Roseburg will shortly start for Philadelphia, where she proposes to graduate as an M.D." (23 December 1873, 1). Later Bethenia learned that the famed Captain George Flavel of Astoria, whom she had held "in great awe" in her early life, had taken notice of her medical school plans. "That woman deserves great praise," Flavel told John Hobson, a close friend. "She has accomplished more through her own efforts than any woman I ever knew" (Owens-Adair 1906, 259).

Although Bethenia had anticipated disapproval from relatives and friends, she was unprepared for the fierce opposition she faced. "My family felt that they were disgraced," she remembered, "and even my own child was influenced and encouraged to think that I was doing him an irreparable injury" (Owens-Adair 1906, 80).

Finally, with George situated with the Duniways in Portland and the Roseburg shop entrusted to a younger sister, Bethenia boarded the California overland stage to begin her long journey to Philadelphia. "The full moment of what I had undertaken now rose before me," she recalled, "and all I had left behind tugged at my heart-strings" (Owens-Adair 1906, 81). She found comfort again in the words of her attorney: "Go ahead. It is in you; let it come out. You will win!"

The "accident of sex" Bethenia had regretted as a child prevented her from enrolling in most medical schools, which barred their doors to women. After 1849, when Elizabeth Blackwell graduated from the Medical College of Geneva, New York, as the first American woman to earn a medical degree, women gained entry to some medical schools. Yet the belief that women were inherently unfit for the study and practice of medicine held sway. Women who studied medicine were ridiculed and harassed, refused attendance at anatomy lectures, and excluded from clinical work and internships. The argument went that biologically, intellectually, and psychologically, women were suited to remain within the domestic, private sphere, the feminine world, and not to enter the public sphere of the masculine world, from which they should be protected. As Barbara Welter wrote in her 1966 study of "true womanhood," the cardinal virtues for women were purity, piety, submissiveness, and domesticity. When Bethenia began her studies in 1874, of 64,414 physicians in the United States, only 544 were women (Walsh 1972, 185–186).

Philadelphia in 1874 was a major center of medical education, boasting the University of Pennsylvania School of Medicine, Jefferson Medical College, and some eighteen other medical institutions. The most prestigious did not admit women students, yet Bethenia knew "a degree from Philadelphia" would have real currency when she returned to Oregon. She decided to enroll in the Eclectic Medical College, where William Lysander Adams was developing a specialty in rheumatism. He, in fact, became Bethenia's preceptor. The curriculum stressed basic science, anatomy, physiology, and experience in clinical study. The lectures Bethenia attended and the textbooks she used were nearly identical to those found in the "regular medical colleges." While the faculty condemned practices such as blood-letting and the use of mineral poisons, they encouraged familiarity with any beneficial treatments found in popular health movement sects, such as homeopathy, electropathy, hydropathy, neuropathy, Thomism, botanic, and chromo-thermalism (Abrahams 1966, 233–235, 546–563).

To complement the school's program, Bethenia attended lectures and clinics at Blockly Hospital twice a week, along with all the other medical students in the city. She conducted a practice for working-class women patients in Boston.

Her thesis, titled "Metritus," was the study of uterine inflammatory disease; she clearly intended to develop a specialty in women's health care, specifically gynecology. At the end of 1874, when she was thirty-four, Bethenia received her medical degree and returned to Roseburg.

The reception Dr. Bethenia Owens received in Roseburg was far from welcoming. An old man had died, and the six physicians who attended him planned an autopsy. As luck would have it, one of the six was Dr. Palmer, who still carried a grudge because Bethenia had successfully inserted the catheter for one of his patients. At Dr. Palmer's scornful suggestion, Bethenia, "the new 'Philadelphia' doctor," was invited by messenger to be present at the autopsy. She arrived at "the old shed, where the corpse lay on a board, supported by two saw-bucks, and covered with a worn gray blanket." Dr. G. W. Hoover asked Bethenia: "Do you know that the autopsy is on the genital organs?" "No," Bethenia answered, adding, "but one part of the human body should be as sacred to the physician as another." Dr. Palmer then objected to Bethenia's presence at a male autopsy, threatening to leave if she remained. She coolly challenged him, asking, "[W]hat is the difference between the attendance of a woman at a male autopsy, and the attendance of a man at a female autopsy?" (Owens-Adair 1906, 83–84). When put to a vote, the majority of the doctors, including her friend Dr. Salathiel Hamilton, did not object to Bethenia's attendance. She remained, and Dr. Palmer retired, "amid the cheers and laughter of forty or fifty men and boys in and outside the old shed." One of the doctors offered Bethenia an old dissecting case, and she asked in surprise, "You do not want me to do the work, do you?" The answer was yes, and Bethenia "took the case and complied." By then, she later recalled, "news of what was going on had spread to every house in town, and the excitement was at fever-heat" (Owens-Adair 1906, 84).

After performing the dissection, Bethenia received three cheers from the audience. Then she made her way along the street, "lined on both sides with men, women and children, all anxious to get a look at 'the woman who dared,' to

"[W]hat is the difference between the attendance of a woman at a male autopsy, and the attendance of a man at a female autopsy?"

see what sort of a strange, anomalous being she was. The women were shocked and scandalized! The men were disgusted, but amused, thinking it 'such a good joke on the doctors.'" Although her brothers Flem and Josiah did not approve of her actions, Bethenia believed they saved her from a coating of tar and feathers. Everyone in Roseburg knew her brothers "would shoot at the drop of a hat," and "they would have died in their tracks" before seeing her "subjected to such indignities, or driven out of town" (Owens-Adair 1906, 84, 85).

Shortly after the autopsy incident, Bethenia realized how difficult it would be to establish a successful medical practice in Roseburg. Moreover, it seemed she was "only 'a thorn in the flesh'" to her family (Owens-Adair 1906, 85). Her dear brother Flem was a recently elected member of the Oregon Senate, and neither he nor the majority of his constituents approved of his sister's "unwomanly" behavior. Bethenia soon closed her millinery business and moved with her younger sister to Portland.

In Portland, Bethenia formed a successful partnership with Dr. Adams, with whom she had studied in Philadelphia. To complement their practice in Portland, located on First Street between Yamhill and Taylor, the two doctors offered electrical and medicated baths, "a new process of treatment," and Dr. Adams used atomizer vapor baths to ease the symptoms of rheumatism and other chronic conditions. Their partnership continued until the spring of 1877, when Dr. Adams relocated at Hood River and eventually founded his own clinic and drugstore.

Although she was occasionally rebuffed and slighted by Portland's old-school doctors, some of whom scorned her as "a bath doctor," Dr. Owens had a profitable practice and felt comfortably settled in Portland. In accord with her "grand scheme" for her son George, he graduated in 1877 from the Medical Department of Willamette University, in Salem, commenced his residency at Good Samaritan Hospital in Portland, and later, with his mother's help, established a drugstore in Goldendale, Washington Territory, followed by a practice in North Yakima.

In time, Bethenia found herself "pining for more knowledge" and determined to treat herself "to a full medical course in the old school and a trip to Europe." Although her medical degree in 1874 was legitimately earned and granted, the Eclectic Medical College of Pennsylvania had been embroiled in a

Dr. Bethenia Owens, ca. 1882.
Photo by Bradley and Rulofson,
San Francisco. CCHS 595.00A.

scandal involving the issue of fraudulent degrees. To avoid any question about her credentials, Bethenia wanted a degree that was "second to none" (Owens-Adair 1906, 88, 90).

Against the objections of family and friends, including Jesse Applegate, she liquidated all her holdings in 1878 and traveled to Philadelphia to invest her $8,000 in a better education. Armed with letters of recommendation from United States senators, governors, professors, and medical doctors, she applied at the renowned Jefferson Medical College, which did not accept women. A kindly professor explained that the board of regents "would simply be shocked, scandalized, and enraged at the mere mention of admitting a woman." The professor suggested the Woman's College as equal to Jefferson College, but Bethenia observed that "a Woman's College out West stands below par." Then he recommended the University of Michigan, at Ann Arbor: "It is a long-term school, and a mixed [coeducational] school, and it is second to none in America" (Owens-Adair 1906, 90–91).

Thus, the University of Michigan became Bethenia's school of choice. She graduated in 1880, at the end of her second year. At the time, she was one of 2,431 women physicians in the United States out of a total of 85,671 (Walsh 1972, 185–186). After a residency in Chicago and a tour of European hospitals, Bethenia returned to Portland and began a successful practice as a physician specializing in the "Diseases of Women, and the Eye and Ear." In 1881, she was the first woman in Oregon to perform a perineal repair operation, for which she received "wide notoriety" and "one hundred dollars in gold twenty-dollar pieces" (Owens-Adair 1906, 527). She soon established a reputation for surgical skill and the comfort she could provide by correcting uterine prolapse, the result of repeated childbearing or gynecological disease. In 1882, the little doctor stood tall when she was honored with induction to the Oregon State Medical Society (Larsell 1947, 286).

To extend medical care to women of all classes, Dr. Owens often took her practice outside her office, making calls in Portland's working-class and red-light districts, and later, as a country doctor, in isolated rural areas of Clatsop County.

❧ ❧ ❧

Bethenia Owens embraced three reform movements—woman's rights, temperance, and eugenics. Beginning in the early 1870s, her involvement in woman's rights and temperance brought her before the public, both as a lecturer and writer. The summer before entering medical school, she reported to readers of the *New Northwest* (15 August 1873) that she remained "firm for the good cause" of woman suffrage and had been elected Worthy Chief Templar of Roseburg's International Order of Good Templars, Lodge No. 5. Later, as a member of the Woman's Christian Temperance Union (WCTU), she served many years as Oregon superintendent of hygiene and heredity. After earning her second medical degree in 1882, Bethenia spoke and wrote extensively on heredity and eugenics until not long before her death in 1926.

 Bethenia Owens embraced three reform movements— woman's rights, temperance, and eugenics.

Drawing upon her own experiences and the strength and examples of women such as Susan B. Anthony and Abigail Scott Duniway, Bethenia was an advocate, not only for woman suffrage, but for women's education, employment, and health, which she linked with the need for year-round, outdoor exercise, including running, skating, and riding astride. She argued that all women should be educated and self-supporting, not dependent on fathers or husbands for their livelihoods, and she supported a bill to raise young women's age of consent for marriage in Oregon from fourteen to sixteen. "The woman that charms the world today," she proclaimed, "is the woman of courage, of original and independent character; not a bundle of dry goods and millinery" (Owens-Adair 1906, 524).

Temperance was a reform interest Bethenia shared with her brother Flem, who founded the *Prohibition Star*. As early as 1870, Bethenia was writing letters to newspaper editors deploring "the influence of rum," but without fully revealing her personal reasons for taking up the cause. In one piece, she wrote: "I, being a woman, and like most women having tasted the bitter fruits of intemperance, more keenly feel the necessity of securing a strict prohibitory liquor law enacted to protect our fathers, husbands, brothers, and sons, who have not within themselves the power of self-protection against this fell destroyer" (Owens-Adair 1906, 364).

In a startling revelation, Bethenia wrote in 1885: "My early life was crushed by this common curse of humanity, alcohol. It robbed my home and childhood of every vestige of beauty and sunshine. It permitted me to grow up in ignorance of the contents of even the primary school books; and not until I had reached womanhood, and had earned money by the hardest manual labor, did I have the opportunity of learning to read and write" (Owens-Adair 1906, 438–439). McFarland (1984, 80–81) speculated that someone in Bethenia's family circle was an alcoholic. She concluded that no evidence identifies the person.

But evidence does exist in writings by Bethenia and her mother after Tom Owens died on January 23, 1873, at Piety Hill, Trinity County, California. Sarah Owens (1906, 161) recalled that her family had lived in their Roseburg home "with little to give us trouble or anxiety, until about 1867, when my son [Solomon] Pierce's health became very poor, and my husband's strength, also, began to fail." The family moved to California, and although the climate was mild, the "two invalids" died and were buried there.

In the version of her autobiography that appeared in Gaston's *The Centennial History of Oregon* (1912, vol. 4, 591), Bethenia said she went to Roseburg in the fall of 1867 "to visit my people at their urgent request," a phrase that does not appear in other published versions of her autobiography. Perhaps the serious illnesses of her father and brother constituted the urgency in calling her to Roseburg, and perhaps the family had faced a crisis that involved financial matters and a decision to move from Roseburg to California.

The most telling explanation for Bethenia's passionate involvement in the temperance movement appears in her essay "Disquisition," written for presentation at the State Temperance Alliance meeting and published on the front page of Abigail Scott Duniway's the *New Northwest* on March 7, 1873, less than two months after Tom Owens' death. "My friends," she began, "you see me as I stand' before you dressed in mourning. Shall I tell you the cause of these dark robes? 'Tis but a little word, but oh, how hard to pronounce! Yes, 'tis that enemy of all womankind, Rum." Then she spoke of her "generous hearted and affectionate father," a "noble and intelligent man," who was fond of alcohol in his youth and later "became a slave to the fell destroyer." She recalled her joy and hope in 1848, when she was only eight, and Tom Owens signed a temperance pledge circulated by their minister at Clatsop Plains. "Young as I was," Bethenia wrote, "I knew that every heart murmured amen, for my noble-hearted father was loved and respected, though given to intoxication."

For six years, from 1848 to 1854, Tom Owens kept his pledge, first at Clatsop and then at Roseburg. But when a boyhood friend "pressed him to take just one drink in remembrance of boyish days, he could not resist." Then, said Bethenia, "for fourteen long years our home was unhappy." Dark clouds hovered, "with no ray of sunshine." She remembered that "after fourteen years of intemperance [1854–1868]," her father "was brought, through the influence of family and friends, to the Church." "But," she asked, "did the purity and influence of the Church drive that demon from his path? No! no! For five years [until late 1872] he kept his vow; then misfortune and disease, which intemperance had left upon him, so prostrated him that this demon of Satan again got control, and to-day he sleeps the sleep of death." The dark secret of the Owens family was at last revealed.

Of all Bethenia's reform efforts, her involvement in the eugenics movement is the most difficult to understand today. Bethenia and other participants in this pseudo-scientific cause of the late nineteenth and early twentieth centuries believed that heredity was the directing force of all life, a law of nature that must be understood in order to protect the nation from the unfit and degenerate. These included habitual criminals, the insane, feeble-minded persons, epileptics, and persons affected with venereal diseases which would weaken their offspring, as well as "sexual perverts" and members of "inferior" races, who allegedly propagated at a faster pace than the "higher" races.

Bethenia was disappointed when eugenics bills failed in the Oregon and Washington legislatures in 1907. But two years later, Washington State passed a punitive castration law for rapists and habitual criminals that remained on the books until 1921, when the state passed an even broader law. A bill passed the Oregon Legislature in 1909 but was vetoed by Governor George Chamberlain. Four years later, under Governor Oswald West, a revised bill, which included castration for same-sex "sexual perverts" (those who committed "sodomy or the crime against nature") became law but was soon repealed by a referendum sponsored by the Anti-Sterilization League. Still, by 1920, two Oregon sterilization laws were on the books. Both were declared unconstitutional by the Circuit Court of Marion County in 1921 and not appealed.

With two publications in 1922, Bethenia campaigned for new eugenics legislation in Oregon. In her pamphlet titled *The Eugenic Marriage Law and Human Sterilization*, she argued for a Eugenic Marriage Law that would determine the fitness of couples to enter into marriage contracts. If deemed "unfit," one or both would have to be "rendered sterile" to receive a license. In her book *Human Sterilization*, she presented arguments on sterilization from various sources, both pro and con, and elaborated on why she supported "humane sterilization" of "the unfit." To protect unborn children, she favored "purification" through vasectomies for unfit men and salpingectomies (ligation of the fallopian tubes) for unfit women; however, for rapists, sodomists, and other "perverts," she advocated castration.

In 1923, the Oregon Legislature passed a new sterilization law that was later amended but continued as final law until revisions were made in 1967. Oregon did not officially abolish its State Board of Eugenics, later called the State Board of Social Protection, until October of 1983.*

In April of 1884, while bustling about Portland in anticipation of Oregon's upcoming vote on a woman suffrage amendment, Bethenia Owens had a chance

---

*In December of 2002, Governor John Kitzhaber apologized on behalf of the state for the forcible sterilization of over 2,600 Oregon residents between 1917 and 1981. Oregon was one of thirty-three states to pass sterilization laws in the first quarter of the twentieth century and the second state to make a public apology.

Dr. Bethenia Owens, early 1880s. These photos were probably taken in Portland, Oregon, where Dr. Owens returned to practice medicine after receiving her second medical degree in 1880. Courtesy of the Oregon Historical Society, CN3 and CN4062 (full-length shot).

meeting that summoned up memories of Clatsop and brought her face-to-face with romance. Seeking out Charles W. Fulton, then state senator from Clatsop, she found herself at a hotel breakfast table in the company of Fulton and three other men from Clatsop—John Adair, who was called "Colonel Adair," and his two brothers. "We made a jolly party," she later wrote, "all talking Woman Suffrage, as we partook of the morning meal" (Owens-Adair 1906, 100).

The amendment went down to defeat the next month, the first of five defeats before Oregon women gained the vote in 1912. But Bethenia's disappointment was eased by her blossoming romance with John Adair, whom she had known as a child on Clatsop Plains. When Bethenia was thirteen, Adair, seven months her senior, "was a large handsome boy of his age, with the most beautiful curly auburn hair imaginable," and she "admired and was quite fascinated with him, then" (Owens-Adair 1906, 100–101).

After she became a doctor, Bethenia was often asked why she did not marry. Her answer was always, "I am married. I am married to my profession" (Owens-

LEFT: Colonel John Adair, age forty-five. A. B. Paxton of Astoria, Oregon, took this photo in July 1884, the month and year of the Owens-Adair wedding. COURTESY OF MARILYN (LEBACK) VAUGHN OF BROWNSVILLE, OREGON. RIGHT: Colonel John Adair, late 1860s to early 1870s. COURTESY OF MARILYN (LEBACK) VAUGHN OF BROWNSVILLE, OREGON.

Adair 1906, 100). In a letter written to Jesse Applegate in 1879, while she was in medical school in Michigan, Bethenia made it clear that she and a Roseburg suitor, probably Asher Marks, had separated because "he never understood me" and "his ideas of woman's position (sphere) do not run exactly in the groove with my own." She added, "I can never give up my freedom, my individuality" (Owens-Adair 1906, 296–297).

The gregarious and charming Adair overcame Bethenia's resistance, and within three months of their reunion, they were married, on July 24, 1884. The wedding, at the First Congregational Church in Portland, was a major social event, with guests from throughout the state. The bride, dressed in an elegant wedding gown of cream-colored, brocaded silk, was forty-four, and the groom, attended by four groomsmen, was forty-five. After a month's honeymoon in San Francisco, the couple returned to Portland, where Bethenia resumed her medical practice with a new, hyphenated name: Dr. Owens-Adair.

Who was this "colonel" who stole Bethenia's heart and prompted her to write: "There were no dark shadows in his pictures, and my love for him knew no bounds" (Owens-Adair 1906, 102–103)? John Adair's title was not related to any rank that he held in the military. McFarland (1984, 137, n. 62) reported that it was family custom to call him colonel, perhaps to distinguish him from his father, who was called "General Adair." In an interview with Fred Lockley (1928, vol. 1, 239–242), Colonel John Adair, the eldest of thirteen children, said he was born in 1839 on the family plantation near Frankfort, Kentucky. His paternal grandfather, John Adair, served as governor of Kentucky and later as a United States senator and congressman. His well-educated father, General John Adair, was appointed Oregon's first Collector of Customs by President Polk in 1848, and the Adair family arrived in Astoria in 1849. General Adair, for whom Bethenia "always had the most profound admiration," and her father, Tom Owens, came from similar backgrounds of wealthy, plantation-holding Kentucky families and were "warm friends" in their shared years at Clatsop (Owens-Adair 1906, 101, 100).

At the age of sixteen, Adair was appointed to the West Point Military Academy by General Joseph Lane, who held strong pro-slavery views and served

General John Adair and his wife Mary Anne (seated at center front) with their family in Astoria the summer of 1886. Colonel John Adair is not in the photo. CCHS 5016.00A.

The home of General John Adair in Upper Astoria, built in 1849. The two-story addition at right, completed in 1855, had the first plastered rooms in Astoria. CCHS 5303.960.

as Oregon Territory's Democratic delegate to Congress. As Oregon's first cadet, Adair was directed to Fort Vancouver, where he met Captain U. S. Grant and Lieutenant Philip Sheridan.

Adair began the five-year curriculum at West Point in the spring of 1856. The 1953 *Register of Graduates* shows that he graduated thirteenth in his class of forty-five cadets in 1861. "Some of the members of my class at once resigned and went south to become officers in the Confederate Army," Adair told Fred Lockley (1928, 241). According to the *Register of Graduates,* twenty-two members of his class fought in the Battle of Bull Run in July of 1861. Rather than joining the Confederate Army or leading Union troops on the battlefield, Adair was ordered to Washington, D.C., and given charge of President Lincoln's guard of twenty men. Although his Kentucky slave-holding background prejudiced him against Lincoln, Adair found it impossible to hate "one of the biggest men mentally and morally I had ever met" (Lockley 1928, 241).

Army records show that Adair was dismissed in 1861. Did President Lincoln grant him his wish to return west rather than fight his own people in the Civil War? No answer is provided in Adair's interview with Lockley, but historians offer explanations. Bancroft / Victor (1888, 456, n. 29) reported that Adair "was commissioned lieutenant of dragoons and ordered to join his regiment at Walla Walla, and afterward to report at Washington, instead of which he deserted, and went to Victoria, V.I. [British Columbia]. He was dismissed from the service." In a similar account, Carey (1935) noted that Adair was ordered to join a company of dragoons, declined the duty, and was removed from army rolls. The *Oregon Statesman* of August 25, 1862, declared on the front page that Adair was "a deserter, and now in the British army, to the everlasting disgrace of the name Adair."

Although the circumstances of Adair's military career remain unclear, faith in his abilities and character was restored by 1874, when he was again in Oregon and accepted appointment as Brigadier General of the State Militia. The same year, with his brother Samuel D. Adair, John Adair established a salmon cannery in Astoria. The brothers enjoyed the decade of the salmon boom on the Columbia River. In 1881 Adair sold his share of the business to his brother William, but he remained in Astoria to continue promoting and investing in real estate. Adair had a particular interest in reclaiming and developing several thousand acres of tideland near Astoria, which he and Samuel had purchased in 1877. Here, the colonel envisioned, farms would flourish and the future townships of Sunnymead, Meriwether, Downs, Warrenton Park, and New Astoria would thrive.

> *"[N]ow that I have a husband whom I love, and who is devoted to me, my life is, indeed, a happy one."*

Not long after their marriage, Adair persuaded Bethenia to invest in these unclaimed tidelands. "Reclamation at that time was very expensive," she recalled, "and little understood." Bethenia was "earnestly advised not to invest in the proposition," but with an annual income of $7,000 from her Portland medical practice, she made the investment (Owens-Adair 1906, 103).

Whatever doubts Bethenia might have had about the investment or her husband's business acumen she set aside in favor of love and romance. In April of 1885, after almost a year of marriage, Bethenia wrote to Inez Adams Parker: "[N]ow that I have a husband whom I love, and who is devoted to me, my life is, indeed, a happy one. . . . [I]t is indeed a great blessing to find one to whom you

Sunnymead Farm, southwest of the present Port of Astoria Airport,

on a hill overlooking the Columbia River and extensive farmlands.

<small>Courtesy of Marilyn (Leback) Vaughn of Brownsville, Oregon.</small>

can at all times turn for consolation and advice." Years later, when she looked back across twenty-one years of marriage, Bethenia admitted that her husband was "usually among the clouds," rarely getting "down to *terra firma*," yet "an optimist of a happy and cheerful disposition" (Owens-Adair 1906, 420, 102).

On January 28, 1887, eleven days short of her forty-seventh birthday, Bethenia gave birth to a daughter, and her "joy knew no limit" (Owens-Adair 1906, 103). The infant was named Mary Anne, probably after Colonel Adair's mother. Within three days, however, the baby died in Portland after contracting pneumonia, and Bethenia entered one of the darkest periods of her life.

She became severely depressed, particularly with Adair far away in Clatsop, trying to reclaim his tideland "with the aid of twenty-five Chinamen." Finally, she told her husband that she would go to Astoria. "I can have a practice anywhere, and I cannot endure our separation, now that our baby is gone" (Owens-Adair 1906, 103, 104). After two years in Astoria, where she rented a house and had a successful medical practice, Bethenia came down with typhus fever.

To aid in her recovery, Adair persuaded her to move to the fresh air at a farm he had purchased near Clatsop Plains, about five miles southwest of Astoria. An eternal optimist, he believed that railroad trains would be running across their land within two years, and he promised Bethenia, "[O]ur fortunes will be assured, and you will never need to work again" (Owens-Adair 1906, 104).

In a "weakened condition," Bethenia agreed, and they moved in July of 1888 to Sunnymead Farm, where they remained for eleven years. Although this was an out-of-the-way place to practice medicine, Bethenia never refused a call, "day or night, rain or shine." Sometimes she traveled by horseback, sometimes by boat, sometimes by foot "through trails so overhung with dense undergrowth, and obstructed with logs and roots, that a horse and rider could not get past; and through muddy and flooded tide-lands in gum boots" (Owens-Adair 1906, 104). During one winter storm, a messenger called for her at four in the morning to hurry to Seaside, fifteen miles away. Bethenia traveled on horseback, with her blankets tied to the saddle and cinch so she would not be blown off. For two hours, the colonel and the messenger cleared a path with axes through the fallen timber, only to emerge from the dark woods to face the full brunt of the angry storm. The trip took seven hours, but Dr. Owens-Adair arrived at her destination.

In addition to her practice as a country doctor, Bethenia was busy with the house and farm, often managing Sunnymead when Adair was away on business. "There was little on the farm I could not do," she wrote. Some days she spent "three to seven hours in the day in the saddle looking after the stock" (Owens-Adair 1906, 108).

At Bethenia's urging, her son George Hill allowed her grandson, Victor, born in 1886, to join the Owens-Adair household in 1888, after the death of his mother, Anna. A bright and lively little fellow, Victor was sunshine for Bethenia, and when his father remarried, she "adopted" him for a time. She also enjoyed the company of a young woman whom she referred to as her "adopted daughter."

About 1876, while practicing medicine in Portland, Bethenia met Mattie (Martha) Belle Palmer, then about fourteen. Mattie's mother Rebecca, suffering from double pneumonia, had been brought in an open wagon and boat from the Fort Vancouver area of Clark County to Bethenia's office. The doctor did not think the woman would last through the night. Before dying, Rebecca Palmer asked Bethenia to take one of her three daughters. Later, the father, Josiah Palmer, introduced the doctor to Mattie, the eldest of the three.

LEFT: Victor Hill, Bethenia's grandson (seated), and John Adair, Jr. (standing at left), ca. 1898, both members of the Owens-Adair household at Sunnymead Farm. COURTESY OF MARILYN (LEBACK) VAUGHN OF BROWNSVILLE, OREGON. RIGHT: Dr. Martha (Mattie) Belle Palmer, late 1880s. COURTESY OF MARILYN (LEBACK) VAUGHN OF BROWNSVILLE, OREGON.

Bethenia recalled that Mattie "was a puny, sickly looking little creature. . . . [S]he stood beside her father, who was also undersized, in her old, faded calico dress, up to her knees, her stockings tied up with strings, her shoes out at the toes, and holding a bundle done up in an old red cotton handkerchief, with a scared look on her pinched little face" (Owens-Adair 1906, 87). Unable to deny the child, Bethenia took her in, educated her, and even sent her to medical school. In 1886, Mattie received her medical degree from Willamette University, but she chose not to practice medicine on her own or to marry, preferring to live with Bethenia and volunteer for the WCTU and various charities. According to Bethenia, Mattie was a home-body and quite shy. She read extensively and was an authority on almost any subject. Bethenia wrote, "Had I had a hundred children, I am sure none could have been more faithful, or loved me better. She was always a sunbeam, not only in my heart, but in my home, as well" (Owens-Adair 1906, 100).

Bethenia loved children, and across the years, she temporarily included younger siblings, her granddaughter Vera Hill, foster children, and nieces and nephews in her household. Her most surprising act of maternal love occurred in 1891 when she was fifty-one years old. "I officiated at the birth of a boy whose mother gave me her child. I officially took the little orphan to my bosom, and gave it a share of my mother-love, and, with my husband's consent, I called him John Adair, Jr." (Owens-Adair 1906, 114).

Who was this "little orphan," the child Bethenia came to call "my boy"? According to McFarland (1984, 126), who interviewed various descendants of John Adair, the child was born on October 7, 1891, at Sunnymead Farm, and his birth was recorded in the Adair Family Bible, in Adair's handwriting, as John Adair, Jr., fourth in the line of John Adairs. McFarland added, "The Adair family has always accepted the fact that Mattie Belle Palmer was the child's mother and that Colonel Adair was his father."

Mattie Palmer continued to live in the Owens-Adair household at Sunnymead for two more years, until her "unexpected" death on October 16, 1893,

Vera Owens Hill, Bethenia's only granddaughter, early 1900s. CCHS 92.96.69.141.

"after a very brief illness" (Owens-Adair 1906, 135). Bethenia and Adair formally adopted her child on April 9, 1898.

There is little doubt that Adair was the father. Could this have been a surrogate motherhood, to which Bethenia agreed, so that Adair might father a son to carry on the Adair name? Did the colonel seduce or rape Mattie? Or did Mattie, who was inexperienced in romance, fall in love with him? Whatever the circumstances surrounding Mattie's pregnancy and the birth of her child, what explanations did Bethenia, the colonel, and Mattie offer to family and friends?

In the original version of her autobiography, published in 1906, Bethenia spoke lovingly of her "adopted daughter" and included excerpts from Mattie's diary and the last letter Mattie wrote to her. In January of 1890, the year before the birth of baby John, Mattie wrote of her happy family circle composed of Bethenia, whom she identified as "Dr.," the colonel, Bethenia's grandson Victor, and Sallie, one of Bethenia's young nieces. "Col. read," Mattie wrote, "and we spent a pleasant evening. Our evenings are always enjoyable, when we are all at home. We are learning many instructive and beautiful things pertaining to life." In her last letter to Bethenia, dated October 10, 1893, two years after the birth of baby John and six days before her death, Mattie wrote from Sunnymead to her "Dear Mother," then attending the Chicago World's Fair. "We are all so glad when your letters come! Victor's eyes get big, and John says, 'Hurrah for mamma and the big fair,' as we have taught him" (Owens-Adair 1906, 133). At the age of two, little John was calling Bethenia "mamma." We have no record of what he called Mattie.

Changes, particularly deletions, in a later published version of Bethenia's autobiography suggest that she decided some topics were better left unmentioned. In Gaston's 1912 version of her autobiography, probably prepared in 1911 by Bethenia, she did not mention Mattie or her adopted son, and she abbreviated her discussion of Colonel Adair. Moreover, she deleted details of her first eleven years at Sunnymead.

In her original autobiography, Bethenia wrote that she suffered both mental and physical anguish at Sunnymead, a condition undoubtedly linked to complicated domestic circumstances, financial worries, and sorrow at the loss of loved ones, including Mattie, brother Flem, Jesse Applegate, and brother-in-law John Hobson. Moreover, problems and losses associated with various land dealings affected family relations. For example, in *Adair et al. v. Adair et al.* (March 7, 1892), Bethenia and the colonel were defendants in a suit "to enforce the specific performance of a written agreement to convey land," brought before the Supreme Court of Oregon by Adair's brother Samuel and wife Mary (*Pacific Reporter*, vol. 29, 193–200). Considering her move from Portland to Sunnymead, Bethenia wrote, "Now, as I look back, I realize that that move was one of the greatest mistakes of my life" (Owens-Adair 1906, 104).

By 1898, although Bethenia had worked steadily for eleven years as a country doctor, Adair had secured little income, and the debt on Sunnymead alone was $24,000. Despite her daily regimen of cold baths and physical exercise, Bethenia's health was undermined by rheumatism, and she was convinced she would "soon become a cripple" if she continued to live in the wet climate at Sunnymead (Owens-Adair 1906, 109).

Bethenia and Adair rented out Sunnymead and moved, in April of 1898, with grandson Victor and John, Jr., to the arid climate of North Yakima, Washington, where Bethenia's son George Hill and his second wife and daughter lived. As Bethenia told the colonel, "I shall make money, and you ought, with your education, to be able to get into some kind of paying business." Welcomed by the citizens of North Yakima and her fellow professionals, Bethenia established a good practice and became president of the Yakima Medical Association. During the summer months, she enjoyed taking her practice to the popular summer resort of Seaside. In the summer of 1900, she earned a post-graduate degree at the Chicago Clinical School and felt "equipped for going on" with her professional work, just what was needed "after those eleven years on the farm" (Owens-Adair 1906, 109, 110).

Adair, however, found no business in North Yakima, and Bethenia recommended that he and John, Jr., who was grieving for the farm, move back to Sunnymead. "If you cannot get into business down there," she told her husband, "you can certainly see that the place is kept up." Bethenia's plan was to work in North Yakima until their properties were self-supporting and they had enough income to live comfortably at Sunnymead. "[T]hen I shall be glad to retire and return home," she said (Owens-Adair 1906, 111).

In June of 1902, Adair and John, Jr., age ten, moved back to Sunnymead. Bethenia continued her country practice, usually doing her own driving, day

Dr. Owens-Adair:
Some of Her Life
Experiences, published
in 1906 in Portland,
Oregon. CCHS 92.096.069.

and night, with her horse and buggy. On October 10, 1905, after earning about $25,000, Dr. Owens-Adair closed her North Yakima office and officially retired at the age of sixty-five. Then, with her good horse Pride, she began the journey home to join her husband and John, Jr., before traveling for an extended stay in San Diego County, California, with Inez Adams Parker.

At the Parker home, Bethenia, who had initially intended to write a book on "medicine from a woman's standpoint," wrote instead "a short, plain, truthful story of my own life," complemented by a collection of writings and letters as well as "sketches of the lives of various pioneers of Oregon, especially those of Clatsop County, which was my first, and is to be my last home." She dedicated the 537-page book to her "beloved mother," Sarah Owens, who lived in Oregon until her death in January of 1908 (Owens-Adair 1906, 113, Dedication). *Dr. Owens-Adair: Some of Her Life Experiences* was published by Mann & Beach in Portland in December of 1906, to positive reviews. The *Morning Astorian* observed: "As one reads, one can hear this good woman talking; . . . there is the same wholesome, straight-forward, convincing intelligence, backed by the realistic charm the truth always contributes to a tale, be it told in speech or written" (Owens-Adair 1922c, 12).

When Bethenia returned to Sunnymead in March of 1907, she found "chaotic confusion, neglection [*sic*] and destruction everywhere" (Gaston 1912, vol. 4, 596). "The barn was unsafe and the house unfit for occupation," she said. "The rats made night hideous." The orchard and grounds were overgrown. Adair had not maintained Sunnymead and had probably moved, perhaps to Astoria.

Bethenia and Adair divided their properties and were divorced. In a partition deed, signed September 30, 1907, Adair kept his reclaimed lands, the property closest to Warrenton, and the subdivision called Sunnymead Addition. Bethenia apparently received $7,500 from Adair, which she deposited in the Astoria Savings Bank, and she kept the property farther south, Sunnymead Farm, and a homesite called Grand View. In her divorce petition filed in Clatsop,

Dr. Bethenia Owens-Adair ca. 1905. This photograph appears
in Bethenia's 1906 autobiography. CCHS 30964.00A.

Bethenia claimed that she lived in fear that the colonel would harm her (Clatsop
County Judgment Roll 4805; Penner 1996, 21). Her husband had become a
"gross habitual drunkard" and, when intoxicated, spoke to her in "abusive and
insulting language." Bethenia was a successful, practicing physician when they
married in 1884, but Adair did not work after their marriage and incurred enormous debts. Judge Thomas A. McBride granted the divorce, and Bethenia was
once again a free woman. The general public knew only of a separation, not a
divorce.

Bethenia preferred not to dwell on this difficult period, writing in her revised
autobiography that "many sorrows" had been "interspersed with the pleasures"

John Adair, Jr., probably about 1910, when he attended Oregon State Agricultural College in Corvallis, Oregon. Courtesy of Marilyn (Leback) Vaughn of Brownsville, Oregon.

of her married life. "Suffice it to say," she continued, "that I have lived through it all and still have my health, and my mind is unencumbered" (Gaston 1912, vol. 4, 596).

After the divorce, Bethenia gave energy to reform efforts and enjoyed the "three lovely farms side by side"—Grand View, Sunnymead, and Park. She restored Sunnymead and built a new home at Grand View, five miles from Astoria and a mile and a half from Warrenton. The front porch and windows offered a commanding view of Youngs Bay and "the lordly Columbia a mile away" (Gaston 1912, vol. 4, 596).

In the 1910 Federal Census for Clatsop, Bethenia Owens-Adair appeared as a physician and divorced head of household. On a neighboring farm, Adair, with his son, John, Jr., age seventeen, appeared as a farmer and divorced head of household. (The colonel was also listed as a lodger with rooms in Astoria.) Adair's health failed a few years later, and he died in Astoria in 1915 after "a lingering illness due to general debility" (*Astoria Daily Budget,* 20 November 1915, 6). Bethenia's quixotic husband died destitute.

Shortly before the colonel's death, John, Jr., was appointed by the court as his ailing father's guardian. Two years later, John, Jr., married Grace Dawson of Clatsop. He appeared in the 1930 Federal Census for Clatsop as a stockman on a cattle ranch, residing with his wife and three children—Florence, Marjorie, and John—in the household of his brother-in-law, Seymour Dawson, a dairy farmer.

Bethenia spent the last years of her life at her farm, where she loved to entertain. At the age of eighty-four, she wrote to Fred Lockley that she could still mount a horse from the ground and lift herself into the saddle (Lockley Papers, 29 December 1924). Rheumatism, she claimed, was a problem that was lessened with exercise; people "rust out" from inactivity.

In time, however, age and physical infirmity took their toll, and her four-hundred-acre farm and dwindling assets became too much to manage. In January of 1925, at her request, Frank Patton, president of the Astoria Bank, was appointed guardian of Bethenia's property, along with attorney Edwin C. Judd.

Bethenia made her last public appearance at the age of eighty-six, for the 1926 dedication of the landmark Astor Column in Astoria. Shortly afterward, on September 11, 1926, she died at home of a heart ailment. The burial and funeral were at Ocean View Cemetery in Warrenton.

In her will, Bethenia included modest bequests for her son George Hill, John Adair, Jr., and her grandchildren, and she asked that the bulk of her estate be used to establish a eugenics institute and to create a public park, named Owens Park, at Warrenton. But because her estate was found deficient to cover outstanding debts, Bethenia's wishes were not fulfilled.

Her burial site remained unmarked until 1975, when the Clatsop County Historical Society placed a headstone at her grave. The dedication of the monument, on July 19, 1975, celebrated Bethenia Owens-Adair's achievements as a feminist, teacher, physician, and reformer. Her epitaph reads simply: "Only the enterprising and the brave are actuated to become pioneers."

Acknowledgments

I am indebted to all those whose research and writing on the life and work of Bethenia Owens-Adair preceded mine and to those who gave so unselfishly of their time and effort to assist with this essay. In particular, I wish to thank Lucy Berkley, formerly with Research Library Photographic Services, Oregon Historical Society; Carol Kirkby McFarland of Arcata, California, who shared valuable research insights; Jena K. Mitchell, Curator, and Karen Bratton, Research Librarian, both of the Douglas County Museum, Roseburg, Oregon; Liisa Penner, Archivist and *Cumtux* Editor, Clatsop County Historical Society, Astoria, Oregon; and Sara J. Piasecki, Head, Historical Collections and Archives, Oregon Health and Science University Library, Portland, Oregon. Many thanks to Marilyn (Leback) Vaughn, who so graciously provided family photographs to help illustrate this essay. And a special acknowledgement goes to Karen Kirtley, Michael Bales, and Steve Forrester, the three who made it possible for Dr. Owens-Adair to step into the twenty-first century.

Sources Cited

See also "Selected Writings of Dr. Bethenia Owens-Adair" (page 193).

Abrahams, Harold J. 1966. *Extinct Medical Schools of Nineteenth-Century Philadelphia.* Philadelphia: University of Pennsylvania Press.

Applegate, Jesse. 1868. A Day with the Cow Column in 1843. *Overland Monthly Magazine* (August).

Bancroft, Hubert Howe. 1886. *History of Oregon, Vol. 1, 1834–1848.* San Francisco: History Publishing Co. [*See also* Frances Auretta Fuller Victor.]

Bowen, William A. 1978. *The Willamette Valley: Migration and Settlement on the Oregon Frontier.* Seattle: University of Washington Press.

Gaston, Joseph. 1912. *The Centennial History of Oregon, 1811–1912.* 4 vols. Chicago: S. J. Clarke Publishing Co.

Larsell, Olof. 1947. *The Doctor in Oregon: A Medical History.* Portland, OR: Binford & Mort.

Lockley, Fred. 1914. Berthine [*sic*] Angeline [*sic*] Owens Adair. In *The Lockley Files: Conversations with Pioneer Women.* 1981. Comp. and ed. Mike Helm. Eugene, OR: Rainy Day Press, 29–32.

_____. 1928. *History of the Columbia River Valley from the Dalles to the Sea.* 3 vols. Chicago: S. J. Clarke Publishers.

Lockley Papers. Special Collections, University of Oregon Library, Eugene, Oregon.

McFarland, Carol Kirkby. 1984. *Bethenia Owens-Adair, Oregon Pioneer Physician, Feminist, and Reformer, 1840–1926.* M.A. Thesis, University of Oregon.

Miller, Emma Gene, ed. 1958. *Clatsop County, Oregon: A History.* Portland, OR: Binford & Mort.

Owens, Sarah Damron. [1906]. My Mother's Story [autobiography of Sarah Damron Owens]. In *Dr. Owens-Adair: Some of Her Life Experiences.* Bethenia Owens-Adair. Portland, OR: Mann & Beach, 144–161.

Penner, Liisa. 1996. Two Divorces: The Shivelys and the Adairs. Clatsop County Historical Society. *Cumtux* 16 (Fall): 18–21.

Register of Graduates, United States Military Academy, 1802–1953. 1953. New York: West Point Alumni Foundation.

Victor, Frances Auretta Fuller. 1886. *History of Oregon, Vol. 1, 1834–1848.* San Francisco: History Publishing Co. [*See also* Hubert Howe Bancroft.]

Walsh, Mary Roth. 1972. *"Doctors Wanted: No Women Need Apply": Sexual Barriers in the Medical Profession, 1835–1975.* New Haven: Yale University Press.

Welter, Barbara. 1966. The Cult of True Womanhood: 1820–1860. *American Quarterly* (Summer): 151–162, 173–174.

Selected Writings of Dr. Bethenia Owens-Adair

Owens-Adair, Bethenia Angelina. 1873a. Disquisition: Essay by Mrs. B. A. Owens of Roseburg, Oregon—prepared to read before the recent meeting of the state temperance alliance, but not delivered on account of the disorganizing secession element that couldn't bear it. *New Northwest* (7 March): 1.

_____. 1873b. Letter from Roseburg: Letter from B. A. Owens. *New Northwest* (15 August): 2.

_____. 1877. Correspondence of the O.S.W.S.A.: Letter from Mrs. B. A. Owens, M.D. *New Northwest* (9 March): 1.

_____. 1879. Letter from Michigan University. *New Northwest* (23 January): 2.

_____. 1881. Woman as a Physician: Essay read by Mrs. Dr. B. A. Owens before the Oregon State Woman Suffrage Association. *New Northwest* (3 November): 1.

_____. 1883. Pilgrim Mothers: Extract from an address delivered by Mrs. Dr. B. A.

Owens at a recent "Liberty Meeting." *New Northwest* (18 January): 1.

____. 1884. Heredity. *New Northwest* (28 February): 1.

____. 1885. Letter from Dr. Owens Adair. *New Northwest* (12 February): 1.

____. 1897. Sarah Damron Owens. *Daily Astorian* (1 August): 6.

____. 1898. Pioneer Women of Clatsop County. *Transactions of the Twenty-Fifth Annual Reunion of the Oregon Pioneer Association for 1897*. Portland, OR: George H. Himes & Co., 77–105.

____. 1901. Mrs. Sarah Damron Adair [should be Owens], Pioneer of 1843. *Transactions of the Twenty-Eighth Annual Reunion of the Oregon Pioneer Association for 1900*. Portland, OR: Himes & Pratt, 65–82.

____. 1904. Letter to the Editor. Portland *Oregonian* (11 March).

____. 1906. *Dr. Owens-Adair: Some of Her Life Experiences*. Portland, OR: Mann & Beach, Printers.

____. 1910. *Human Sterilization*. Warrenton, OR: n.p.

____. 1922a. *The Eugenic Marriage Law and Human Sterilization: The Situation in Oregon*. Salem, OR: published by the author, 22 December 1922. Accompanied by the text of two bills to be introduced into the Oregon Legislature in 1923.

____. 1922b. *Human Sterilization: It's [sic] Social and Legislative Aspects*. Portland, OR: Metropolitan Press.

____. 1922c. *A Souvenir: Dr. Owens-Adair to Her Friends, Christmas, 1922*. Salem, OR: Statesman Publishing Co.

____. n.d. Bethenia A. Owens-Adair. Miscellany. University of Oregon Medical School, Portland, Oregon. Northwest Collection.

____. Bethenia Owens-Adair Papers, 1864–1921. Three folders. Oregon Historical Society Research Library.

Silas Bryant Smith

By Stephen Dow Beckham

Silas B. Smith led a remarkable life. Unlike several hundreds of children born to Native American mothers and fathers involved in the Pacific Northwest fur trade, Smith became a farmer, attorney, author, and civic leader. Meriwether Lewis and William Clark—explorers who dealt with Clatsop chief Coboway, Smith's grandfather—would probably have expressed astonishment that this man from the mouth of the Columbia River would follow a course so different from that of his maternal ancestors. In spite of his accomplishments, however, Smith chose to stay in the Clatsop homeland for most of his adult life.

Silas B. Smith, grandson of Clatsop chief Coboway and son of Solomon and Celiast Smith. Photo by A. B. Paxton of Astoria, ca. 1890. Courtesy of Dick Basch. Depping Collection, CCHS.

Remarkable forces shaped Silas B. Smith. He had parents of determination and character. He took the most of opportunities when they beckoned to him. He had a sense of civic responsibility that propelled him to public service, and a love of history that inspired his commitment to put pen to paper and publish information of interest to others. He displayed ambition and tenacity in seeking justice for the tribes at the mouth of the Columbia River. Smith made his most enduring contribution as architect of Indian tribal land claims, seeking remuneration from the federal government for lands lost in the influx of white settlers.

✣ ✣ ✣

Smith was born on September 22, 1839, on Chehalem Creek in what later became Newberg, Oregon. At the time his father, Solomon Howard Smith, worked for Ewing Young in construction and operation of a water-powered sawmill that cut lumber for buildings on nearby French Prairie and in the Chehalem Valley (U.S.C.C. 1902, 222). A former fur trapper who engaged in the trade in the Southwest and California, Young had settled in Oregon. When he announced his intention to operate a still and sell alcoholic beverages, Hudson's Bay Company officials and Methodist missionaries diverted him. They sent Young in 1837 to California to purchase cattle and drive a herd, initially a thousand head, north to Oregon. Young had hired Smith in 1836 to cut boards for fences, barns, corrals, and oak flooring (Holmes 1967, 138–139).

Silas Smith's mother, originally known as Celiast, carried the baptismal name Hélène, or Helen. Like other children of prominent and wealthy Clatsops,

Solomon H. Smith and his wife, Celiast (Hélène, or Helen). From *History of the Pacific Northwest: Oregon and Washington,* vol. 2, Portland, Oregon: North Pacific History Co., 1889, opposite p. 110. CCHS COLLECTION.

her head was flattened in infancy on a cradleboard. She and her sisters, Yiamust and Kilakotah, were destined to lives dramatically different from those of other women in the tribe (Evans 1889, vol. 2, 570–572).

Solomon Howard Smith was born in 1809 in Lebanon, New Hampshire. He attended school in Norwich, Vermont, and studied medicine with an uncle. But he was forced to take a job as a clerk in Boston after an investment in cod fishing off Newfoundland failed. By 1832, he was eager for a new start. He joined a group who emigrated overland to Oregon Country with Nathaniel Jarvis Wyeth, a successful Boston ice merchant. Wyeth had decided to invest his capital and compete against the Hudson's Bay Company fur trade business. Their overland journey was fraught with hardship: hunger, desperate winter conditions, and confusion about the route of travel (Munnick 1968, 399–407).

Wyeth's Columbia River Fishing and Trading Company established Fort William on Sauvie's Island at the confluence of the Willamette and Columbia Rivers. In spite of starting an ambitious trapping and trading program, Wyeth lacked sufficient resources, including personnel, to compete with the well-entrenched Hudson's Bay Company. In 1836, he closed operations and returned to Boston. Smith remained in Oregon.

John McLoughlin, Chief Factor at Fort Vancouver, hired Smith to replace John Ball as teacher in the fort's new school. Smith found himself faced with a polyglot group of students: white, Indian, Hawaiian, Polynesian, and those of mixed ancestry. Soon Smith became interested in Hélène, the "wife" of Basile Poirier, the post baker. Smith's ardor quickened when word reached the fort that Poirier, who had three children by Hélène, also had a wife in Canada.

Hélène Poirier and her surviving sons, François and Alexandre Poirier, left the fort and moved to French Prairie in the northern Willamette Valley to the household of Joseph Gervais, a French-Canadian who had married Hélène's sister, Yiamust. Another sister, Kilakotah, also lived at French Prairie and was successively the wife of William Matthews, James McMillan, and Louis LaBonté.

Smith followed Hélène, and he accepted a job to teach in nearby Fairfield at the first school in Oregon (Lee and Frost 1844, 132; Munnick and Warner 1972, A-76). After a short time, the couple were married by Rev. Jason Lee, a Methodist missionary who had also traveled with Wyeth. Henceforth she was known as Helen Smith.

In May 1840, when Silas Smith was about eight months old, he traveled with his parents and Rev. Daniel Lee, Jason Lee's nephew, to the mouth of the Columbia River to await the arrival of the *Lausanne*, a ship bringing new personnel and supplies to support ambitious plans for expanding Methodist missions in the Oregon Country. This was probably Silas Smith's first visit to his mother's homeland. His father, Solomon Smith, liked what he saw. In August that same year, inspired by the prospect of the Methodists opening a Clatsop Plains mission, the family moved permanently from French Prairie to an initial claim on Neacoxie Creek, a small, sluggish stream that for many years ran north from Cullaby Lake but more recently flows south into the Necanicum River.

Another missionary, Joseph Frost, visited the Smiths in early September. He wrote:

> Here we found the Clatsop Indians waiting for the commencement of their second salmon season, the season in the Columbia having closed in August. And here we found Mr. Smith, who had laid up the body of a log-cabin, about fifteen feet square, and was living in it without floor or roof (Lee and Frost 1844, 275).

In 1841, Smith moved his family north approximately eight miles to a claim on the Skipanon River. Frost noted: "In November Mr. Smith, my old neighbour, removed to the plain, where he has no neighbours except our cattle and horses" (Lee and Frost 1844, 310).

Here Smith broke ground and began farming; he confronted chilly weather and poor soil. Frost went to the Smith claim on March 5, 1842, and later wrote: "Visited Mr. Smith upon the Plain, and found him very much discouraged. Surely he has difficulties to pass through of which those in the civilized world know nothing" (Lee and Frost 1844, 315).

Because of these conditions, Smith found that raising livestock and operating a dairy were more productive than farming. The same year he purchased horses and cattle from the estate of Ewing Young and, with missionary Frost, drove them over the Coast Range via Tillamook to establish herds at the mouth of the river.

Silas B. Smith and his sister Charlotte Smith, ca. 1880. CCHS 10.049.

After gold was discovered in California, Solomon Smith found a ready market for butter from his dairy. In 1849 he opened a mercantile store at Skipanon (a small community on the northern end of the Clatsop Plains near present-day Warrenton) to supply other residents settling on the Clatsop Plains. Passage of the Oregon Donation Land Act enabled Smith to secure the land at no cost. In 1851, he leased a sawmill on the Lewis and Clark River. Although he cut and sold some lumber, he soon abandoned the business and returned to full-time farming (Evans 1889, vol. 2, 569). Conditions were challenging in the 1840s. The Smith family, though connected to the local tribal community, lived an isolated existence. The Methodist mission did not prosper and was eventually abandoned. At one point, it is said that Helen Smith saved the life of Rev. Daniel Lee by wresting a gun from the hands of Kotata, an enraged Clatsop man who threatened to murder him. This incident, first reported in print in 1887, received no mention in Lee's diary. Historian David Peterson-del Mar has suggested the incident is "too romantic and too dramatic to be true" (Peterson-del Mar 1995, 16).

Tragedy struck the family, too. Helen Lavinia Smith, born in 1837, died at age fourteen when she fell from a horse (Munnick and Warner 1972, A-76). Alpheus Dexter Smith died in infancy, and Henry Smith died at age eleven. Besides Silas, the Smiths had three surviving daughters: Josephine Smith, Agnes Smith, and Charlotte P. Smith.

Solomon Smith was a staunch supporter of public schools and served for a number of years on school boards in Clatsop County. In 1874 he was elected to the Oregon State Senate. He died in 1876 while serving in Salem and was survived by his widow and four adult children (Evans 1889, vol. 2, 569).

Helen Smith died in 1890 (Peterson-del Mar 1995, 20). She and her husband were buried in the Clatsop Plains Cemetery adjacent to Gray Memorial Church, site of the Methodist mission in the 1840s.

☙ ❧ ☙

Silas B. Smith attended the first school on the Clatsop Plains. Rev. Josiah L. Parrish taught the session during the winter of 1844–1845. Smith did not identify the location, but it was likely the Clatsop Mission founded by the Methodists, since Parrish came to Oregon to work for Rev. Jason Lee and to convert the Indians.

Silas Smith wrote:

> The Morrison and Smith children attended, and perhaps some others.
> Mr. W. W. Raymond, who had removed to Clatsop from Salem after
> the dissolution of the mission there, opened the second school at
> our place in the winter of 1846–47. This was quite a large school for
> this new settlement. He was succeeded after the first quarter by Miss
> Elmira Phillips, who continued to conduct the school for at least

six months longer. In the winter of 1849–50 W. H. Gray organized a boarding school at his place (the old mission place), the Rev. Lewis Thompson being teacher; children from Astoria and other parts of the county came hither, seeking the Pierian spring (Smith 1899c).

In his "Educational History of Astoria, Oregon," John Minto remarked that School District No. 1 in Clatsop County was established in 1854. He noted: "There are no records in existence" (Minto 1903, 25). Silas Smith's account of 1899 thus covered the earliest history of education in Clatsop County.

In 1866, his father decided to send Silas Smith to New Hampshire for more education. Although it is rumored that he went east to enroll in the program for Indian boys at Dartmouth College, no record confirms this supposition. Possibly Silas Smith attended an academy. Next he studied law with William N. Blair; later he entered law practice in Gilford, New Hampshire.

Smith married Mary Hannah Swain, who was born in 1844 in Meridian, New Hampshire, the daughter of George W. and Elizabeth Swain. In 1871 the

SILAS B. SMITH,
SKIPANON, OR.

MRS. S.B.SMITH,
SKIPANON, OR.

Silas B. Smith and his wife Mary Swain Smith of Skipanon, Oregon. From *History of the Pacific Northwest: Oregon and Washington,* vol. 2, Portland, Oregon: North Pacific History Co., 1889, opposite p. 110. CCHS COLLECTION.

couple settled in Missouri, where he was admitted to the bar (U.S.C.C. 1902, 223). Their first child, Agnes G. Smith, was born in 1872. After the birth of their daughter, the Smiths moved to Oregon and settled on the Clatsop Plains. Four other children—Goldwin Smith, Starr T. Smith, Laconia Smith Oman, and May Smith Wallingford—were born in Oregon. In Clatsop County, Smith worked as a farmer at Skipanon and a lawyer in Astoria.

His farming was unremarkable, but his work as a lawyer was unique. Smith became a member of the Oregon bar in January 1876 and was most likely the first Native American on the West Coast to practice law (U.S.C.C. 1902, 222). Although the 1870 Federal Census in New Hampshire identified Smith as white, he and his children were identified as Indian in Oregon in the census a decade later (Bureau of the Census 1880).

Silas Smith had a deep interest in the history and culture of the Chinookan tribes of the Columbia River. Working with his mother, he compiled cultural lore. In 1881 he responded to questions from Charles J. Smith of Brookfield, Washington, about fish such as salmon that leave the Pacific to breed in rivers. Smith wrote descriptions of the migratory fish, gave their Chinookan names, and discussed the dates of their appearance in fresh water. His account was published in 1882 in the *Smithsonian Miscellaneous Collections* (Smith 1882).

As a well-known and informed resident with Native American connections, Smith fielded numerous questions when, in the latter half of the nineteenth century, residents and tourists at the mouth of the Nehalem River found beeswax, fragments of Chinese porcelain, timber, and other evidence of a shipwrecked Spanish galleon. Euro-American settlement commenced in Tillamook County in the 1850s. While the southern third of the county remained within the Coast Reservation until 1865, seekers of donation land claims, homesteads, and purchases of land from the General Land Office settled at the Nehalem estuary and Tillamook Bay.

Impoverished and enduring a subsistence lifestyle in a relatively isolated region, the early residents mused about prospects of buried treasure. Hulking Neahkahnie Mountain, towering over the shoreline, seemed an ideal setting for pirates to bury looted treasure. Or maybe the riches were the salvage from a vessel bound on the great, circuitous route across the North Pacific. Incomplete information about the sailing of the Manila Galleon (1565–1815), loss of several of the ships carrying cargoes from the Philippines to New Spain (Mexico), and rumors that Francis Drake may have sojourned during the summer of 1577 on the coast of Oregon fed the imagination.

Silas Smith gave concrete information about this little-known history in "Tales of Early Wrecks on the Oregon Coast, and How the Bees-wax Got There," a fascinating essay that appeared in the first volume of *Oregon Native Son* (1899a). The account confirmed that Smith was a student of history and also was familiar with the oral traditions of the Clatsop and Nehalem Indians, who told of shipwrecks and survivors. He wrote:

> But tradition among the Indian tribes at the mouth of the Columbia river and vicinity tell[s] us that long prior to that time their shores had been visited by at least three other vessels; that is to say, the treasure ship at Echanie [Neahkahnie] mountain, the bees-wax ship near the mouth of the Nehalem river and one other, just south of the mouth of the Columbia river. The two last becoming wrecks on the ocean beach at the places named, evidences of which facts of a more or less conclusive character can be adduced to establish the truthfulness of such statements.
>
> The treasure ship did not become a wreck; she dropped anchor as she approached land and sent a boat ashore with several men and a large chest or box. The box was taken up on the southwest face of the mountain above the road and there buried. And some say that a man was then and there killed and buried with the chest. Then some characters were marked on a large stone which was placed on the spot of burial, and the men then returned to the vessel, when she again put to sea. The treasure character of the deposit is an inference of the whites and the alleged manner of entombment (Smith 1899a, 443).

The account inspired several generations of treasure-hunters to probe Neahkahnie Mountain. There is a strong probability that Smith was motivated to write about this subject by Thomas H. Rogers' novel *Nehalem: A Story of the Pacific, A.D., 1700*, published in 1898, and subsequently reprinted as *Beeswax and Gold: A Story of the Pacific, A.D. 1700* (1929). While Rogers' account was fanciful, Smith's account was historical, tapping both oral tradition and documentary information.

In 1899 Olin D. Wheeler, working closely with the publicity office of the Northern Pacific Railroad, was the first to retrace most of the route traveled by the Lewis and Clark Expedition. As the centennial of their expedition approached, Wheeler was aware of growing interest in the Corps of Discovery and the Louisiana Purchase. Here was an ideal opportunity to promote railroad tourism tied to the heritage of the American West. When he reached the mouth of the Columbia, he sought information about the location of Fort Clatsop, where the expedition had wintered. His quest led to Silas B. Smith.

By 1899, Smith was a well-known and respected elder among the Clatsop Indians. He had lived on the Clatsop Plains for fifty-nine years. His essay, "History of Chief Comcomley," published in the *Oregonian* of December 18, 1899 (Smith 1899b), demonstrated thorough knowledge of local history. When Wheeler arrived, it was inevitable that local residents directed him to Smith.

After their meeting, Smith took Wheeler and George H. Himes of the Oregon Historical Society to the west bank of the Lewis and Clark River and the donation land claim of Carlos Shane. An overland emigrant of 1846, Shane had

Group that identified the site of Fort Clatsop, photographed June 9, 1900.
Silas B. Smith is at far left, and Carlos W. Shane (in long coat) is near center.
Preston W. Gillette is at right with his son. CCHS 11190.796.

filed on a property he consistently identified as "Lewis & Clarke Encampment, Lewis & Clarke River" in correspondence with Surveyor-General John B. Preston and territorial governor John Gaines (Genealogical Forum of Portland, Oregon, 1959, 42; Shane 1852a, 1852b). Wheeler hired George M. Weister, a landscape photographer from Portland, to document his investigations. The photographs show the site covered with a heavy growth of bracken fern. Wheeler subsequently wrote:

> This spot was named Fort Clatsop, after a tribe of Indians in
> whose territory it was situated and its identity and history have
> been satisfactorily preserved. The chief of the Clatsops was called
> Comowool [Coboway] by Lewis and Clark, and he was a frequent
> and welcome visitor at the fort during the winter, and when Fort
> Clatsop was abandoned in 1806, the Captains presented the fort to
> Comowool, who used it as a fall and winter residence for many years
> (Wheeler 1904, vol. 2, 194).

In 1899, Shane said: "I built a house on the land in 1851 and occupied it until 1853. A few feet from where I built my house were at that time the remains of two of the Lewis and Clark cabins. They lay east and west, parallel with each other, and ten or fifteen feet apart" (Wheeler 1904, vol. 2, 198). Shane said that when he cleared his farm, he burned the remains of the old fort (Wheeler 1904, vol. 2, 198).

Smith's help in identifying the Fort Clatsop site and his early membership in the historical society, founded in 1898, led to the state's first historic preservation project. The Committee on Memorials of the Oregon Historical Society visited both the purported site of Fort Clatsop and the Lewis and Clark Salt Works in June 1900. In the party were L. B. Cox, William Galloway, Carlos W. Shane, Preston W. Gillette, Silas B. Smith, and others. Smith, Shane, and Gillette* were pioneer settlers of Clatsop County.

---

*Preston Wilson Gillette (born in Ohio in 1825) traveled overland to Oregon in 1852 and in May 1853 settled on the Lewis and Clark River in Clatsop County, where he established a nursery. In 1862 and 1864 he represented Clatsop County in the legislature, and in 1864 he became collector of customs in Astoria. In 1867 Gillette sold his property and settled in Portland, where he was yet living in 1911 (Gaston 1911, *History of Portland*, vol. 3, 110–115).

The committee's minutes noted: "Acting under the direction of Shane and Gillette your committee marked off the site of the old fort as near as can now be determined, and with what your committee believes to be substantial accuracy, located the positions of the two cabins which were occupied by Lewis and Clark and their followers" (File folder "Fort Clatsop," Oregon Historical Society Library, Portland, OR).

As part of its documentation, the Committee on Memorials secured affidavits from knowledgeable persons. Silas W. Smith gave his statement on June 15, 1900, noting: "My mother frequently told me that the buildings at the old fort were occupied by my grandfather and his family during the hunting season for ten or fifteen years after they had been given to him, and she also told me that in one of the cabins a large stump stood, which the Lewis and Clark men had cut off square at the top and used for a table" (File folder "Fort Clatsop," Oregon Historical Society Library, Portland, OR).

Shane signed his affidavit the same day, and Preston W. Gillette executed his the following day.

By December 1901, the Oregon Historical Society was negotiating for the purchase of three acres. To their dismay, the Society's officers learned that the deed reserved to the Oregon Pottery Company the right of removing clay and thus potentially destroying the historic site. The issue was finally resolved, and in March the next year, the Oregon Historical Society paid $250 for the land. In 1928 it purchased an additional two acres. The Society's goal at the Fort Clatsop site was to erect in 1905 "an imposing and enduring monument to this great achievement in our national history and to the memory of the brave men who accomplished it" (File folder "Fort Clatsop," Oregon Historical Society Library, Portland, OR). While it preserved the site thanks in part to Smith's help in identifying the location and raising public interest, the Society was unable to erect the monument, presumably because of lack of funds.

Smith was also instrumental in locating the site of the "Salt Cairn" or Salt Works at nearby Seaside, which his mother had pointed out to him. During the winter of 1805–1806, Lewis and Clark stationed a patrol at the north end of Tillamook Head to boil sea water in order to produce salt needed to preserve fresh-killed elk meat. Wheeler, photographer Weister, Himes of the historical society, and Smith visited this site on August 28, 1899. Subsequently the Clatsop

Tsin-is-tum (Jennie Michel) at the site of the Lewis and Clark Salt Works
in Seaside, Oregon, ca. 1903. CCHS 11191.005.

woman Tsin-is-tum (Jennie Michel) put her "X" on an affidavit that stated: "A few days ago I went to the place where Lewis and Clark's men made salt with Silas B. Smith, George Noland, L. B. Cox, William Galloway and others. I had often been to this place with my mother when I was a girl and a young woman picking *esulth* (kinnikinnick) and *quin-quin* (salal) berries" (Wheeler 1904, vol. 2, 205–206).

Today Fort Clatsop and the Salt Works are protected as heritage sites. Both are part of the Lewis and Clark National Historic Park administered by the National Park Service.

※ ※ ※

As the first Native American active in the Oregon Historical Society, Silas Smith joined the ranks of distinguished contributors to the early issues of its *Quarterly* magazine. His essay "Primitive Customs and Religious Beliefs of the Indians of the Pacific Northwest Coast" (1901) was published alongside the essays of Dr. Frederick George Young, historian at the University of Oregon;

Frances Fuller Victor, author of several volumes in Hubert Bancroft's *History of the Pacific States;* and poet-essayist Joaquin Miller.

Smith's article challenged several stereotypes about Northwest Coast Indians and about the Chinookans in particular. He explained that the process of head-flattening neither blunted intelligence nor imposed pain on infants. He addressed the proclivity of writers to speak of the tall and noble Indians from east of the Cascade Mountains and the "squat bodies and bowlegs of the coast Indians." Smith wrote, "In reality, the bowlegs, so far as these people are concerned, is a myth." He explored the issue of slavery and noted that "almost every leading family held from one to half a dozen slaves, and some of the chiefs having even many more." Smith also discussed "first fruits" ceremonies, special rites that ensured the return of salmon.

> When the species of wild raspberry, which abounds in the coast region of Oregon and Washington, first ripens in the spring, the salmon, when caught, are laid with their heads pointing up stream, and then a berry of this variety is placed in the mouth of each fish, to remain there, however, for only a limited space of time, and hence the name of the salmon berry, which it now universally bears. From the observance of this ceremony the early traders on the Columbia River, who witnessed the same, gave the berry that name. This rite, however, is only a propitiatory offering to the divine influences which are supposed to control the migration of the salmon (Smith 1901, 259).

Smith concluded his article with the Clatsop tale "The Legend of the Surf." The literary account, set in a transition time of humans, talking animals, and monsters, explained the distant roar of the ocean. Those living on the Clatsop Plains knew the approach of stormy weather when they heard the roar from the south, fair weather when the roar came from the northwest, and a change in the weather when it came directly from the west. These were the voices of Cheatco, a monster doomed to attend to the duties of the Thunder God. "So when storms threaten," recounted Smith, "you will hear his angry tones in the south, and when the clouds begin to roll away you will notice the song of his milder mood in the north" (Smith 1901, 264–265).

Silas Smith's Indian heritage and legal knowledge led to his most notable accomplishment. In 1868 Congress invoked the sovereign immunity of the United States in the matter of Indian lawsuits. This meant that the only way a tribe could sue the federal government—for any errors or breaches of trust responsibility or treaty guarantees—was to secure an act of Congress. Persuading a congressman to introduce a bill that would allow a tribe to sue the government was highly unpopular. At the time, public opinion expressed little sympathy for Indians. Many believed they were a "vanishing race."

In spite of those attitudes, the lack of strong political connections, and distance from Washington, D.C., Silas Smith embarked on a campaign for justice. Aware of the Bowman Act of March 3, 1883, and its broadening of jurisdiction of the Court of Claims (established in 1855), he filed complaints against the United States for the taking of Indian lands at the mouth of the Columbia River without ratified treaties. On June 7, 1897, he persuaded Congress to appropriate $10,500 to pay the Naalem (Nehalem Band) of Tillamooks for their lands. Although years would pass before the payment was made, Smith had successfully secured the first land claims award to any Pacific Northwest tribe (U.S. Congress 1897, vol. 30, 78; U.S. Congress 1907, 1).

On May 1, 1899, thirty-seven members of the Lower Band of Chinooks signed a contract with attorneys in Astoria and Washington, D.C., to file their land claims case. The signatories included Mary (Marie) Rondeau Ducheney Preble Kelly, a granddaughter of Chief Comcomly and contemporary of Chief Coboway. These Chinooks lived along the north bank of the Columbia River from Cathlamet to Pillar Rock, at Chinook and Ilwaco, and most particularly at Bay Center on Willapa Bay. The Lower Band of Chinooks contracted with Silas B. Smith and Harrison Allen in Astoria and Charles C. Lancaster and John T. Dewees in Washington, D.C. Allen was then the Astoria city attorney, later district attorney for Oregon's Fifth District, and ultimately in private practice in Portland. Because the Clatsops and other bands were also co-plaintiffs, it is likely that the other tribes entered into comparable agreements with the same attorneys (U.S.C.C. 1902; Carey 1922, vol. 3, 470).

The Senate, first session, fifty-ninth Congress, authorized the U.S. Court of Claims to hear the cases of the Clatsop, Nehalem Band of Tillamook, Cathlamet, Lower Band of Chinook, Wahkiakum Band of Chinook, Wheelapa (Willapa) Band of Chinook, and the Nuc-quee-clah-we-much—peoples living in the vicinity of the mouth of the Columbia River. The lawsuit claimed that aboriginal lands were taken without ratification of their treaties. Each of these tribes had signed treaties with Anson Dart, Superintendent of Indian Affairs, in 1851 in the Tansy Point Council at the north end of the Clatsop Plains. The treaties reserved the Indians' rights to hunt, fish, graze, and gather on the lands that were formerly theirs. When the treaties were forwarded to Washington, D.C., the Senate ignored them and ordered all printed as "Confidential." This meant that for decades they were invisible. Unratified, their provisions of reserved rights of hunting, fishing, grazing, and gathering were meaningless. The government and settlers appropriated all the Indian lands ceded and reserved in the Dart treaties (U.S. Congress 1912b, 3).

The lawsuit progressed slowly. In January 1902, Benjamin Beekman, a Portland attorney, traveled to Astoria to depose twelve plaintiff witnesses. The purpose was to explore issues related to the claim of the Lower Band of Chinooks. Six witnesses were tribal members; six were pioneer residents of the Lower Columbia River or Clatsop County officials. Beekman questioned each closely about the number of Indian villages, resources of the land, and aboriginal "use and occupancy" of the territory in the Lower Band's claim area: Pacific County, Washington.

Silas Smith, though a Clatsop and an attorney involved in the litigation, was also deposed. He spoke of memories from childhood, when he lived among his mother's people and the Lower Band of Chinooks in the 1840s and the 1850s. Recalling their traditional lodges, he said:

> The houses that the Indians were then occupying were mostly built of
> cedar planks two or three inches thick and from 2 to 3 feet wide, and
> some of them perhaps 20 feet long, all split out from cedar timber,
> and they were built with posts, the roofs being made from planks, and
> the insides were partitioned off into beds and bunks, and oftentimes,
> partitioned off through different fires.

Some houses would have three or four fires, perhaps more, and each fire would be for the accom[m]odation of a family living in the lodge; and maybe two or three or four families—and perhaps more—would live in a single house. These houses were quite large—40 or 50 or 60 feet long, and maybe 25 feet wide and perhaps wider (U.S.C.C. 1902, 226).

Indian claims cases were low priority and often prolonged. Smith did not live to see the outcome of the case he initiated. Following his death in 1902, the litigation continued its sluggish course in the U.S. Claims Court. When it became apparent that the tribes had a clear claim to the land, the Justice Department negotiated a settlement. In anticipation of this event, Dr. Charles McChesney, of the Bureau of Indian Affairs, visited tribal members in 1906, gathered information on family histories, executed affidavits, and produced rolls of the plaintiff tribes. McChesney interviewed Smith's son, Goldwin T. Smith, and Smith's sister, Charlotte (Smith) Effler, both of whom provided family histories (McChesney 1906, 37–38).

The tribal claims and family histories were published in the *Congressional Serial Set*. McChesney never met Silas Smith, but he noted the assistance of the surviving attorney: "I am indebted to Mr. Harrison Allen, of Astoria, Oreg., attorney for the Lower Chinook and Clatsop Indians, for much valuable assistance and courtesy shown me. Mr. Allen has done much work for these Indians before the Court of Claims and elsewhere, for which he has yet received no compensation" (McChesney 1906, 3).

In 1907 Congress made an initial appropriation to settle the litigation. Finally, in 1913, fourteen years after the case was authorized, the Secretary of the Treasury released $66,000 for per capita payments to the plaintiffs: $10,500 to the Nehalem Tillamook Tribe; $15,000 to the Clatsops; $1,500 to the Nuc-quee-clah-we-much; $7,000 to the Cathlamet Band of Chinooks; $7,000 to the Wahkiakum Band of Chinooks; $5,000 to the Wheelapa Band of Chinooks; and $20,000 to the Lower Band of Chinooks of Pacific County, Washington. The sum of $66,000 included money reserved for attorney fees to be determined by the Commissioner of Indian Affairs (U.S. Congress 1912a, 535).

Silas Smith did not live to see this token settlement for the taking of his mother's ancestral lands. He succumbed to the ravages of tuberculosis on

August 23, 1902, in Astoria. The *Oregonian* of August 28, 1902, ran a notice of his passing with a portrait and the headline: "One of the Most Prominent Men in Clatsop County." The obituary noted: "Mr. Smith was a man of strict adherence to the cause of temperance. He was everywhere recognized as a learned lawyer and able speaker, and he was closely identified with several of the pioneer societies of the state" (Anonymous 1902a). The *Morning Astorian* of August 24, 1902, referred to Smith as "a learned lawyer and a successful orator," "a man of rare moral fibre . . . and a hater of sham and deceit" (Anonymous 1902b). The Oregon Pioneer and Historical Society conducted his funeral services, paying tribute to the man believed to be Clatsop County's oldest resident at the time of his death (Anonymous 1902c).

A man of Smith's many accomplishments could have settled anywhere in the country. Yet Silas B. Smith chose to stay in his Clatsop homeland. For most of his adult life, he lived a few miles from the villages where his people had traded with the American Corps of Discovery a hundred years earlier.

Sources

Anonymous. 1902a. "One of the Most Prominent Men in Clatsop County," *Oregonian* (Portland, OR), August 28.

_____. 1902b. [Obituary of Silas B. Smith], *Morning Astorian* (Astoria, OR), August 24.

_____. 1902c. [Obituary of Silas B. Smith], *Astoria Daily Budget* (Astoria, OR), August 23.

Bureau of the Census. 1850. Sixth Census of the United States, Clatsop County, Oregon Territory. Microcopy 437, Roll 742, RG 29: Records of the Bureau of the Census, National Archives, Washington, DC.

_____. 1860. Seventh Census of the United States, Clatsop County, Oregon. Microcopy 6753, Roll 1055, RG 29: Records of the Bureau of the Census, National Archives, Washington, DC.

_____. 1870. Eighth Census of the United States, Gilford, Belknap County, NH. Microcopy 593, Roll 836, RG 29: Records of the Bureau of the Census, National Archives, Washington, DC.

_____. 1880. Ninth Census of the United States, Clatsop County, OR. T-9, Roll 1080, RG

29: Records of the Bureau of the Census, National Archives, Washington, DC.

____. 1900. Twelfth Census of the United States, Clatsop County, OR. T-623, Roll 1346, RG 29: Records of the Bureau of the Census, National Archives, Washington, DC.

____. 1910 Thirteenth Census of the United States, Clatsop County, OR. T-624, Roll 1278, RG 29: Records of the Bureau of the Census, National Archives, Washington, DC.

Carey, Charles. 1923. *History of Oregon,* vol. 3. Chicago and Portland: The Pioneer Historical Publishing Company.

Engeman , Richard. 2006. Interview with Stephen Dow Beckham, June 13. MS notes in possession of Stephen Dow Beckham, Lake Oswego, OR.

Evans, Elwood. 1889. *History of the Pacific Northwest: Oregon and Washington,* 2 vols. Portland, OR: North Pacific History Company.

Genealogical Forum of Portland, Oregon. 1959. *Genealogical Material in Oregon Donation Land Claims,* vol. 2. Portland, OR: Genealogical Forum of Portland, Oregon.

Holmes, Kenneth L. 1967. *Ewing Young: Master Trapper.* Portland, OR: Binford & Mort, Publishers.

Lee, Daniel, and Joseph Frost. 1844. *Ten Years in Oregon.* New York City: J. Collord.

McChesney, Charles E. 1906. *Rolls of Certain Indian Tribes in Oregon and Washington. House Document No. 133,* 59 Congress, 2 Session. Washington, DC: Government Printing Office.

Minto, John. 1903. The Educational History of Astoria, Oregon. Portland, OR: *Oregon Historical Quarterly.*

Munnick, Harriet Duncan. 1968. Solomon Smith, *The Mountain Men and the Fur Trade of the Far West.* LeRoy R. Hafen, ed. Glendale, CA: Arthur H. Clark Company.

Munnick, Harriet Duncan, and Mikell DeLore Wormell Warner. 1972. *Catholic Church Records of the Pacific Northwest: Vancouver Volumes I and II and Stellamaris Mission.* St. Paul, OR: French Prairie Press.

Peterson-del Mar, David. 1995. Intermarriage and Agency: A Chinookan Case Study. *Ethnohistory*, vol. 42, no. 3, 130.

Shane, Carlos W. 1852a. Letter of May 18 to John Preston. Miscellaneous Letters Received, 185153, Box 49, 1: Item 192. RG 49: Records of the Bureau of Land

Management, National Archives, Seattle, WA.

_____. 1852b. Letter of May 24 to Jno. P. Gaines. Miscellaneous Letters Received, 185153, Box 49, 1: Item 195. RG 49: Records of the Bureau of Land Management, National Archives, Seattle, WA.

Smith, Silas B. 1882. On the Chinook Names of the Salmon in the Columbia River. *Proceedings of the National Museum, 1881. Smithsonian Miscellaneous Collections*, vol. 4, 391–392.

_____. 1899a. Tales of Early Wrecks on the Oregon Coast, and How the Bees-wax Got There. *Oregon Native Son*, vol. 1, 433–446.

_____. 1899b. History of Chief Comcomley. *Oregonian* (Portland, OR), December 18.

_____. 1899c. Tales of Early Times in Oregon. *Oregonian* (Portland, OR), December 18.

_____. 1901. Primitive Customs and Religious Beliefs of the Indians of the Pacific Northwest Coast. Portland, OR: *Oregon Historical Quarterly,* vol. 2, 255–265.

U.S. Congress. 1897. *Statutes-at-Large.* Vol. 30, 78. Washington, DC: Government Printing Office.

_____. 1907. *Lower Band of Chinook Indians of the State of Washington. Senate Document No. 188,* 59 Congress, 1 Session. Washington, DC: Government Printing Office.

_____. 1912a. *Statutes-at-Large.* Vol. 37, 535. Washington, DC: Government Printing Office.

_____. 1912b. *Final Settlement with Tillamook Indians for Certain Oregon Lands. Senate Report No. 503,* 63 Congress, 2 Session. Washington, DC: Government Printing Office.

U.S. Court of Claims (U.S.C.C). 1902. Testimony taken in No. 10,441, *Lower Band of Chinook Indians of the State of Washington v. United States.* MS typescript, Oregon Historical Society, Portland, OR.

Wheeler, Olin D. 1904. *The Trail of Lewis and Clark, 1804–1904: A Story of the Great Exploration Across the Continent in 1804–06; with a Description of the Old Trail, Based Upon Actual Travel Over It, and of the Changes Found a Century Later.* 2 vols. New York and London: G. P. Putnam's Sons, The Knickerbocker Press.

Molding Astoria—
The Role of Two Editors

By Sandra Haarsager

*It is rightly named, for the paper is devoted
almost exclusively to the material,
intellectual, and moral interests of Astoria.*
—Rev. Isaac Dillon on the new
Tri-Weekly Astorian, 21 October 1873

How a community unfolds in time, how it views its horizons, depends in part on its press coverage and what is reflected back to residents. As editors and publishers, two men in Astoria, Oregon, helped to shape the city and its image. Products of different times and standards, they chronicled events for what became the *Daily Astorian* while also engaging in political crusades for causes they championed.

DeWitt Clinton Ireland established an enduring newspaper when Astoria was a frontier outpost. Merle R. Chessman, caught up in the Depression and World War II, steered the community through tumultuous times. Both men were experienced in print journalism before they took on responsibilities in the city where the Columbia River and Pacific Ocean meet. Both were tried, literally, by fire—conflagrations that destroyed much of Astoria's business community. They were expert communicators, provocative and independent, and not above being outrageous in order to garner attention. They were also complex individuals. One vilified Chinese residents and was accused of beating his wife and drinking too much; the other stood up to threats and demands of a resurgent Ku Klux Klan in Oregon. "Somehow they gave their newspapers the rocket fuel to get off the ground," *Daily Astorian* editor and publisher Steve Forrester said in a

2006 interview. One did it by creating something from nothing at the edge of a continent, while the other did it with an outpouring of intellectual energy and leadership in support of the newspaper and the community.

DeWitt Clinton Ireland, born in Vermont in 1836, came to Oregon in 1862 at age twenty-six. His father was born in England and his mother in Connecticut. Ireland, red-headed and restless, worked in Portland as a reporter

DeWitt Clinton Ireland, editor of the *Tri-Weekly,* then the *Morning Astorian,* the *Weekly Astorian,* and the *Daily Astorian* newspapers, ca. 1874.

for the *Oregonian* before starting his first newspaper in Oregon, the *Enterprise*. The *Oregonian* noted the development: "We have before us the prospectus of a new paper to be issued at Oregon City on the 27th of next month. . . . This new journal will be conducted by Mr. D. C. Ireland, for the past three years the local reporter of the *Oregonian*. It will be issued weekly and will contain twenty-eight columns" (*Daily Oregonian,* September 24, 1866).

Ireland bought the press and type of the defunct *Marine Gazette* (1864–1866), founded in Astoria by W. W. Parker, to use in Oregon City. The subscription rate was $3 a year. The *Oregonian* of October 29, 1866, deemed the new paper "first-rate" and a "candidate for popular favor." Because of its smaller type, it conveyed more news than the similarly sized Corvallis *Gazette*.

Ireland's rarely neutral political preferences often got him into trouble. In Oregon City, his editorial policies and politics eventually created enemies, and his financial backers sold the paper out from under him after he lost support of the town's merchants.

Ireland returned to Portland with his wife, Olive (Livy), and three children, Alba James, Sarah Lillie, and Henry, and became editor of the new Portland *Bulletin*. In a few years, that paper, too, was sold. In conflict with the new owners, Ireland left their employ in 1873.

Community leader Adam Van Dusen invited him to Astoria, which had no newspaper at the time, and Ireland accepted the offer. The community he found in 1873 was a village of fewer than a thousand inhabitants, built largely on wooden pilings, with docks and businesses jutting out over the water where the hillside met the river's edge. A new era in his life began with the creation of the *Tri-Weekly Astorian,* which became the *Morning Astorian* three years later, the town's first daily newspaper. Revenues failed to meet expectations, and a month later the four-page daily became a weekly. Commercial printing income, in the form of labels for canned salmon, brought enough prosperity to support daily publishing about the time Ireland added politics to his portfolio. Ever restless, he sold the paper in 1881, but he had made his mark on Astoria.

Merle A. Chessman, by contrast, had deep roots in the community. He was editor and publisher of the *Astorian* for nearly three decades, having spent his entire professional life at the Pendleton *East Oregonian* or the *Astorian*. In 1930 the *Astorian* was sold to the owners of the competing *Astoria Evening Budget,* which included Merle Chessman and publishers of the Pendleton paper. The merged paper became the *Astorian-Budget*, its name until 1960, when it became the *Daily Astorian*.

What made a frontier newspaper successful?

Journalism historian Barbara Cloud (1992) cited several factors in her study of frontier newspapers between 1846 and 1890: a market of literate readers with a minimum county population of 2,500, availability of credit, railroad connections, presence of a stabilizing female population, and solid advertising receipts, all while keeping costs low. Most newspapers started with fanfare but failed after a year or two. The newspapers that were moderate politically and most strongly connected to their communities had the most staying power. Support from commercial printing was another important factor.

The tone of frontier publishing, especially in the West, often meant the publisher's tongue was solidly planted against his cheek. "If anybody has lost a cold, they can find one at this office. We won't require payment for this notice if they will take it away" (*Astorian*, December 27, 1873). Humor, sarcasm, outright advocacy, and sometimes personal invective shared space in the news columns. Editors favored elaborate practical jokes, and Ireland was no exception. The *Weekly Astorian* of June 18, 1874, ran this story involving a prominent citizen.

A few days ago some bright but naughty boys borrowed two eggs from the hennery of Capt. H. A. Snow, and after boiling them in a calico bag, returned them to the nest. The boiling process left the eggs covered with the pretty figures of the calico, and the excited owner exhibited these curiosities far and near, and sought in vain for an explanation for this "curious freak of nature." Whether an ineffectual attempt to hatch a calico chicken revealed to the Captain the stupendous joke or not cannot be told, but the hen fancier's enthusiasm has subsided. When anybody says "calico chickens" to Capt. Snow he immediately remembers he has an appointment to keep. Capt. Irv. Stevens is accused of putting up this job on Snow.

Newspapers of this era fostered community relationships as they reported on the events of the day. Where connectedness in the twenty-first century is found on computer screens and through cell phones, connectedness in the late nineteenth and early twentieth centuries depended on published accounts of comings and goings in hospital and hotel registries, accounts of who entertained whom each week, and reports on club and lodge activities. The introduction to a typical article, "Died Alone" (*Astorian,* December 10, 1873), read as follows:

> It is very seldom that a public journalist is called upon to detail a
> more sorrowful circumstance than the following which occurred in
> Pacific county last week. The death of an aged and esteemed citizen,
> in a manner unaccountable, alone by the roadside, exposed to the
> elements of chill Winter, with no kind hand to minister to his dying
> wants.

The direct and personable, sometimes smiling style of address included the ads, which were often tucked into the news text. A news item near the masthead in the same 1873 issue read: "Gray and Donaldson are fattening a lot of splendid geese, chickens and turkeys for a week from next Thursday. Call and take your pick now." A display ad read: "Bramel's Coffee Stand, Now Open. The Public now supplied with a superior quality of hot coffee, cakes, oysters, pig's-feet, confectionery, cigars, tobacco, pipes, Notions, etc."

Ireland's Astoria was new and raw. Docks over water had become streets, later connected by wooden bridges. Initially privately owned, they had been taken over by the city. Street names were complex Anglicizations of the names of regional Indian leaders. The newspaper offices were established in the Monitor Building, a rickety two-story wooden structure built on pilings, with a Chinese wash house in the rear. A chair without a seat over a hole in the dock furnished a crude toilet. At least it was centrally located, as Roger Tetlow noted in his well-researched, fictionalized biography of Ireland (1975). At the time, Astorians read the *Oregonian,* the Oregon City *Enterprise,* or other nearby papers for news, but these papers didn't have much to say about Astoria.

Ireland recognized the commercial opportunities in the city and persuaded a couple of Astoria's business leaders, who wanted the paper established, to put up the necessary $500 surety bond for registration with the Secretary of State. City leaders graciously made him secretary of the equivalent of the Chamber of Commerce, with an advance to cover his initial expenses (*Astorian,* September 4, 1873). He was involved in the community from the start.

Using a San Francisco firm and a line of credit, he ordered a press and type for the paper's debut. He hired Fidella (Del) Ferguson, an experienced printer with whom he had earlier worked in Portland. Later they added an apprentice, Frank Baltes, who went on to establish a printing firm in Portland with Ireland. Newsprint, always a concern to a publisher, was produced in Oregon mills and readily available. In what was known as "trade-outs," Ireland began exchanging future advertising for needed services, such as rides to Portland on the Oregon Steamship Navigation Company line. He made a number of paid-in-advance advertising sales.

His family had not yet joined him, and he stayed in the popular Occident Hotel. He and Ferguson managed to turn the old Monitor Building into a workable office for what became the *Tri-Weekly Astorian,* although the structure fell into the river in 1876, shortly after they abandoned it for better quarters (Tetlow 1975, 36). Ireland faced a facilities hazard few early publishers faced—loose logs and debris in the bay in bad weather or the floodtides of spring crashing against the pilings that held up the building, threatening to throw the plant and its small staff into the murk.

When they installed glass in the office door, with the newspaper masthead painted on it, Ireland had an 1873 dime embedded in the "O" of "Office." He said a dime was all he had when he came to start the paper, and he had sunk his entire fortune into the enterprise. The door with its unusual marker was installed in new *Astorian* offices a few years later.

After their first advertising sales, Ireland and company produced a marketing prospectus for the paper. A manifesto defining the purpose of the community newspaper, it was reprinted in the *Astorian* on July 3, 1873: "The paper will be independent of politics in all its views, expressed or implied, and will be conducted with the aim in view to make it wholly and solely devoted to the best interests of this state." He concluded with this description of his personal commitment:

With the view of supplying this want, the undersigned has concluded to enter the newspaper work at this venerable old city, on the banks of one of the loveliest rivers entering any ocean, and relying for my support upon an appreciative people among whom I am not as a stranger, having been connected with the press of the state for ten years, it is with the utmost confidence of success that I issue this brief outline of the purposes actuating me, and solicit your patronage.

The prospectus ended with subscription and advertising rates and Ireland's name.

His business off to a propitious start, Ireland sought a house to accommodate his family, finding one initially at Cass and Court Streets (today Tenth and Franklin Streets) on a hill above the docks (Tetlow 1975, 40). His house at 989 Franklin Street, a simple, one-story wood frame building, still stands. At that point his family consisted of wife Livy, said to be frail and beset with unnamed illnesses, and children DeWitt, Lillie, Harry, and a baby, Gustav Rosenk, who may have been the namesake of another woman's family. (Historian Liisa Penner identified a woman in Astoria with the maiden name Rosenk, arriving in 1875,

DeWitt Clinton Ireland's home in Astoria, which still stands on the southwest corner of Tenth and Franklin. CCHS 31036.960.

who had been born in Minnesota, where the Irelands lived.) Ireland's eldest son, Alba James, was not with the family at this point. His mother, Ireland's first wife, died of tuberculosis at age twenty-six in New York in 1861; Ireland married Olive six months later in St. Paul. James Alba, who may not have been welcome in Ireland's second family, chose to live mostly in Minnesota, then in Michigan with Ireland's parents.

The night five hundred issues of the paper's first edition sat awaiting distribution the next day, Ireland and two of his backers—Adam Van Dusen and Capt. J. G. Hustler—brought out bottles of sparkling champagne in celebration. Although his wife was reportedly a teetotaler, he gained a reputation as a drinker, not an uncommon pastime in a town that soon developed dozens of saloons catering to the seaport trade.

On the morning of July 1, 1873, Ireland opened his office doors and began selling newspapers, the city's first since 1866. They sold out by noon.

TRI-WEEKLY ASTORIAN.

| Vol. 1. | ASTORIA, OREGON, JULY 1, 1873. | No. 1. |

Masthead for D. C. Ireland's *Tri-Weekly Astorian,*
first published on July 1, 1873. CCHS COLLECTION.

The first edition of the *Tri-Weekly Astorian* comprised four pages and five columns. Vol. 1, No. 1, was roughly ten by thirteen inches, typical for the times and technology, and sold for 10 cents a copy or $5 a year. Ten lines of advertising cost $2.50. "Any friend who feels an interest in the prosperity of this region, is authorized to act as Agent for this paper, in procuring subscribers," Ireland wrote.

News items were headed "City Intelligence," "Common Council," "Street Work," "High Tariffs," "Chowder Club," and "Fireman's Ball." A report on ship traffic said, "The Puritan of Boston came through, carrying flour and lumber for Hong Kong." The paper noted that locks at the falls of the Willamette had been completed, and farmers were pleading for a large wharf and warehouse at Astoria instead of the current small warehouses. Boosting Astoria over Portland as the best place to load ocean-going ships became a theme that ran for decades.

The paper included church notices, bits on current topics, club and lodge news. The fifth and last column carried news of the weird and interesting— "Wild Plants Domesticated," about cabbages, and "Water in the Atmosphere," about the tons of vapor above the earth—along with puzzles, doggerel verse, and jokes. "Scandalous! The friendship of two ladies is always a plot against a third one," read one. "Three years is the average life of feminine school-teachers. After that they get married," read another. Although Ireland came to support women's voting rights, he included sexist bits of humor for his readers' entertainment.

The first issue also contained dozens of ads Ireland had sold. His $5 subscriptions were selling as well, and the *Astorian*'s claim to the lucrative legal and judicial advertising for Clatsop County came through by August, further solidifying the newspaper's success as a business.

Ireland's maiden efforts gained the notice of regional papers, including Portland's *Oregonian* and *Bulletin*. On July 9, 1873, the *Morning Oregonian* praised the upstart in a way that presaged coming battles:

> The first number of the *Tri-Weekly Astorian* made its appearance yesterday. Its name indicates its character, as it is to be issued each Tuesday, Thursday, and Saturday, and, judging by the number before us, is very *Astorian* in its tone, strongly advocating the superior advantages of Astoria over all other points on the Northwest Coast as the site of the great commercial entrepot and center of the future. Mr. Ireland, editor and publisher of the *Astorian* is too well known to the people of Oregon as a newspaper man to need an introduction at our hands, and we doubt not he will make his paper a success. His first number was racy, newsy, and neat. We like its appearance and wish it prosperity. *Oregonian*.

From the beginning, Ireland directed practical city planning. Early in his tenure as publisher, he visited what was known as Upper Town, cut off from Lower Astoria by an unusable trail along Scow Bay. At a time when a town's permanence depended on the locus of state and federal buildings, Upper Town had lost out on the location of a customs house and courthouse, leaving lingering resentments. Yet there was a thriving settlement in Upper Town, with a large leather factory, many Scandinavians, and opportunity for more commerce for the *Astorian*. Ireland successfully pushed for the construction of a bridge to connect the two settlements.

The first winter was difficult for the fledgling paper. The national financial collapse of 1873–1874 cut into advertising sales, and Astoria's huge bay froze over, making it impossible for the *Astorian* to get newsprint and other necessary supplies. Ireland put out a small "Ice-O-Lated" edition lamenting that a prosperous burg such as Astoria could be so cut off from Portland and the sea, when that could be remedied by forty miles of telegraph lines and sixty miles of railroad. He pushed hard for both developments.

In a progress report to readers (August 13, 1874), Ireland drew a figurative line in the sand around the *Astorian*'s fortunes and Astoria's future:

> We are working out our salvation no longer with fear and trembling
> of Portland, or any man in that town. The institution is free from debt,
> has a paying patronage, and is receiving from 10 to 16 subscribers
> weekly. We need all the patronage we can get, to enable us to advance.
> We now employ two presses, and have a third one in the office, but
> must have a machine press for the newspaper this fall.

Ireland was creative in raising operating capital. He vigorously pursued job printing, the salvation of many an early publisher, ordering small presses and type from San Francisco in the hope of stealing business that routinely went to Portland. He lowered his advertising rates for the city and county if they placed all their advertising with him. He even opened a real-estate office in his building, though he found this sideline unprofitable and soon gave it up. Despite his efforts, market conditions declined and expenses rose. The *Tri-Weekly Astorian* was reduced to a weekly early in 1874.

Tragedy struck the Ireland family in 1874. Baby Gustav Rosenk died in May. Six months later, Olive filed a petition for divorce. The dark side of the publisher emerges in this roughly transcribed text of the complaint filed in circuit court at Astoria:

During the last year the Deft. [D. C. Ireland] has been guilty
of intolerable cruelty and inhuman treatment and her son
[indecipherable] of indignities towards this plaintiff, rendering her
life burdensome, committed on or about the 31st day of Oct. 1874 in
Astoria, the said deft. assaulted and beat the plaintiff in the presence
of other persons, bruise and [indecipherable] plaintiff so that she
has been sick, sore and lame. The 26th of Oct. 1874 he assaulted her
throwing blocks of wood at her in a most violent and inhumane
manner and threatened to murder her and called her a god-damned
bitch. They have three children living with them, Lillie 10 years, Harry
7, DeWitt 4. The defendant has deserted her and the children and
refuses to provide her with food or clothing. Complaint date Nov. 14,
1874. Transcription of Judgement Roll #1957 at the Clatsop County
Courthouse in Astoria, D. C. Ireland file, Clatsop County Historical
Society.

A drunken rage? A regular occurrence? The exaggerations of an irate spouse?
The circumstances are not clear from this distant perspective. Nevertheless,
Ireland gained a reputation as a wife-beater. The divorce never took place, and
roughly one year later, son Clinton Leonard was born. Another son, Francis
Connor, followed.

In 1877, Ireland began a campaign for a community hospital in Astoria.
"Almost every day the private purses of our liberal citizens are appealed to for
aid to some worthy distressed individual," he wrote. "Sailors find no home here,
citizens no place of refuge" (*Astorian*, July 11, 1877).

Ireland continued to hammer at the need for a facility. Finally, in 1880 a
group of Catholic nuns came to investigate a site for a hospital. Ireland backed
a subscription drive that netted $1,700 to help the sisters found St. Mary's
Hospital. In his newspaper, he predicted that the hospital, offering the best of
medical care as well as the "bracing effect of sea breezes," would attract many
patients from the interior and soon rival St. Vincent's of Portland.

Ireland used his paper to push for still another symbol of community prosperity and sophistication—the opera house. He understood the role of culture
and ritual participation in creating a sense of community. He also plugged the

development of an Astoria brass band and the opening of a vocal studio and dance academy.

By 1875, the *Astorian*'s fortunes had improved, but the paper remained a weekly. For timely news and information, a telegraph line was essential in remote western towns. A line from Portland to Astoria was finally completed in 1876, and on May 1 of that year, Ireland realized his ambition and printed the first *Daily Astorian*. Again, sister papers lauded the publication. Financial support remained insufficient, however; by mid-June, the paper was again a weekly.

Economic salvation came to the *Astorian* in the form of job printing. From Chicago, Ireland acquired equipment capable of printing the thousands of multi-colored labels attached to cans of salmon processed at Astoria. By then the city produced over 400,000 cases of salmon a year, requiring some 19 million labels.

A Bumble Bee brand label for the Columbia River Packers Association, ca. 1920. CCHS 04.049.008.

✲ ✲ ✲

In 1876, Ireland declined a proposed nomination as an Independent candidate for the Oregon Legislature to represent Clatsop and Tillamook Counties. Three months later, he was approached to run for mayor of what had become a larger town with the ills typical of a growing seaport, and he became the town's fourth mayor in August of 1876. Itinerant labor in the burgeoning canneries, immigrants who did not readily assimilate, and sailors looking for recreation had led to the growth of businesses the community professed to condemn, even as some members greatly profited from them. In editorials Ireland attacked the city's deterioration:

> Gentlemen, do for heaven's sake build us something in Astoria besides
> brothels and their attendant iniquities. We have had quite enough of

them. Put your money into dwelling houses for respectable people who would come here for their permanent homes were it not for the growing and paralyzing influences of this immoral element (quoted in Tetlow 1975, 121–122).

Astoria lacked effective fire protection and suffered from inadequate sewage and garbage disposal. Abigail Scott Duniway, publisher of the weekly human-rights newspaper *New Northwest,* minced no words after a visit to the city:

Astoria is very little for its age, and certainly the dirtiest town of its size we ever saw anywhere. There are evidences, however, that its second growth has commenced. The streets, hotels, and private houses are alike full of strangers, and were real estate held at its legitimate worth, many valuable buildings would soon take the place of the decaying vegetable matter and decomposing sturgeons upon the river banks. . . . As it is, you strain your breath through your handkerchief and fasten your thoughts as best you can upon the blue headlands in the distance (*Weekly Astorian,* August 28, 1875).

Ireland quickly responded that the problem was temporary and due to a decomposing whale that had washed upon the beach below Duniway's room. The nuisance had been removed.

Shortly after Ireland became Astoria's mayor in 1876, he again tried to establish a daily morning paper; but his new duties, including serving as secretary to the Board of Pilot Commissioners meeting in Salem, delayed that step. Later he became absorbed in the construction of new quarters for the newspaper. Ireland signed a five-year lease with entrepreneur George Flavel for property at Cass and Squemocqha Streets (today Tenth and Commercial), leasing out part of the building to recover some of the costs. He also ordered a steam-powered press.

On April 7, 1877, Ireland addressed his readers directly. "Well, here we are at last, and the *Astorian* greets its readers today for the first time from under its own roof. This week we have barely time to make the announcement, and if the present edition does not meet your expectations, attribute the deficiencies to business of other nature. But we are at home and that is our compensation."

The *Astorian* newspaper office located at Tenth and
Commercial Streets, 1879. CCHS 15141.900.

The *Astorian* office, ca. 1879. CCHS 5684.400A.

A milestone for the city, heralded by the paper, came in 1877—the first telephone line: "Astoria has got it at last. It broke out between Probb and Fulton's office and the Astorian office one day last week." By then the small city also had forty saloons (Van Dusen Scrapbooks, 104, 113).

Also in 1877, a fire that began in one of the saloons swept through several blocks of the city. At 2:30 p.m. on June 2, Ireland sent a telegram announcing, "Astoria is in flames. Four blocks are in flames, and the whole city is bound to go south of the Parker House. A hard wind has been blowing and is still prevailing." As mayor, he sent another telegram to Portland's Mayor Chapman asking him to "dispatch with all speed two steam fire engines on the fastest boat to [Astoria's] assistance" (*Morning Oregonian*, June 4, 1877). The Kinney Bros. Cannery was saved, but every building on the north side of Concomley Street was consumed. A shift of wind kept the damage from being worse, sparing the Parker House and the Occident Hotel. This fire was a harbinger of flames to come. In 1879 a smaller fire destroyed a store, then in 1883 a larger fire left dozens in Astoria homeless. Ireland kept up a crusade for improved fire-protection equipment and staffing.

Ireland and his wife Livy suffered a life-changing blow in September of 1878. Eleven-year-old Harry, on an excursion with friends at a ranch three miles away on Youngs Bay, was kicked in the head by a horse he had gone to retrieve. His friends found him dead in the grass. For more than two years after Harry's death, Livy seldom left their house.

One of the many roles publishers assume is to protect the town against outsiders. Ireland saw the Chinese as a threat to Astoria's future and attacked them in print.

The Chinese arrived in Astoria in 1876 when cannery owner Ed Hume began importing them to work in his business. At the peak of the salmon industry, more than two thousand Chinese did the hardest labor in the canneries, cutting, gutting, sorting, and canning. The federal Exclusion Act of 1882 slowed the immigration. But a significant population remained until after the 1890s, sometimes smuggled in through Canada to work in the canneries.

Chinese cannery workers in Astoria, ca. 1915. CCHS 30173.330.

A Chinese dragon was the highlight of the 1900 Regatta parade in Astoria. CCHS 1520.100.

The Chinese population, always predominantly male, shrank rapidly after the turn of the century due to declining salmon runs, especially after the 1922 fire destroyed their meager homes and several canneries. Technology also reduced the need for their labor. New cannery equipment was called the "iron chink" in back-handed recognition of the role the Chinese had played in salmon processing to that point.

Ireland came to resent the unfamiliar language and ways of the Chinese (dubbed "Celestials" in editorials), deplored their frugality in sending their meager wages to China, and feared their presence in the city would grow. He wrote these caustic words about the wash-house business in the back of the newspaper's first home:

> To "smell hell," rent the front room of a building occupied by Celestials, and stay there during the celebration of the Heathen New Year. If you don't conclude that the reeking fumes of the damned are around, with the stifling and sulfurous air permeating every crack of the partitions, and imagine yourself in hell, we give up (quoted in Tetlow 1975, 89).

Many residents of Astoria became deeply prejudiced against the Chinese. Local unions, knowing the Chinese would work for less pay and were unlikely to strike, tried to limit how many Chinese could work in a cannery. The Chinese were denied police protection. Ireland didn't create the unease, but he amplified the perceived Chinese threat and thus discouraged further immigration. As Liisa Penner wrote in the introduction to the 1990 *Chinese in Astoria, Oregon, 1870–1880,* "Ireland hammered into the consciousness of the Astorians that Chinese were dangerous; they were less than human; they could never be assimilated into the rest of the population, they would subvert the youth; they would spread disease and pestilence." Prejudice, social segregation, and declining economic opportunity led to their gradual disappearance as a community.

❧ ❧ ❧

Ireland promoted the virtues of Astoria and Clatsop County in newspapers outside the region and in circulars heralding the seaport and industries. He defended local control of pilotage and towage through the Columbia's mouth and minimized the dangers of the Columbia River bar, for which he was bitterly criticized in Portland. The series of causes he exhorted the community to support included the construction of schools. "Give us good schools, gentlemen," he wrote, "and you can build up a desirable city from the start, upon a foundation as enduring as time itself" (*Astorian*, June 8, 1878). The public school buildings he advocated did not come in his time, but were built from plans developed while he was publisher.

He did much to shape Astoria physically. Ireland was principally responsible for the roads to Upper Astoria, to Nehalem and Forest Grove, and to what is now Warrenton and Seaside. He led efforts to bring the telegraph and railroad to town, to dike the lowlands and enhance agricultural production, and to keep the Customs Office in Astoria. His civic leadership knew few limitations. He helped secure government appropriations to improve navigational aids and lighthouses, to modernize the fire department and reduce city fire hazards, to upgrade and light streets, and to raise walkways above muddy streets. He campaigned for improved water and sewage systems, new city facilities, and penalties for those who supplied alcohol to minors. He also printed reminiscences of early settlers that contributed significantly to Oregon's historical record.

In 1879, Ireland declined to run for a second successive term as mayor. But he was again approached by city standard-bearers. He entered the race reluctantly and was swept into office, where he remained until he sold the *Astorian* in 1881.

Somewhere along the line, Ireland began to enjoy politics and the power inherent in the role he could play. In 1880, he hosted a visit by President Rutherford B. Hayes. He used the occasion, as Chessman would do decades later with Franklin D. Roosevelt, to lobby for federal attention to Astoria's problems, such as the difficulty of getting in and out of the city across the bar where the Columbia River flowed into the sea. After an extended visit to the East Coast, he was chosen as an Oregon committeeman and helped to nominate Chester Garfield for president at the 1880 Republican National Convention in Chicago.

By then Astoria was prospering. The city had some forty canneries annually producing 500,000 cases of canned salmon, each containing forty-eight, one-pound tins. The canneries employed two thousand workers at the height of the

View of Astoria to the northwest, ca. 1890s. CCHS 114.900.

Upper Astoria looking west, showing canneries along the riverfront, ca. 1908.

PHOTO BY E. A. COE. CCHS 7578.900A.

season. The town's waterfront consisted of wood wharfs and canneries perched on pilings, sometimes connected by wooden walkways. An obliging eight- to ten-foot tide usually took away sewage and offal. The wharves backed onto steep hillsides dotted with a growing number of Victorian-era houses in period styles such as Gothic revival, Italianate, and Queen Anne. Scandinavians and Greeks had their own communities, as did the Chinese, who continued to do the hardest work in the canneries.

Problems in the Ireland household worsened. Livy, who had lost two children as well as the companionship of her husband, became a kleptomaniac, embarrassing Ireland by taking small things from stores around Astoria (Tetlow 1975, 160–161). The situation was burdensome not only for Ireland, but also for their daughter Lillie, then sixteen, who had to assume many household duties and care for her ailing mother. Ireland often went around town paying merchants for what Livy had stolen. His deteriorating family life was a major factor in his decision to sell the newspaper.

@ Halloran wrote in his diary that Ireland "was a gross-minded common-place creature who 'got drunk,' beat his wife, was 'bad.'" @

Among the powerful enemies Ireland had collected over the years was the family of H. B. Parker, a police judge and owner of commercial stables who ran a cigar and liquor store in town, one of the businesses affected by reform ordinances Ireland helped to push through. Parker, with others, recruited former teacher Joseph F. Halloran in a scheme to force Ireland aside and acquire the paper. In 1881, J. F. Halloran and a partner bought the *Astorian* for $8,000 in gold coin.

Halloran's view of Ireland varied sharply from that of the many Astorians who held him in high esteem. Halloran wrote in his diary that Ireland "was a gross-minded common-place creature who 'got drunk,' beat his wife, was 'bad,' generally was tolerated by the tough element and was despised by the decent people; he was 'for sale' all the time to all men and essayed to be a political boss on a small scale: he had no business ability and was always in debt" (Halloran diary). In his diary, Ireland's successor, who had negative views aplenty, referred to Astoria as "an isolated community, amphibious, uncouth and unattractive."

DeWitt Clinton Ireland, Astoria newspaper editor and publisher, ca. 1886.

❧ ❧ ❧

In his farewell address to the community he had helped to build, D. C. Ireland wrote:

> My connection with the *Astorian* ceases with this edition: I cannot say
> without regret. Future editions of the paper, and all future business
> in connection therewith, will be entrusted to other hands; not new
> hands, because my successors are men of experience, whom it will be
> found do not lack the ability to carry this establishment on in the tide
> of success which attends it (*Astorian,* September 30, 1881).

Not everyone welcomed the change in the paper's leadership. Halloran noted the "manifest hostility displayed by Ireland's followers" (Halloran diary).

The *Astorian* of that time was the only paper on the Lower Columbia, covering the counties of Clatsop and Tillamook in Oregon and Wahkiakum and Pacific in Washington State. Ireland left the new owners with a paid daily circulation of three hundred, a weekly circulation of one thousand, and a two-story, well-equipped office and printing plant. This was a significant achievement during the eight years the *Astorian* belonged to D. C. Ireland.

At loose ends for a while after the sale, Ireland found life with Livy ever more difficult. On his behalf, two friends filed a complaint in the county court-house at Astoria charging Livy with insanity. After hearing testimony from local doctors, the judge ordered her committed to an asylum in Portland. She was later transferred to an institution at Salem, where she died alone in 1900.

After selling the newspaper, Ireland worked for a short time as supervisor of a salmon cannery on the Fraser River in British Columbia, Canada. Later, hiring two former employees away from the *Astorian,* he formed a printing company on Front Street in Portland and launched the Portland *Commercial Herald* in March of 1883. It could not effectively compete with the already established *Journal of Commerce* and soon shut down. He briefly published a weekly in McMinnville called the *Yamhill Daily Reporter.* Dreaming of starting up again in Astoria, in 1890 he launched the Astoria *Express,* which had a still shorter lifespan.

In the meantime, Astoria's export business had grown. Londoners enjoyed Oregon fruit, Germans put Oregon hops in their beer, and South Africans used Oregon flour in their bread. Oregon fir made the masts "from which floated the flags of France and Russia and England," Halloran wrote in his diary (174). Prosperity attracted newspaper startups. Soon the *Budget* was established and lasted long enough to be merged with the *Astorian.* In the fast-growing towns of the American West, creations, consolidations, and closures of newspapers were common.

By 1890, Astoria had eight thousand residents, a street railway line, two electric lines, and twenty platted additions to the city; twenty-one companies were incorporated within the city (*Astorian*, quoted in "Spirit of the Northwest Press," *Morning Oregonian*, January 5, 1890). The city and its paper had moved beyond Ireland and his style of business. He decided to leave the town he had helped to create, once and for all. He edited the *Chronicle* of The Dalles for

Masthead of the *Evening Astorian-Budget.* CCHS COLLECTION.

View of Astoria looking to the east, ca. 1894. CCHS 946.900.

a time, then moved briefly to the Wasco *Sun.* Eventually he bought the *Moro Observer* in Sherman County with his sons Francis and Clinton. Slowly they beat the competition until theirs was the only paper left, by then called the *Sherman County Observer.* Daughter Lillie ran Ireland's household during all these years, but eventually she married and moved to Portland.

In December 1912, the year after Astoria celebrated its centennial, Ireland had a stroke that left him weak and paralyzed. On January 10, 1913, his paper the *Sherman County Observer* observed his passing:

> Mr. Ireland retained all the faculties of his mind, except for brief
> intervals, until less than three hours of his passing away. His was a
> genial, generous, sunny disposition; he was a kind father; he always
> tried to interest his fellow men in the better and more material

objectives of life; even the suffering of dumb animals always brought a responsive sympathetic attempt at relief.

Ireland was buried at Zion Memorial Park Cemetery in Canby, Oregon.

Merle Chessman was one of three men at the Pendleton *East Oregonian*—a small paper on the opposite side of the state—who took the risk of purchasing the *Astoria Evening Budget* in 1919, six years after Ireland died. He moved from Pendleton and served as the editor and publisher at Astoria for nearly three decades, until his son took over his responsibilities. During those years, Chessman faced an array of challenges that threatened to sink Astoria's fortunes.

The Great Astoria Fire broke out before dawn on December 8, 1922. Chessman stood on the flat tar roof of the *Evening Budget*'s new building at

The great fire of December 8, 1922.

Downtown Astoria after the great fire of December 1922. Photos by Frank Woodfield, Astoria, Oregon. CCHS 21091.935 (above) and CCHS 30464.935 (below).

View of Astoria to the southwest from the corner of Thirteenth and Duane
Streets, ca. 1925, showing reconstruction of Astoria after the devastating 1922 fire.
The offices of the *Astoria Evening Budget* are visible at right front. CCHS 1196.900.

Twelfth and Exchange, trying to protect it from encroaching flames, as his wife
and young children watched from an upstairs apartment on Grand Avenue.

"Dad was standing on top of the building with a hose, keeping it wet so it
wouldn't burn," his daughter told a reporter in 1999. "When the fire got close
to a Standard Oil tank that was nearby, the fire department cut the water off."
Chessman jumped to safety as they watched "the whole town burn," including
his paper's new plant (*Daily Astorian,* September 9, 1999, 1A, 10A). In two-
inch-high letters, the *Oregon Journal* headline of the day read "27 Astoria Blocks
Wiped Out" (Van Dusen Scrapbooks, 81).

The fire started in a restaurant and pool room. Desperate firefighters used
dynamite to raze buildings and halt the progress of the fire, but to no avail. The
wooden pilings that had supported Astoria for decades had been covered over
with pavement on Commercial Street, and the open space acted as a flume, carrying oxygen and spreading flames in all directions. From Eighth to Fifteenth,
from Waterfront to Exchange, the heart of Astoria was destroyed. Chessman
became a central figure in the city's recovery.

Chessman was born in 1886 in Alsea, Oregon, moving soon to Springfield, where his father co-owned a grocery store. Chessman aspired to become a teacher and attended the University of Oregon, graduating in 1909. To pay for it, he secured bank loans and in summers worked on a combine in eastern Oregon. One summer he wrote an ode to the hard work, "The Shortest Route to Hell," which described the heat, dust, and long hours connected to harvesting.

Seeking summer employment, Chessman met in 1909 with E. B. Aldrich, publisher of the *East Oregonian*. Aldrich, impressed, hired him for the summer then asked him to stay on. Chessman canceled a fall teaching contract at Fossil, Oregon, and for the next eight years served as reporter, telegraph editor, and city editor for that paper. He cut his teeth on local news, social news, sports, business, agriculture, and other beats. In 1911 he married his high-school girlfriend, Daphne Leasure. They had a daughter, Peggy (Margaret), in 1914, followed by a son, Robert, in 1921.

Chessman took a leave of absence in 1917 to supervise county war bond drives and to administer the food distribution program. He also worked for the Red Cross. His own family suffered medical crises after minor surgery for his wife turned into a disaster. An unexpected delay in the surgery resulted in fever and infection, leaving Daphne hospitalized for twelve months. Chessman bicycled to the hospital daily before working a night shift at a bottling company, a second job he took on to help pay the mounting medical costs. In an article their daughter wrote for the Clatsop County Historical Society, she describes seven harrowing box-car trips to Portland for more surgery and bone grafts for his invalid wife (Lucas 1986).

In 1919, three *East Oregonian* principals contracted to buy the *Astoria Evening Budget*, offering Chessman a chance to become part-owner and move to Astoria as editor with Lee Drake as manager. Chessman relished the challenge. He was able to double circulation and gross revenues in a relatively short time; later he bought out Drake's interest in the paper.

As publisher, Chessman was quick to decry city incompetence and outright corruption. He and others led a successful drive to establish a city charter and

Merle R. Chessman, publisher of the
Astoria Evening Budget, ca. 1940.
Daily Astorian Collection, CCHS
07.060.011.

city manager plan, which voters backed. Flush with success, the partners bought land on Exchange Street between Eleventh and Twelfth for a new plant for the paper.

A defining moment in Chessman's long career came with the rise of a reinvigorated Ku Klux Klan (KKK) following World War I. In Oregon as elsewhere, the Klan of the 1920s attracted members by labeling and denouncing not only blacks but Catholics, Jews, communists, socialists, and most immigrants. In their view, white, native-born sons were the true Americans. In the 1920s, Astoria's immigrant population was Oregon's highest, with 60 percent of the population of some 14,000 having at least one parent who was foreign-born. In contrast, Oregon overall in 1920 was 85 percent white and native-born. The Klan's promise to corral "alien" forces struck a chord in the city. Before the Klan faded by 1928, more than two thousand citizens of Astoria had joined (McLain 2003, sections 1, 4, 5).

The KKK's racism was born of a paranoia among small-town Protestants against Bolsheviks (including any "radicals," such as labor organizers) and Irish-Catholic immigrants, as well as the Eastern Europeans, Italians, and Jews who

A Ku Klux Klan meeting in Astoria, ca. 1922. CCHS 3503.54.

came in significant numbers to this country in the decades around the turn of the century. Newspapers and nativists often reinforced cultural and ethnic stereotypes, and the KKK used falsehoods and misinformation campaigns to spur the fears.

Known historically for their white hoods and sheets and sometimes violent raids, the KKK gained support in places like Astoria through their beneficent support of community causes, often through Protestant churches. Members typically monitored and targeted bars and nightclubs, violators of the Sabbath, scandalous behavior, bootleggers, and other perceived threats to the social order, along with the "alien element." They capitalized on secrecy and hierarchy and used tools such as boycotts and propaganda to apply pressure on those who would not yield. In Astoria and elsewhere, they made charitable contributions with grand entrances and flourishes.

National Klan leader Fred Gifford, via the Portland-based Good Government League, urged Klans throughout Oregon to propose slates of officers for the November 1922 elections. The Astoria Klavern hand-picked candidates for mayor, constable, and city, port, and county commissioners, as well as candidates for the senate and the house.

Chessman had to walk a narrow path with this powerful and growing organization. He could stomach some of the Klan's candidates, but he made it clear to readers that the Good Government League was associated with the KKK. In carefully worded editorials he recognized the "patriotic purposes" of the organization and the appeal it had for many reputable citizens. But he denounced the Klan's political agenda and its manipulations. The news columns of the *Budget* were open to Klan coverage, he concluded. But editorially, the *Budget* answered only to its sincere convictions and to its readers.

Chessman's attacks on Klan activities were condescending and intellectual, written in a tongue-in-cheek style reminiscent of Ireland's work. For example, after anti-Catholic attacks led to the resignation of the Catholic Chamber of Commerce president and removal of Catholic school board members, Chessman wrote: "Carry on Knights of the Ku Klux Klan! Carry on until you have made it impossible for citizens of foreign birth, of Jewish blood or of Catholic faith to serve their community or their country in any capacity, save as taxpayers" (*Budget*, January 30, 1922, 4). His words infuriated those on the receiving end of his barbed pen.

The Klan's members often sparred among themselves, but they united in growing anger at Chessman's stance and the paper's power to point the finger at them. They used boycotts and bans, letters to his partners in Pendleton, letters to the editor denouncing him, and threats to start a competing paper. Ultimately they demanded that either Chessman be fired or the *Budget* be sold to the Klan.

Chessman's opposition to the Klan was dangerously out of step with prevailing attitudes in his community.

On June 30, 1922, local leader E. P. Hawkins wrote to Aldrich complaining of the Klan committee's "unanimous disapproval of the attitude assumed by Mr. Chessman . . . who in the recent past, so freely, caustically and sarcastically expressed his views of an adverse nature regarding such organizations. . . . The committee also realizes that the editorials of a newspaper are not only one of the most potent factors in molding public sentiment of a community, but that they express the very heartthrobs of the paper itself, and are read more generally, perhaps, than any other part of a small daily, except the local news" (Hawkins 1922–1923).

Chessman did what he could to placate the Klan without compromising his beliefs. On July 9, Chessman reassured Aldrich. "As I wired you Thursday evening, the [Klan's] new paper committee has called off its plans and lifted the ban on the *Budget*." He worried about the perception that the *Budget* had backed off and reported a rumor already circulating that the Klan had "licked the s.o.b. who is editor of the *Budget* so that he won't dare to open his mouth against the city administration or klan either."

He also worried about the paper's credibility and his own. "If the committee in its report to the klan makes it appear that the *Budget* has pledged a friendship to the organization and the members in turn spread such a report around, I can foresee grief ahead," he wrote, adding that another of the rumors held that Aldrich himself was a Klan member.

Chessman's opposition to the Klan was dangerously out of step with prevailing attitudes in his community, as the results of the November 1922 election demonstrated. The Klan slate was elected to office. In Astoria, however, at least two of the men elected later abandoned the Klan and its dictates.

On March 23, 1923, Lem Dever, editor of the Klan's Portland-produced paper the *Western American,* expressed grudging respect to Chessman in a letter. "We have been trying to hate each other, and I guess we do, but I recognize you as a fighter worthy of respect, and I hope the feeling is reciprocated." But in an advertisement of October 26, 1923, the Klan again attacked the *Budget* and Chessman as not "on the list of our friends" for its almost daily malicious "falsehoods" about the Klans in Astoria and nearby.

When the Editor of any paper is so YELLOW that he will Krawl on his Knees to Keep the support of Klansmen and agree to refrain from slandering their great and patriotic order, and then later allow himself to be reinfluenced to print the lying propaganda of the Roman Catholic church is not WORTHY of any consideration by WHITE FOLKS.

The ad then lists and refutes five recent *Budget* headlines. It concludes: "Then why does he do it? Not to change the subject, but we wish to know if the *Budget* had enough money to rebuild after being burned out in the recent fire?" The last sentence could be read as an oblique threat (Chessman file, Clatsop County Historical Society).

Scandal, infighting, and the gradual dissolution of the KKK at both the state and the national level spelled the end of the Oregon Klan before the end of the decade. In later years, Chessman grappled with new enemies.

He vigorously defended Astoria from what he saw as another external threat, the Communist Party, which came to town in the 1930s. A petition to create the party in Oregon was circulated in Astoria in 1934, gaining 220 signatories. Chessman printed their names as he editorialized against the evils of Communism, joining other editorial writers in labeling their efforts as seditious.

One of the men negatively affected was John T. Lassila. He alleged that he lost his job at the Pillsbury Flour Mill as a result of being personally identified and sued Chessman and his paper for libel. Circuit Judge Howard Zimmerman upheld the right of the newspaper to criticize a political organization and ruled that an individual member of the group cannot be libeled in an attack on the organization.

Nothing further came of the suit. Chessman's daughter later wrote that "following expiration of the time for an appeal, it was revealed that every attorney in Clatsop County had sent a written communication to Chessman endorsing his stand on Communism, applauding his courage and volunteering services in defense of his action free of charge" (Lucas 1986, 9).

In the hard economic times of the 1930s, Chessman fought another threat to Astoria in the form of union violence. In 1935 a jurisdictional dispute between the Sawmill and Timberworkers Union and the Pulp, Sulphite, and Paperworkers made Astoria and nearby Seaside the scene of beatings and even deaths. Chessman editorially excoriated both unions and their members' occasionally violent tactics. Once again he was threatened with boycotts and violence. According to his daughter, Chessman took to keeping a revolver in his desk drawer, although he never had occasion to use it (Lucas 1986, 10). She added that although her father had many intense verbal confrontations, the presence of a rather large circulation manager, "Big John" Verschueren, outside his door, helped to calm tense situations when arguments erupted.

Chessman wrote what became a widely reprinted editorial in response to union violence:

> This newspaper is not interested in which union is right in its claim
> for jurisdiction or whether either is. The quarrel between them is
> penalizing an industry, a whole community and hundreds of men
> who need employment and whose families are suffering from the
> long controversy. We are only interested in maintaining law and order
> and insuring peace and security for the law-abiding citizens, whether
> union member or not, whether laborer or employer, and regardless of
> race, religion, color or political belief (quoted in Lucas 1986, 10).

❀ ❀ ❀

By 1925, Astoria had 16,000 people and a tax valuation of $10.8 million, with a remarkable $4.45 million in bonded indebtedness. It also had 4,100 homes wired for electricity, 2,903 phones, 427 students in high school, eleven churches, and three theaters ("Facts Concerning Astoria," Van Dusen Scrapbooks, 107). Chessman was president of the Astoria Community Chest organization in 1927.

During the Great Depression, tax delinquencies in Astoria reached 75 percent, and by 1929 two of the city's banks closed. The town could barely support one newspaper. Demonstrating faith in the future of the community, in 1930 Chessman and his Pendleton partners bought the *Morning Astorian* first established by Ireland, combining it with the *Budget* into the *Evening Astorian-Budget*, later called simply the *Daily Astorian*.

Chessman used the *Astorian-Budget* as a bully pulpit, supporting progressive and sometimes unpopular causes. He argued for the creation of the Oregon Coast Highway Association to complete a four-hundred-mile roadway along Oregon's beautiful coastline. After two years of an organized lobbying effort, Highway 101 segments were linked via a tunnel at Arch Cape at a cost of $20 million.

Chessman was then tagged to lead a drive to replace the ferries where rivers bisected the highway, requiring Public Works Administration funding and support from the Oregon Legislature. At an expense of more than $4 million, bridges were built over the Rogue, Umpqua, Alsea, Yaquina, Siuslaw, and Coos Rivers, forever changing the speed of travel and commerce in Oregon. Chessman later fought to make the bridges toll-free, which the Oregon Legislature accomplished in 1936.

Flush with success, Chessman led a city campaign for a bridge to Washington State across the wide mouth of the Columbia at Astoria, which he believed would enhance tourism and thus the city's economy. A study by the Army Corps of Engineers deemed the project feasible and not a hindrance to river traffic. The bridge was not completed until 1966, but Chessman and his allies had laid the groundwork for what became a four-mile span between Oregon and Washington.

Chessman was appointed to the Oregon Fish Commission in 1936. His commitment to community service was deep and wide-ranging. His daughter wrote that in 1936 alone, he was president of the University of Oregon Alumni Association, its Dad's Club, and the Oregon State Editorial Association. In addition he was on the Oregon Wildlife Conservation Commission, the Oregon State Geographic Board, and after 1940, the Oregon Fisheries Commission. Locally, he served as president of the Rotary Club, headed the Clatsop County Historical Society, chaired the county library board, and belonged to the Masonic, Elks, and Woodmen of the World lodges. A lifelong Republican, he was also independent, choosing to back Roosevelt early on.

As early as the 1920s, Chessman recognized the critical role federal support could play in Astoria's future. Among the causes for which he worked tirelessly were returning nearby Fort Stevens to active military status after a twenty-year hiatus and restoring a jetty at the northern entrance of the Columbia. A principal effort was the development of Tongue Point as a submarine and aviation base. In the anxious days before World War II, Chessman wrote dozens of editorials on the subject and trekked to Washington, D.C., five times on behalf of the cause, meeting with President Roosevelt and Senator Charles McNary of Oregon in 1938. In 1939 Congress approved the proposal. The site became a naval air station and was critical to patrolling the West Coast after December 7, 1941. After World War II, it became moorage for cargo and transport ships, eventually becoming a Job Corps Center.

In 1942 state senator Frank Franciscovich died, and both the Republican and the Democratic central committees of Clatsop County recommended

Merle Chessman, center, presided as toastmaster when the Army-Navy "E" awards were presented to workers in Westport and Wauna, Oregon, ca. 1944, to encourage production of war materials. CCHS 040.060.061.

Chessman to fill out the term. Chessman stood for Astoria in the halls of the Oregon Legislature. In 1945, he was largely responsible for a bill that broadened the fishing commission's powers and increased its funding. Earlier he had helped to organize the Columbia Basin Fisheries Development Association to protect the fishing industry against the inroads of dams being built on the Columbia, which became an increasingly controversial issue in the region.

In 1946, the Republican Party nominated him for election to the Oregon Senate. He refused to run a campaign or raise money—he felt that his record of service was enough for voters to evaluate. Supporters organized an advertising campaign for him, and he won.

Chessman's time in the senate was short. During the 1947 session of the Oregon Legislature, he was felled by a brain tumor. He had surgery but never recovered consciousness. Three months later he died, at the age of sixty.

Out of respect, Astoria's downtown stores were closed during his funeral at the First Presbyterian Church, which was attended by friends and dignitaries from across the state. He was survived by his wife Daphne, son Robert, daughter Peggy (Mrs. Robert) Lucas, and three grandchildren. His son Robert, twenty-six years old when Chessman died, led the paper from 1947 to 1960.

Robert Chessman, ca. 1955. Image courtesy of Peggy Chessman Lucas.

Ireland, Chessman, and their newspapers left a legacy that can be seen on the roads, docks, and sidewalks of Astoria and in its confident sense of itself. They made their newspapers a force for the community, and their small community a force in Oregon. "They stood for something," *Daily Astorian* publisher Steve Forrester noted in a 2006 interview; they used their powers of persuasion to realize their vision of what was good for the community.

The role of community newspapers has diminished in the age of the Internet. But it is important to recognize the role of editorial leadership in molding communities such as Astoria. Both Ireland and Chessman helped to build the city we know today.

Works Cited

Aldrich, E. B. 1922–1923. Correspondence to Merle Chessman and Lee Drake. Clatsop County Historical Society Archives.

Chessman, Merle. Ephemera file. Clatsop County Historical Society Archives.

Cloud, Barbara. 1992. *The Business of Newspapers on the Western Frontier*. Reno: University of Nevada Press.

Halloran, Joseph F. Transcription of Joseph Francis Halloran's diary. Typescript. Clatsop County Historical Society Archives.

Hawkins, E. P. 1922–1923. Correspondence to E. B. Aldrich and Merle Chessman. Clatsop County Historical Society Archives.

Ireland, DeWitt Clinton. Ephemera file. Clatsop County Historical Society Archives.

Lucas, Peggy Chessman. 1986. Merle Chessman, Editor, Statesman. *Cumtux*, Clatsop County Historical Society Quarterly, vol. 6, no. 4, p. 315.

McLain, Annie. 2003. *Unmasking the Oregon Klansman: The Ku Klux Klan in Astoria, 1922–1925*. Master's thesis. Retrieved 13 January 2006, from http://www. pacificu.edu/as/history/students/mclain.cfm.

Penner, Liisa. *DeWitt Clinton Ireland (1836–1913), Oregon Newspaperman*. Manuscript, Clatsop County Historical Society Archives.

_____. 1990. *Chinese in Astoria, Oregon, 1870–1880: A Look at Local Newspaper Articles, the Census, and Other Related Materials*. Astoria: privately printed.

Tetlow, Roger T. 1975. *The Astorian: The Personal History of DeWitt Clinton Ireland, Pioneer Newspaperman, Printer, and Publisher*. Binford & Mort, Portland, 1975.

Tri-Weekly Astorian, Morning Astorian, Weekly Astorian, Astoria Evening Budget, Astorian-Budget, and *Daily Astorian.* 1873–1999. Astoria Public Library and University of Oregon Archives.

Van Dusen Scrapbooks. Astoria Public Library.

The Salmon Kings

By Liisa Penner

L ittle more than a decade after the race for gold in California mountain streams ended, another quest for riches began seven hundred miles away in the Columbia River. The Salmon Rush jolted Astoria to life from 1866 to 1899,

Top: Horse seining for salmon on a sand bar in the Columbia River, ca. 1920. CCHS 1056.310. Above: A horse-seining group, ca. 1905. The man standing in the center of the boat wearing a cap and holding the big salmon is Chris K. Henry, who began fishing on the Columbia River in 1883 and fished summer and fall for sixty years until he retired in 1943. He was married to Louise Elliott, the great-great-granddaughter of Chinook chief Comcomly. CCHS 3493C.310.

HORSE SEINING

TOP: Horse seining on the Columbia, ca. 1938. On a sand bar exposed by the tide, one set of horses anchors the net, which waiting skiffs pull out into the river in a broad semicircle then attach to another pair of horses that pull the net and the catch to the sand bar. These fishermen are standing on a sand bar lifting the net to keep salmon from escaping. The process of horse seining was outlawed in Washington in 1934 and in Oregon in 1948. CCHS 21054.310. ABOVE: Columbia River fishing fleet during the Regatta at Astoria, ca. 1907. PHOTO BY O. W. WHITMAN, ASTORIA, OREGON. These boats were known as the "Butterfly Fleet" because they resembled butterflies when their two triangular sails were spread out. CCHS 15571.315.

CANNERIES

TOP: Canneries in Upper Astoria in the 1880s: White Star Packing Company, Smith Cannery, and Hanthorn Cannery. PHOTO BY PARTRIDGE, PORTLAND, OREGON. CCHS 07.060.007. LEFT: Children as well as adults worked in the packing room of an Astoria cannery, ca. 1910. CCHS 12343.330. BELOW: Women about to fill cans with salmon pose for the photographer, ca. 1915. CCHS 31058.330.

triggering a booming canning industry that transformed huge fish runs into fortunes of gold and reshaped the city.

Like the hardy and ruthless men who became lords of the Gold Rush, a roundtable of rival Salmon Kings armed with hard fists and nimble minds dominated the canneries, boats, and traps that blanketed the river. Calling a truce once a year, they quietly met on the waterfront to fix the price they would pay legions of fishermen. (It was less than a dollar for a monster Chinook.) Setting the price artificially low kept the unruly fishermen in their place.

The fishermen, hailing mostly from Scandinavia and the Balkans, plied their nets from vessels vulnerable to the Columbia's capricious weather. The boats often were no match for gales, especially when caught between a fast-flowing spring flood and wall of ocean breakers. Dozens drowned in a severe storm in 1880, although the exact total was never determined. But more were waiting to fill their jobs. For the April-to-August season, fishermen might earn a lucrative $100 a month, boat pullers $70, and Chinese cannery workers $40 to $50.

Cannery owners hoped to make a hundred times more than the fishermen. Not all succeeded, because canning operations blossomed and died at an astonishing pace. But for those who outsmarted and outlasted the competition, each salmon was cash with fins. While most cannery owners were not wealthy by East Coast standards, they could afford mansions. Captain John West was prominent enough to have a town named after him—Westport.

None would have thrived without a new technique to preserve food in sanitary cans and a far-flung craving for protein-rich salmon. Fast-sailing ships sent much of the early catch to Britain and Australia. In later years, a U.S. market for salmon developed as a huge influx of Catholic immigrants sought an affordable alternative to red meat on Fridays.

Many men tried to capitalize on those developments, but few could claim the title of Salmon King. Here are snapshots of some of the most notable.

Hume Brothers

Despite their prominence among the Salmon Kings, no town is named after the quartet, only an insignificant Astoria street. In 1882, William Hume described how the Maine clan's salmon enterprise started in California a dozen years after the discovery of gold in the Sierra Nevadas:

Top Left: Cannery at Eagle Cliff, Columbia River, Washington Territory, ca. 1897. This was the first salmon cannery in the Pacific Northwest, established in 1866 by William and George Hume and Andrew Hapgood. Photo by John W. Tollman and Frank H. Canaris. Courtesy of the University of Washington. UW12686. Top right: William Hume (1830–1902). Image scanned from Courtland L. Smith, *Salmon Fishers of the Columbia*, Corvallis, OR: 1979, p. 19. Above Left: Joseph Hume operated a cannery in Astoria in the late 1870s and early 1880s. Image scanned from Courtland L. Smith, *Salmon Fishers of the Columbia*, Corvallis, OR: 1979, p. 19. Above Middle: George W. Hume, ca. 1870. CCHS 26087.00H. Above Right: Robert D. Hume was a salmon cannery owner and operator on the Columbia River until 1877, when he moved to the Rogue River and established another cannery. Image scanned from Leigh Hadley Irvine, *A History of the New California: Its Resources and People*, New York: The Lewis Publishing Company, 1905.

My father one day received a large order for nets from some California people. . . . I concluded that fish must be plentiful in a country where they needed so many nets, and I made up my mind to visit the coast at once. . . . [I]n 1863, or thereabouts, I commenced to fish on the Sacramento River. Accordingly in 1864, A. S. Hapgood who is now dead and myself entered into partnership to do a general canning and fishing business. Hapgood was a tinner by trade and he thoroughly understood the art of making tin cans, and I knew how to fish (*Daily Astorian*, May 18, 1882).

When gold mining's environmentally devastating effects reduced the Sacramento's salmon runs, the Humes and Hapgood relocated to the Columbia, where salmon were plentiful. They established the first salmon cannery in the country in 1866, forty miles east of Astoria at Eagle Cliff, near the eastern border of what is now Wahkiakum County in Washington. By 1881, the Humes owned almost half of the thirty-five canneries on the Columbia. In 1884, three Humes-owned canneries operated in Astoria at what is today Fourteenth Street and Marine Drive, Twelfth and Marine, and near Second Street.

Astoria Canneries

While others had canneries nearby, John Badollet, George W. Warren, John Hobson, Henry S. Aiken, and Christian Leinenweber established the first in present-day Astoria in 1873, known as Badollet & Co. In 1874 Booth & Co.

Joseph G. Megler, pioneer cannery man along the Columbia River, at Brookfield in the Washington Territory. CCHS 12275.00M.

ASTORIA CANNERIES - THE KINNEY CANNERY

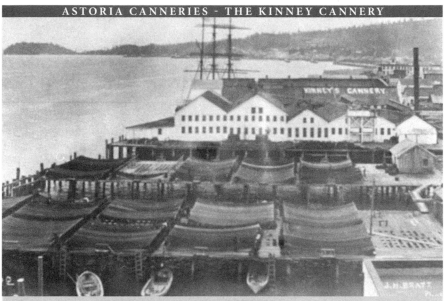

Top: The Kinney Cannery, later the Columbia River Packers Association, ca. 1893. Photo by J. H. Bratt. CCHS 274.330. Left: Marshall J. Kinney at the 1897 Astoria Regatta. Courtesy of the Gearhart Heritage Committee, Gearhart City Hall. Bottom: An old Kinney Cannery label later used by Bumble Bee Seafoods, ca. 1960. CCHS 91.070.40.

GUSTAV HOLMES

Top: Gustav Holmes with his family, ca. 1888. CCHS 3891.00H. ABOVE: The Gustav Holmes house, built in 1892 at 682 Thirty-Fourth Street, Astoria. CCHS 5744.960.

began operations, and Marshall J. Kinney the next year. (Kinney's cannery eventually produced 75,000 cases of salmon a year, possibly a record.)

Together these men proved that canneries situated near the river's mouth could earn more than those upstream. In 1883, twenty-four canneries operated in the Astoria area between Smith Point and Tongue Point, jutting out over the river like so many crooked teeth.

The Salmon Kings typically built large, elegant houses in Astoria but based their lives in California. Any children were usually born there. Those corresponding to this composite include the Humes, Kinney, John Devlin, J. O. Hanthorn, Joseph G. Megler, B. A. Seaborg, Crossman Timmons, G. W. Sanborn, William Barker, Eben W. Tallant, Gustav Holmes, Benjamin Young, and Samuel Elmore.

Samuel Elmore

Serving as a Union lieutenant after enlisting underage in the Wisconsin Infantry in 1864, Samuel Elmore pursued Confederate guerrillas through Kansas and Missouri. His bold, sometimes bloodthirsty, and avidly Republican disposition served him well until a violent accident many years later.

After the Civil War, Elmore continued west. By 1875 he was working in California as a commission agent for Robert Hume, from whom he acquired a taste for the salmon business. He visited Astoria to investigate the trade and leased a cannery from Joseph Hume. But Elmore had bigger ambitions. He took over the failed Union Packing Company Cannery, built in 1881 and owned and operated as a cooperative by ten Finnish fishermen. Under Elmore's management, the cannery, namesake for the area of Astoria known as Uniontown, was an unqualified success. The original building fronted Bond Street across from Flavel Street. In 1895, Elmore built an adjacent structure jutting over the Columbia. Added onto over the years, it became known as the Elmore Cannery, a name that persisted decades after his death.

For a number of years, Elmore had urged cannery owners to consolidate operations. The result was the Columbia River Packers Association, often referred to as the CRPA or "Combine." Formed in 1899, the group represented seven companies with ten canneries on the river. The group chose Elmore as vice-president and general manager. Able to work more efficiently by sharing operations, the association shut down excess facilities and made the Elmore

SAMUEL ELMORE

LEFT: Samuel Elmore, ca. 1900. COURTESY OF THE OREGON HISTORICAL SOCIETY. CN008060/BB006518.

BELOW: Office of Elmore, Sanborn & Co., "Commission Merchants & Packers of Canned Salmon." Detail from a lithograph by Bruce Wellington Pierce, published ca. 1890 by J. W. Stengele as "View of Astoria in 1890." CCHS COLLECTION.

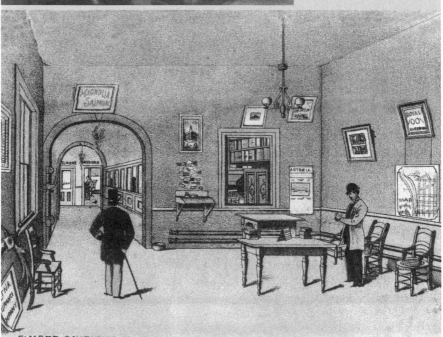

ELMORE, SANBORN & CO., COMMISSION MERCHANTS & PACKERS OF CANNED SALMON.

SAMUEL ELMORE

Salmon Canning, Astoria, Oregon.

RES. S. ELMORE 1908

Top: The Elmore Cannery in Astoria, ca. 1910. Fishing boats await the next trip out on the turbulent Columbia for a load of salmon. CCHS 15347.330. Above: Former home of cannery owner Samuel Elmore and his family, 1899. The building still stands on the northwest corner of Fourteenth and Grand in Astoria. CCHS 052.001.032.

Cannery its center of operations. The group also expanded capacity by adding more canneries upriver and in Bristol Bay, Alaska. In 1910, the group began the Bumble Bee brand of salmon, the best known of scores from the Combine's canneries, and added tuna in the 1930s. Elmore's concept had grown into one of the largest commercial forces on the Columbia, producing seafood eaten around the world. The Elmore plant earned distinction as the longest continuously operated cannery in the United States and was designated a National Historic Landmark on November 13, 1966. It closed in 1980. In 1993, fire destroyed what remained of the building.

Elmore also had political and other business interests. He owned a cannery at Kernville on Siletz Bay in Lincoln County and invested in two ships that bore the family name. Starting in 1890, he owned and operated the *Astorian* newspaper for four years. He served as mayor for about a month in 1891 and was a member of the Astoria Water Board that built the city's water system and reservoir.

Elmore, who wintered with his family every year in Oakland, began spending more and more time in California, and relinquished control of the Combine's day-to-day operations. About 1906, Elmore, his wife Mary, their three daughters, and two servants moved to a large house on the northwest corner of Fourteenth Street and Grand Avenue in Astoria (now the Elmore Apartments). In 1910, he was named president of the Port of Astoria. Later that year, while in California with his family, Elmore and a married woman with whom he had been spending considerable time took a drive in his new car. They approached a rail crossing where brush hid an oncoming train. Both were killed instantly. Elmore left an estate of about $360,000, equal to $16 million today.

Benjamin Young

A symbolic bookend to Elmore, Young was born in Malmo, Sweden, in 1843. He spent years as a poor sailor before entering the freight business in San Francisco, where he earned enough cash to join the Salmon Rush in 1874. With others, he organized the Fishermen's Packing Company and later the Scandinavian Packing Company.

Young branched out geographically, starting canneries on the Fraser and Skeene Rivers in British Columbia and investing in a cannery on the Nushagak

BENJAMIN YOUNG

LEFT: Benjamin Young and his wife, ca. 1885. CCHS 28189.00Y.

BELOW: Benjamin Young with his family, ca. 1900. CCHS 4377.00Y.

The Benjamin Young house on Duane Street, ca. 2000. Reprinted with permission from Kenneth Naversen's *Beautiful America's Northwest Victorians* (Beautiful America Publishing Company, Woodburn, Oregon, 2001).

River at Bristol Bay, Alaska. After selling his Canadian interests in 1891, he helped to organize the Astoria Savings Bank and invested in railroads and steamboats. The lone Democrat among the Salmon Kings, he lobbied the Oregon Legislature to outlaw fish traps. "Personally," he wrote, "I think the only legitimate form of fishing is with gillnets and I consider all traps, wheels, etc. simply slaughtering pens" (*Astoria Evening Budget*, February 16, 1895). The Legislature agreed but not until 1927, sixteen years after Young's death.

Describing Young as a developer of Astoria, a contemporary said: "Notwithstanding his genial manner he is business from head to foot, and having followed a fixed purpose and principle is the recipient of a well-merited reward" (Hines 1893, 468).

Young died in Los Angeles in 1911 at a hotel where he liked to spend the winters. His children and grandchildren lovingly cared for the Astoria house he built in 1888 until it passed out of their hands. Once topped with a golden salmon weather vane, the house still overlooks the Columbia River at 3652 Duane Street, a reminder of the bygone days of the Salmon Kings.

Young and his wife Christine, also from Sweden, had seven children. Their son Johan, a lawyer, was elected in 1899 to represent Clatsop County in the Oregon Legislature but died the next year. Their oldest child, Clara, became a physician in 1907 and later married another doctor, Eldred Waffle. She taught nurses at St. Mary's Training Center for sixteen years and became known as Astoria's baby doctor. Several generations of Astorians may remember her daughter Josephine Waffle Swanson, a Regatta Queen, teacher at Astoria schools, and popular columnist for the *Astoria Budget*.

Salmon fed the fortunes of ten or more investors, men who in turn envisioned a new future for the mouth of the Columbia River. They invested in banks, wharves, sawmills, railroads, and ships that contributed to Astoria's growth into the largest and most important city on the coast of Oregon and Washington by the start of the twentieth century.

Works Cited

Astoria Evening Budget. "The Fish Question." February 16, 1805.

Daily Astorian. "Origin of the Salmon Fishery." May 18, 1882.

Hines, H. K. *History of Oregon.* Lewis: Chicago, 1893.

Acknowledgments

I would like to acknowledge my debt to Bruce Berney, former director of the Astoria Public Library, for his years of work toward developing a comprehensive index to the Astoria newspapers. This is the single most important resource available to those who want to write on local subjects. I would also like to thank Matt Winters and Michael Bales for their work on "Salmon Kings."

About the Authors

STEPHEN DOW BECKHAM is the Pamplin Professor of History at Lewis & Clark College. Born in Coos Bay, Oregon, Prof. Beckham received his Ph.D. from UCLA and has taught for the past forty-one years. His teaching and research topics include Native Americans, the history of the American West, and environmental history. A former Oregon Professor of the Year and recipient of the American Historical Association's Distinguished Teaching Award, he is the author of essays in three volumes of the *Handbook of North American Indians* and several books. His titles include *Oregon Indians: Voices from Two Centuries* (2006), *Astoria Column* (2004), *The Literature of the Lewis and Clark Expedition* (2003), and *Lewis and Clark: From the Rockies to the Pacific* (2002). Prof. Beckham has served as curator and author of numerous museum exhibits and television programs, including The History Channel, CBS, and Oregon Public Broadcasting.

SANDRA HAARSAGER wrote extensively about Pacific Northwest history, specifically the books *Organized Womanhood: Cultural Politics in the Pacific Northwest, 1840–1920* and *Bertha Knight Landes of Seattle: Big City Mayor*. She also published several book chapters and journal articles. An award-winning writer, she was a reporter, editor, and columnist for a number of years. Dr. Haarsager lectured frequently on women's unrecognized roles in creating the communities of the Northwest and taught courses in journalism, culture, and mass media as a professor at the University of Idaho at Moscow. She gained her Ph.D. in American Studies from Washington State University and a master's in Public Administration from Boise State University. After an extended illness, Dr. Haarsager died in October 2007. This book is dedicated to her memory.

LIISA PENNER was born in Finland to a Finnish native and her American husband. She moved to the U.S. as a child, eventually coming to Astoria in 1951. After graduating from Astoria High School, she attended the University of Oregon, where she received her Master's Degree in Anthropology. Upon returning to the Astoria area, she became active in the Clatsop County Genealogy Society, working with its members to produce several books of local research materials. About the same time she began working with the collections at the Clatsop County Historical Society and was given the task of monitoring accessions and responding to queries. Discovering a serious need for making historical source material available for researchers, she began collecting, abstracting, and printing up this material. She has worked as editor of the historical society's quarterly *Cumtux* since 1992, publishing over seventy issues of the magazine. Penner is now Archivist for the Clatsop County Historical Society at the Heritage Museum.

ROBERT MICHAEL PYLE was born and raised in Colorado and took his Ph.D. in conservation biology at Yale. He has published hundreds of essays, stories, and poems, and fourteen books including *Wintergreen, The Thunder Tree, Where Bigfoot Walks, Chasing Monarchs, Walking the High Ridge,* and *Sky Time in Gray's River;* as well as *Nabokov's Butterflies* and *The Butterflies of Cascadia.* Pyle has won the John Burroughs Medal for Distinguished Nature Writing, a Guggenheim Fellowship, three Washington Governor's Writers Awards, a Pacific Northwest Booksellers Award, the Harry B. Nehls Award in Nature Writing, and the National Outdoor Book Award for Natural History Literature. His latest title, *Mariposa Road: The First Butterfly Big Year,* was published by Houghton Mifflin Harcourt in fall of 2010. For thirty years Bob has lived along Gray's River, a tributary of the Lower Columbia River, with botanist and weaver Thea Linnaea Pyle.

FREDERIK L. SCHODT is a writer, translator, and interpreter based in San Francisco, California. He has written extensively on Japan, and on the relationship between Japan and America. His books include *Manga! Manga! The World of Japanese Comics* (Kodansha International, 1983), *Inside the Robot Kingdom: Japan, Mechatronics and the Coming Robotopia* (Kodansha International, 1988), *America and the Four Japans: Friend, Foe, Model, Mirror* (Stone Bridge Press, 1994), and *Native American in the Land of the Shogun: Ranald MacDonald and the Opening of Japan* (Stone Bridge Press, 2003). *Native American in the Land of the Shogun* was selected by the American Library Association's *Choice Magazine* as one of the outstanding academic titles of 2004. In 2009, Schodt was awarded the Order of the Rising Sun, Gold Rays with Rosette, by the Japanese government. His website is http://www.jai2.com.

JOHN TERRY is a veteran Oregon journalist whose professional career has spanned more than forty years, at the old *Salem Capital Journal* and later at the *Oregonian*. During his tenure at the Salem newspaper, he won top honors for column and feature writing from the Oregon Newspaper Publishers Association. In 1976 he moved to the *Oregonian*, where he served as photo editor, regional editor, assistant news editor, and national/international copy editor. In 1997 he began a weekly column, "Oregon's Trails," dealing with state and regional history, which he continues in retirement.

JEAN M. WARD is Professor Emerita of Communication and cofounder of the Gender Studies Program at Lewis & Clark College, where she taught and held various administrative posts for forty-two years, from 1964 to 2006. Born in Eugene, Ward received her Ph.D. from the University of Oregon. Her research and writing focus on the lives and rhetoric of Pacific Northwest women, and she has a special interest in reform leaders such as Bethenia Owens-Adair. Two of her books, both co-edited with Elaine A. Maveety, are *Pacific Northwest Women, 1815–1925: Lives, Memories and Writings* (1995) and *"Yours for Liberty": Selections from Abigail Scott Duniway's Suffrage Newspaper* (2000). She was a contributor and participant in Oregon Public Broadcasting's *Oregon Experience* production in 2006 on the life and work of Abigail Scott Duniway, and she has contributed essays on Oregon women to the Oregon Historical Society's online *Oregon Encyclopedia*. Dr. Ward is currently editing the 1877–1878 journal of Dr. Mary A. Thompson, one of Portland's early women doctors.

WILLIAM F. WILLINGHAM is a historian who has written widely in the fields of Pacific Northwest history, historic preservation, historic architecture, and water resources development. He contributed a lengthy introduction and historical overview to *Pendleton Round-Up at 100: Oregon's Legendary Rodeo* (2009). His most recent books are *Starting Over: Community Building on the Eastern Oregon Frontier* (2005) and *The Classic Houses of Portland, Oregon, 1859–1950* (co-author, 1999). He has also written numerous scholarly articles, reviews, and professional papers and has published in such scholarly journals as the *Oregon Historical Quarterly*, the *Public Historian*, and the *William and Mary Quarterly*. Dr. Willingham received his B.A. from Willamette University in 1966 and his Ph.D. in American History in 1972 from Northwestern University.

Index